READERS' GU

CONSULTANT E

Published

Lucie Armitt	George Eliot: *Adam Bede – The Mill on the Floss – Middlemarch*
Paul Baines	Daniel Defoe: *Robinson Crusoe – Moll Flanders*
Richard Beynon	D. H. Lawrence: *The Rainbow – Women in Love*
Peter Boxall	Samuel Beckett: *Waiting for Godot – Endgame*
Claire Brennan	The Poetry of Sylvia Plath
Susan Bruce	Shakespeare: *King Lear*
Sandie Byrne	Jane Austen: *Mansfield Park*
Alison Chapman	Elizabeth Gaskell: *Mary Barton – North and South*
Peter Childs	The Fiction of Ian McEwan
Christine Clegg	Vladimir Nabokov: *Lolita*
John Coyle	James Joyce: *Ulysses – A Portrait of the Artist as a Young Man*
Martin Coyle	Shakespeare: *Richard II*
Justin D. Edwards	Postcolonial Literature
Michael Faherty	The Poetry of W. B. Yeats
Sarah Gamble	The Fiction of Angela Carter
Jodi-Anne George	Chaucer: The General Prologue to *The Canterbury Tales*
Jane Goldman	Virginia Woolf: *To the Lighthouse – The Waves*
Huw Griffiths	Shakespeare: *Hamlet*
Vanessa Guignery	The Fiction of Julian Barnes
Louisa Hadley	The Fiction of A. S. Byatt
Geoffrey Harvey	Thomas Hardy: *Tess of the d'Urbervilles*
Paul Hendon	The Poetry of W. H. Auden
Terry Hodgson	The Plays of Tom Stoppard for Stage, Radio, TV and Film
Stuart Hutchinson	Mark Twain: *Tom Sawyer – Huckleberry Finn*
Stuart Hutchinson	Edith Wharton: *The House of Mirth – The Custom of the Country*
Betty Jay	E. M. Forster: *A Passage to India*
Aaron Kelly	Twentieth-Century Irish Literature
Elmer Kennedy-Andrews	The Poetry of Seamus Heaney
Elmer Kennedy-Andrews	Nathaniel Hawthorne: *The Scarlet Letter*
Daniel Lea	George Orwell: *Animal Farm – Nineteen Eighty-Four*
Philippa Lyon	Twentieth-Century War Poetry
Merja Makinen	The Novels of Jeanette Winterson
Jago Morrison	The Fiction of Chinua Achebe
Carl Plasa	Toni Morrison: *Beloved*
Carl Plasa	Jean Rhys: *Wide Sargasso Sea*
Nicholas Potter	Shakespeare: *Antony and Cleopatra*

Nicholas Potter	Shakespeare: *Othello*
Berthold Schoene-Harwood	Mary Shelley: *Frankenstein*
Nick Selby	T. S. Eliot: *The Waste Land*
Nick Selby	Herman Melville: *Moby Dick*
Nick Selby	The Poetry of Walt Whitman
David Smale	Salman Rushdie: *Midnight's Children – The Satanic Verses*
Patsy Stoneman	Emily Brontë: *Wuthering Heights*
Susie Thomas	Hanif Kureishi
Nicolas Tredell	F. Scott Fitzgerald: *The Great Gatsby*
Nicolas Tredell	Joseph Conrad: *Heart of Darkness*
Nicolas Tredell	Charles Dickens: *Great Expectations*
Nicolas Tredell	William Faulkner: *The Sound and the Fury – As I Lay Dying*
Nicolas Tredell	Shakespeare: *Macbeth*
Nicolas Tredell	The Fiction of Martin Amis
Matthew Woodcock	Shakespeare: *Henry V*
Angela Wright	Gothic Fiction

Forthcoming

Pascale Aebischer	Jacobean Drama
Simon Avery	Thomas Hardy: *The Mayor of Casterbridge – Jude the Obscure*
Annika Bautz	Jane Austen: *Sense and Sensibility – Pride and Prejudice – Emma*
Matthew Beedham	The Novels of Kazuo Ishiguro
Jodi-Anne George	*Beowulf*
William Hughes	Bram Stoker: *Dracula*
Matthew Jordan	Milton: *Paradise Lost*
Sara Lodge	Charlotte Brontë: *Jane Eyre*
Matthew McGuire	Contemporary Scottish Literature
Timothy Milnes	Wordsworth: *The Prelude*
Steven Price	The Plays, Screenplays and Films of David Mamet
Stephen Regan	The Poetry of Philip Larkin
Michael Whitworth	Virginia Woolf: *Mrs Dalloway*
Gina Wisker	The Fiction of Margaret Atwood

Readers' Guides to Essential Criticism
Series Standing Order
ISBN 1-4039-0108-2
(*outside North America only*)

You can receive future titles in this series as they are published by placing a standing order. Please contact your bookseller or, in the case of difficulty, write to us at the address below with your name and address, the title of the series and the ISBN quoted above.

Customer Services Department, Macmillan Distribution Ltd
Houndmills, Basingstoke, Hampshire RG21 6XS, England

Shakespeare
Henry V

Matthew Woodcock

Consultant editor: Nicolas Tredell

palgrave
macmillan

First published 2008 by
PALGRAVE MACMILLAN
Houndmills, Basingstoke, Hampshire RG21 6XS and
175 Fifth Avenue, New York, N.Y. 10010
Companies and representatives throughout the world

PALGRAVE MACMILLAN is the global academic imprint of the Palgrave Macmillan division of St. Martin's Press, LLC and of Palgrave Macmillan Ltd. Macmillan® is a registered trademark in the United States, United Kingdom and other countries. Palgrave is a registered trademark in the European Union and other countries.

ISBN-13: 978-0-230-50079-2   hardback
ISBN-10: 0-230-50079-X   hardback
ISBN-13: 978-0-230-50080-8   paperback
ISBN-10: 0-230-50080-3   paperback

This book is printed on paper suitable for recycling and made from fully managed and sustained forest sources. Logging, pulping and manufacturing processes are expected to conform to the environmental regulations of the country of origin.

A catalogue record for this book is available from the British Library.

A catalog record for this book is available from the Library of Congress.

10   9   8   7   6   5   4   3   2   1
17 16 15 14 13 12 11 10 09 08

Printed and bound in China

For Katherine, Oliver and Lucy

CONTENTS

to be observed or reconstructed by critics. Focuses on A. P. Rossiter's account of ambivalence in Shakespeare's histories; Harold C. Goddard's incisive identification of ambivalence and irony in *Henry V*; S. C. Sen Gupta and Robert Ornstein's theories on the importance of drawing attention back to the play's aesthetic qualities; and Norman Rabkin's essay on how *Henry V* forces its audience to choose between diametrically opposed, irreconcilable interpretations.

Discusses Stephen Greenblatt's influential New Historicist essay 'Invisible Bullets' and the presentation of subversion in the play; Jonathan Dollimore and Alan Sinfield's Cultural Materialist essay on how *Henry V* implicitly reveals the workings of Elizabethan ruling ideology; Lance Wilcox, Jean E. Howard and Phyllis Rackin's feminist accounts of how power in the play manifests as violence exerted over female bodies; Graham Bradshaw's critique of materialist approaches to the play; and Tom McAlindon's revisionist attempt to preserve a positive interpretation of Henry through attention to Shakespeare's constructive use of paradox and oxymoron.

Explores a number of ongoing debates in *Henry V* criticism and considers how Claire McEachern, Alison Thorne and Philip Schwyzer locate the play in relation to early modern ideas about an English or British national imagined community; discusses how critics such as David J. Baker, Michael Neill, Andrew Murphy and Christopher Highley trace Shakespeare's response to the Elizabethan colonization of Ireland; and, through drawing on scholarship by Theodor Meron, Steven Marx, R. A. Foakes and John S. Mebane, examines how *Henry V* continues to invite speculation and discussion about the justification of war.

Continues to look ahead to future criticism on *Henry V* and some of the challenges and caveats to consider.

ACKNOWLEDGEMENTS

Anyone working on *Henry V*'s reception history is indebted to Joseph Candido and Charles R. Forker's exhaustive *Henry V: An Annotated Bibliography* (New York: Garland, 1983). Richard Dutton's essay in Stanley Wells (ed.), *Shakespeare: A Bibliographical Guide* (Oxford: Oxford University Press, 1990), pp. 337–80, and Emma Smith's introduction to her *Shakespeare's Histories*, Blackwell Guides to Criticism (Oxford: Blackwell, 2004) have also proved immensely useful in helping to place *Henry V* scholarship within the wider critical landscape for all of Shakespeare's history plays.

I would like to thank Nicolas Tredell for approaching me initially to write this book and for his guidance throughout its production. I am also grateful for assistance from the staff at the Bodleian Library, Cambridge University Library and the Shakespeare Centre Library. Thanks also go to Andrew King, Helen Cooper, Ben Sharpe and Amy Gasper for various forms of help and support during this project.

NOTES ON THE TEXTS

All quotations from *Henry V* are from Gary Taylor (ed.), *Henry V*, The Oxford Shakespeare (Oxford: Oxford University Press, 1982), unless stated otherwise. For consistency, Taylor's spelling of Katherine of Valois as 'Catherine' has been emended throughout my text. Citations and quotations from all of Shakespeare's other works are from Stanley Wells, Gary Taylor, John Jowett and William Montgomery (eds), *The Oxford Shakespeare: The Complete Works*, 2nd edn (Oxford: Oxford University Press, 2005). Capitalization and italicization in quotations from earlier sources has been silently modernized where necessary. In order to ensure the accuracy and context of the major critical studies discussed in this Guide I have worked predominantly from the original texts, although many of the key passages from the critics discussed here can be found in an accessible form in Michael Quinn (ed.), *Henry V: A Casebook* (London: Macmillan, 1969).

Introduction

Henry V is the last in a series of eight plays about English history of the period 1398–1485 that Shakespeare wrote during the 1590s. The first tetralogy, including some of Shakespeare's earliest writings, portrayed the calamitous reign of Henry VI (1421–71), the escalation of the so-called Wars of the Roses between the houses of Lancaster and York and the accession of Henry Tudor as Henry VII (1457–1509) following the defeat of Richard III (1452–85) at Bosworth field in 1485. After writing a stand-alone play about King John (1166–1216) and very likely having a hand in one about Edward III (1312–77), Shakespeare returned to the roots of the mid-fifteenth-century political turbulence and his second tetralogy depicted Henry Bolingbroke's deposition of Richard II (1367–1400), Bolingbroke's troubled reign as Henry IV (1366–1413) and the youthful adventures of his son Hal, the future Henry V (1387–1422), both in taverns and on the battlefield. *Henry V* is perhaps the best known and most popular of all of Shakespeare's English histories. It contains some of Shakespeare's most rousing, patriotic speeches and projects the eponymous hero as a model of chivalric kingship, skilled and courageous military commander, shrewd orator and well-supported ruler of a unified, ordered realm. But as the following chapters reveal, the glorious, honorific image is only part of the story, however beguiling and attractive it may be for audiences and commentators alike. The play also confronts the nature and challenges of rule, the justice of foreign conflict and both the cost and legacy of war; it visits those places never ordinarily seen by jingoistic civilians. The critic Edward Berry certainly does not exaggerate when he calls *Henry V* 'by far the most controversial of the histories'.[1] As many of the critics and editors discussed in this Guide demonstrate, the play inherently seems to force its audiences and readers into various forms of partisanship, into adopting polemic, often polarized critical positions regarding the play and its hero.

THE POLITICS OF HISTORIOGRAPHY

To contextualize the survey of *Henry V*'s critical history that follows, one should begin by relating the practice of criticizing Shakespeare's play to the wider controversy surrounding historiography in the early modern period. Lines of enquiry pursued from the seventeenth century onwards about Henry, Shakespeare and Tudor politics have their origins in sixteenth-century questions about the practice of recording the lives of historical persons. The play's active critical history is in part a response to the fact that historiography, including the writing of historical drama, was a particularly politically charged, ideologically conditioned activity in the early modern period. The accession of Henry VII gave a new impetus to historical writing in England as successive Tudor monarchs sought to contrive a mythical heritage for themselves as a legitimate ruling dynasty by constructing a line of descent stretching from King Arthur down to the sixteenth century. Genealogy and historiography were pressed into the service of political legitimation and panegyric, and *The Faerie Queene* (1590; 1596) by Edmund Spenser (c. 1552–99) was one of the most developed examples of the many literary treatments of the Tudors' mythical British origins. Interest in the study of national 'antiquities' – including topography, archaeology, chorography, heraldry, as well as what nowadays would be classed as local history and folklore – was also fed by a new national self-consciousness occasioned in no small part by the English Reformation and separation of the Church of England from papal Rome. Mythical British history and the study of chronicles of the post-Norman Conquest period were employed to both counter Catholic claims of papal sovereignty over the English church and assert that Christianity was established in England long before Roman missionaries arrived in the sixth century. The history of Henry V also had a particular genealogical connection to the ruling dynasty in Shakespeare's day as Elizabeth I (1533–1603) was descended from the line of Owen Tudor (c. 1400–61) and the king's widow Katherine (1401–37).

Early modern historiography was grounded upon the idea that the past provided lessons and role models for the present. When Shakespeare and his contemporaries chose to deal with real historical subjects in their works, however, artistic choices also had political implications, and topical points of reference and application could prove dangerous. As Sir Walter Ralegh (c. 1552–1618) observed in his monumental *History of the World* (1614): 'who-so-ever in writing a moderne Historie, shall follow truth too neare the heeles, it may happily strike out his teeth'.[2] This particularly proved to be the case in 1599, the year in which *Henry V* was first staged. In February, the lawyer John Hayward (c. 1564–1627) published his prose history *The First Part of the Life and Reign of King Henry IV*, which dealt extensively with Richard II's deposition and debated the legitimacy of usurping the throne from an unfit ruler. What made Hayward's history particularly controversial was his Latin dedicatory epistle to Robert Devereux, the second Earl of Essex (1567–1601). Essex rose to power during the 1590s as a royal favourite at the Elizabethan court.

His active, martial posturing and calls for a holy war against the Spanish, who had been engaged in a bitter conflict with the Dutch in the nearby Netherlands for the last 25 years, hearkened back to the militant Protestant pseudo-chivalry of the Earl of Leicester (1533–88) and Sir Philip Sidney (1554–86), whose widow Essex married. He appeared to represent the answer to popular concerns about the royal succession and the aging queen's growing unpopularity. Hayward's dedication naturally invited comparison between Essex and Bolingbroke, implicitly gesturing towards the courses of action that could be taken. In July 1599 Hayward was questioned by the Privy Council and imprisoned in the Tower of London. The same year, responding to both the Hayward affair and more widespread popular enthusiasm for satirical writing that had been developing throughout the decade, the Archbishop of Canterbury, John Whitgift, (c. 1530–1604) and Bishop of London, Richard Bancroft (1544–1610), imposed an order including the direction that 'noe English historyes be printed excepte they bee allowed by some of her maiesties privie Counsell'.[3] Texts on English historical subjects attracted the most careful scrutiny and, on occasion, censorship during the late Elizabethan and early Jacobean periods. Lines from the scene depicting the king's deposition in Shakespeare's *Richard II* (1595–6) were cut from all printed versions of the play until 1608. Topical allusions in the play were acted upon, literally, in February 1601 when Essex's supporters arranged to stage 'the killing of Richard II' at the Globe theatre the night before the earl's abortive attempt to rouse London citizens into supporting a *coup d'etat*. Essex was arrested, tried and executed within the month.

Thus even in Shakespeare's day, historical drama was consciously constructed and presented as a site for critical controversy. Indeed, a number of modern critics have argued that a significant element of early modern historical drama's content was a reflective commentary upon the history play form itself. Ivo Kamps, writing in 1996, maintains that a perennial theme of historical drama is the production and uses of histories themselves, and in particular, the partial, provisional and 'man-made' nature of history-making and the attendant questioning it invites.[4] Paola Pugliatti in *Shakespeare the Historian* (1996) echoes such sentiments in arguing that Shakespeare's plays set out multiple perspectives, judgements and experiences of historical events, just as a historian sifts and orders their documents and evidence, and then sets this out to their reader for evaluation. As we shall see, such a practice manifests itself in *Henry V* through Shakespeare's use of multiple languages and registers in the play and the ambivalence generated by the Chorus's often contradictory (and contradicted) view of historical events when set alongside actions dramatically represented within the main scenes.[5]

THE HISTORICAL HENRY V

It should also be noted that the historical Henry V himself was a site of controversy from his very earliest textual representation in fifteenth-century chronicles, biographies and literary accounts. Henry is fashioned as the model of a pious ruler and exemplar for future generations in contemporary Latin sources such as the 1417 *Gesta Henrici Quinti* ('Deeds of Henry V'), the metrical life *Liber Metricus* by Thomas Elmham (1418) and Tito Livio's *Vita Henrici Quinti* ('Life of Henry V') that was written in 1437–8 at the behest of Henry's brother Humphrey, Duke of Gloucester (1391–1447).[6] Perhaps not surprisingly, however, there is a great difference between English and French sources in the picture of Henry that emerges in fifteenth-century accounts of the battle of Agincourt (25 October 1415) and the French campaigns as a whole. The former tell of Henry's benevolence and clemency to the French population while the latter depict the terror and brutality of the king's conquest and occupation. As his reign progressed, commentators at home also began to criticize Henry for the great cost of the French wars. The Welsh chronicler Adam of Usk (c. 1350–1430) complained in 1421 that

■ the lord king is now fleecing anyone with money, rich or poor, throughout the realm, in readiness for his return to France. Yet I fear, alas, that both the great men and the money of the kingdom will be wasted in the enterprise. No wonder, then, that the unbearable impositions being demanded from the people to this end are accompanied by dark – though private – mutterings and curses, and by hatred of such extortions.[7] □

Similarly, in an anonymous dream-vision poem called *The Crowned King* included in a mid-fifteenth-century miscellany, a clerk figure petitions the king about tax increases incurred by the commoners to 'susteyne his werres', reminding him that his people's love is a more valuable treasure for him to seek.[8] As will be shown, the cost of war – in both human and financial terms – is a recurrent feature of criticism on and *in* Shakespeare's plays.

THE STRUCTURE OF THIS GUIDE

Critics and editors frequently comment upon and lament the perceived homogeneity of criticism on *Henry V*. Too often the play is thought to invite rather less than adventurous lines of enquiry centred on King Henry himself and, for all its latter-day popularity on the stage and screen, it is viewed as a simplistic, uninspirational conclusion to Shakespeare's own exploration of monarchy identified in both tetralogies. Joseph Candido and Charles R. Forker affirm, in the introduction to their annotated bibliography for *Henry V* (1983), that while the play does attract an active, often heated critical commentary, this is less 'various or inventive' than that for other Shakespearean plays.[9] Many play editions or essay collections characterize *Henry V* criticism as being, for the most part, a polarized debate on whether Henry is 'good' or 'bad' as a person and/or king, and use this as the model for their own short reception histories. For the Oxford Shakespeare editor Gary Taylor, the play divides critics simply between those in favour of Henry and those who favour pacifism, the centrality of war in *Henry V* shaping the direction of responses along preordained lines.[10] It is undeniably true that a vast amount, indeed perhaps the majority, of criticism on *Henry V* has been primarily character-oriented, reflecting an ongoing obsession among audiences and scholars with every nuance of Henry's personality, psychology, politics, motivations and morals. There is a danger, however, that such a reductive approach to the play's critical history encourages an overly simplified response for future critics and students.

The aim of this Guide is to provide a detailed narrative and analytic overview of some of the key critical positions adopted in the ongoing controversy about *Henry V* between the seventeenth and twenty-first centuries. It will examine the most significant ideas and preoccupations of the play's critical history, tracing the development of major critical currents and attempting at each stage to stress the subtlety and variety of criticism on *Henry V*. It *will* perforce revisit debates centred on Henry but aims to use earlier criticism productively and do justice to the many critics who have broken away from the polarizing, binary approach. Unlike Candido and Forker's bibliography, this Guide employs an accessible chronological narrative and, rather than seeking to be dispassionately exhaustive and all-inclusive, aims to describe and offer critical value judgements on a representative selection of *Henry V* criticism. A Guide of this size cannot pretend to cover every topic or period of the play's reception, and for reasons of space, there is less discussion of criticism that simply revisits accepted positions in ongoing debates without itself contributing much that is new or contentious. I have also had to restrict discussion of wider thematic studies that relate *Henry V* to a governing thesis on Shakespeare's treatment of kingship across the histories more than they analyse individual properties of the play itself.[11] While this Guide does not to attempt to offer any extended form of performance history, stage and screen adaptations are mentioned as and when they relate to major critical debates on *Henry V*. Those interested further in the play in performance are directed to the studies by James Loehlin (1996) and Emma Smith (2002).[12]

The first chapter of this Guide addresses some of the most elementary, though greatly contested, questions relating to the form and composition of *Henry V*, exploring controversies concerning its date, sources and textual ontology. It begins by considering how the play may be dated by an allusion to Essex's 1599 expedition to Ireland and then turns to the changing ways in which modern critics and editors, including Annabel Patterson, Andrew Gurr, Gary Taylor and T. W. Craik, have discussed the political and aesthetic implications of Shakespeare's choice of sources. Inexorably connected with the two preceding topics, the issue of the relative merits of the Quarto and Folio texts has attracted extensive critical attention during the late twentieth century consonant with increased interest in individual sites of performance and presentation. The final section of this chapter charts the debate concerning the status of the Quarto and the key ideas presented by Taylor and Gurr.

Chapter 2 looks at seventeenth- and eighteenth-century responses that begin to judge *Henry V* according to neoclassical critical principles, and the successive attempts by a variety of commentators to form new ways of viewing, editing and applying the play, starting with John Dryden (1631–1700). Attention then turns to eighteenth-century commentaries by Nicholas Rowe (1674–1718), Charles Gildon (1665–1724), Alexander Pope (1688–1744), Lewis Theobald (1688–1744) and Thomas Hanmer (1677–1746), and their respective visions of how the play ought to have been written. Of particular concern for many eighteenth-century critics was the role of the Chorus and its professed attempt to apologize for the limitations of the early modern stage. The Chorus continued to trouble Shakespeare's greatest eighteenth-century editor, Samuel Johnson (1709–84), and his commentary on the play also reveals a preoccupation with the fate of Falstaff, a topic that re-appears consistently in *Henry V* criticism for the following two centuries. The chapter concludes by examining the relationship between eighteenth-century critical concerns and contemporary attempts to 'improve' *Henry V* according to neoclassical dramatic tastes written by Roger Boyle, Earl of Orrery (1621–79) and Aaron Hill (1685–1750).

Chapter 3 begins with two early nineteenth-century Romantic critics, August Wilhelm von Schlegel (1767–1845) and William Hazlitt (1778–1830), and their reactions to eighteenth-century scholarship. While Schlegel offers new ways of conceiving the unity of *Henry V*, Hazlitt launches a notoriously aggressive attack on the king's character itself and, in doing so, establishes an influential precedent both for character-centred readings of the play and, albeit later in the play's critical history, for anti-Henry interpretations. The chapter then moves on to look at two German critics, Hermann Ulrici (1806–84) and Georg Gottfried Gervinus (1805–71), and their treatment of history and nationhood in *Henry V*. This is followed by discussion of the play's first historicist interpretation, offered by Richard Simpson (1820–76). Character criticism remains a central component of nineteenth-century scholarship, and the chapter explores both the positive responses to Henry by Edward Dowden (1843–1913) and R. G. Moulton (1849–1924), and the more negative critique of William Watkiss Lloyd (1813–93).

The emphasis on character also informs *Henry V* criticism of the early twentieth century and Chapter 4 opens by examining the pro-Henry patriotic interpretations of Sir Sidney Lee (1859–1926), Felix E. Schelling (1858–1945) and J. A. R. Marriott (1859–1945). In exploring the depths of Henry's character, many of the critics discussed in this chapter also address the question 'what makes a good king?' and begin to confront the notion that effective rulers are not always bound to idealized standards of moral integrity. The most influential essentialist character critic A. C. Bradley (1851–1935) identifies that a good king and a good man are not necessarily the same thing. Even more scathing towards the play and its hero is Gerald Gould (1885–1936), and this chapter examines at length both the tenor and legacy of his anti-Henry reading. Gould's essay reminds us that the play is about justifying, fighting and winning war, and that *Henry V* carries with it all of the reasoned and emotive controversy surrounding modern warfare. The 'king versus man' question continues on into mid-century criticism and frames the essays of John Palmer (1885-1944) and Una Ellis-Fermor (1894–1958), both of which appear in 1945 but are discussed here due to their thematic coherence with Bradley and Gould's work.

Chapter 5 concentrates on a number of critics writing during the 1940s that use *Henry V* in different ways to talk about historical contextualization, both at the point at which the play was composed and during the Second World War. After considering the patriotic critical appropriation of *Henry V* by G. Wilson Knight (1897–1985), which appeared in the same year as the well-known cinematic adaptation by Laurence Olivier (1907–89), attention turns to E. M. W. Tillyard (1889–1962) and one of the most influential studies of Shakespeare's histories ever written. The chapter charts how Tillyard and Lily B. Campbell (1883–1967) develop a historicist mode of criticism as they attempt to reconstruct how *Henry V* engaged with the world view of Elizabethan politics and philosophy. Further sections then discuss how the editors of two important post-war critical editions, John Dover Wilson (1881–1969) and J. H. Walter, offer an extended defence of Henry's character and explore how the play can be better understood as a form of dramatic epic.

While historicism remains, to the present day, a major influence in *Henry V* criticism, there is a danger that attempts to reconstruct the play's historical and ideological context, or to fit the play to such a reconstruction, not only risk reductivism and over-simplification but ignore its formal and aesthetic aspects. Chapter 6 considers how a number of critics during the 1950s–1970s respond to ambivalence and doubleness in *Henry V* and identify how Shakespeare actively complicates an unequivocal interpretation of Henry throughout the play using parody, parallelism and alienation devices (such as the Chorus) to foster our own interrogative response both to the play and its hero. The chapter begins by looking at two pairs of critics whose reactions against historicism complement each other and draw out the value of one another's works within the play's critical tradition. The essay on ambivalence by A. P. Rossiter (d. 1957) is juxtaposed with that of Harold C. Goddard and although the former largely fails to see the potential of his model of dramatic irony and ambivalence for new interpretations of *Henry V*, his essay performs a vital role in informing the direction and vocabulary of later readings that foreground Shakespeare's conscious use of ambiguity. The chapter then reviews the work of S. C. Sen Gupta and Robert Ornstein who each challenge earlier critical approaches and draw attention back to the play's aesthetic qualities. It then concludes by discussing Norman Rabkin's essay on the onus placed upon the audience to select between diametrically opposed, irreconcilable interpretations of *Henry V*. Rather than viewing the play simply as a passive embodiment of Tudor orthodoxy, the critics discussed here remind us of the aesthetic, dramatic dimension, and of how Shakespeare plays with history and its interpretation.

Chapters 7 and 8 discuss a range of critical works produced during the later twentieth century and early twenty-first century, and adopt a broadly thematic approach to illustrate the increasing diversity evident in modern treatments of the play. Chapter 7 begins by analysing two highly influential essays of the 1980s by Stephen Greenblatt, Jonathan Dollimore and Alan Sinfield that break away from pro- and anti-Henry interpretations and, using a mixture of selective close reading and wide-ranging recourse to contextual historical materials, attempt to suggest instead how Shakespeare exposes but also perpetuates the operation of the dominant political power or ideology in Elizabethan England. Both essays exemplify the renewed attention that critics give to the material conditions in which early modern literature was produced and presented. Materialist criticism – a term which encompasses both American New Historicism and its British counterpart Cultural Materialism – effectively becomes the dominant critical paradigm in literary studies from this point onwards though its shortcomings are continually challenged by successive generations of critics, each as committed as the last to interrogating and recalibrating the perceived relationship between formal and contextual analysis. The discussion of power in *Henry V* seen in Greenblatt, Dollimore and Sinfield's essays also meshes with critical debates about how Shakespeare portrays Henry's campaign as a struggle to both exclude effeminacy and the feminine and gain mastery over women's bodies. The feminist interpretations by Lance Wilcox, Jean E. Howard and Phyllis Rackin, characterize the king as a would-be rapist and use the most negative terms imaginable to present an anti-Henry reading that indicts the patriarchal social structure he represented and, at least in part, still represents. Attention then turns to a pair of critics – Graham Bradshaw and Tom McAlindon – who counter the claims of Greenblatt, Dollimore and Sinfield and propose their own theories on how reductive analyses of *Henry V*'s subversive potential consistently fail to appreciate the play's complex, exploratory nature.

Chapter 8 examines three major, interconnected topics that have all featured to some degree in earlier *Henry V* scholarship but which have come to dominate late twentieth- and early twenty-first-century criticism. Each of the chapter's three sections introduces some of the key figures that continue to engage in ongoing and newly emerging debates. The chapter begins by surveying the work of Claire McEachern, Alison Thorne and Philip Schwyzer, who have explored how Shakespeare comments reflexively in *Henry V* on the process of remembering and reproducing historical events, and intersects with early modern ideas on the formation of English and British nationhood. It then examines essays by David Baker, Michael Neill, Andrew Murphy and Christopher Highley, who each offer different perspectives on how *Henry V* relates to the Elizabethan colonization of Ireland. The chapter's final section considers one of the most significant and enduring areas of critical interest on *Henry V*: how Henry goes about justifying war. The idea of just war features throughout twentieth-century criticism but it is afforded particular resonance during the early twenty-first century by the ongoing conflicts in Afghanistan and Iraq. The section discusses studies by a number of critics, including Theodor Meron, Steven Marx, R. A. Foakes and John S. Mebane, offering contributions to the debate on the justice of Henry's claim to France and subsequent campaign that will surely continue to inform *Henry V* criticism in the immediate future as Shakespeare scholarship responds to modern international politics. The Conclusion to this Guide continues to look to the future and briefly considers potential directions and challenges for further studies on *Henry V*.

This Guide's broadly chronological organization should not be interpreted as implying that *Henry V*'s critical history adopts a progressive, evolutionary trajectory. Nor is it suggested here that earlier generations failed to adequately understand Shakespeare and the play but that we do so now. As we shall see, critics and commentators emphasize different aspects of the play at different times in response to a range of aesthetic and political factors, conditions and trends. Dover Wilson offers an apposite observation on how each age takes what it needs from Shakespeare according to changing circumstances when he remarks how the playwright 'mirrors in his plays all sorts and conditions, not only of men and women, but also of national and social moods, so that any day one of them may suddenly become topical, even to the inflaming of political passions'.[13]

CHAPTER ONE

Making the Text: Date, Sources, Textual History

This chapter examines several connected areas of critical controversy relating to how and when *Henry V* was composed and presented. There have been many conjectures about the date and initial context of performance, the sources Shakespeare used in the play's composition and the relationship between the Quarto text of 1600 (and its subsequent reprints) and 1623 Folio. This chapter considers some of the more technical issues that underlie much of the play's later critical history, for example, dating criteria and textual scholarship, which are often glossed over by students and commentators coming to the play for the first time. It sets out to elucidate different critics' understanding of the story behind Shakespeare's text and highlights the subjective, creative element frequently applied in reconstructing such a story. It provides, therefore, a series of salutary examples of how many of the tenets commonly accepted as incontrovertible facts about the play and its origins are grounded upon reasoned conjectures about textual and contextual materials, individual and collective value judgements and fervent critical debate.

DATE AND CONTEXT

Shakespeare's *Henry V* is one of a number of plays about the English king to appear on the popular stage in the 1580s and 90s. The anonymous *Famous Victories of Henry the Fifth* (printed 1594, though first performed nearly a decade earlier) dealt both with Henry's youthful wildness in London taverns and his successful reign as king, focusing especially upon victory at Agincourt. The play provided both the structure and selected narrative material for Shakespeare's two *Henry IV* plays (1596–7) and *Henry V*. *Pierce Pennilesse* (1592) by the writer and pamphleteer Thomas Nashe (1567–1601) includes a comment celebrating earlier dramatic treatments of Henry's reign: '[w]hat a glorious thing it is to have Henry the Fifth represented on the stage, leading the French king prisoner, and forcing both him and the Dolphin [Dauphin] to swear fealty'.[1] (Neither the *Famous Victories* nor Shakespeare's play includes such episodes.) The diary of theatre manager Philip Henslowe (c. 1555–1616) also mentions a new play about Henry V that appeared in 1595. As James Shapiro notes in his micro-history *1599: A Year in the Life of William Shakespeare* (2005), Shakespeare obviously had it in mind to write a play on Henry V's reign from 1596, when he made the decision to stretch the narrative materials found in the *Famous Victories* over three plays.[2] Shakespeare promised to return to Henry's story in the epilogue to *2 Henry IV*: 'our humble author will continue the story with Sir John in it, and make you merry with fair Katherine of France; where, for anything I know, Falstaff shall die of a sweat' (Epilogue, 25–8).[3] But as will be seen in later chapters, critics such as Samuel Johnson and A. C. Bradley were censorious about Shakespeare's very limited treatment of Falstaff in *Henry V*.

The decision to write about Henry V, on the part of Shakespeare and his contemporaries, was perhaps understandable given the martial preoccupations of the 1590s, as Andrew Gurr writes:

■ It was a military decade, starting with vivid memories of the Armada of 1588 heightened by a renewed Spanish attempt at invasion in 1592, and marked by the long campaigns that had begun across the North Sea in the 1580s, where English armies were aiding the Protestants of the Netherlands against their Spanish masters.[4] □

There is one particular military expedition that provides important contextual evidence for dating *Henry V*. The Chorus to Act five invites the audience to imagine Henry's triumphant return following victory at Agincourt:

■ But now behold,
In the quick forge and working-house of thought,
How London doth pour out her citizens.
The Mayor and all his brethren, in best sort,
Like to the senators of th'antique Rome
With the plebeians swarming at their heels,
Go forth and fetch their conqu'ring Caesar in –
As, by a lower but high-loving likelihood,
Were now the General of our gracious Empress –
As in good time he may – from Ireland coming,
Bringing rebellion broached on his sword,
How many would the peaceful city quit
To welcome him! □

(5.0.22–34)

The 'General' here has long been identified as the Earl of Essex, who left London on 27 March 1599 to put down the rebellion in Ireland headed by Hugh O'Neill, second Earl of Tyrone (c. 1540–1616). As such, it is the only explicit, non-dramatic reference to a contemporary event found anywhere in Shakespeare's canon.[5] By July 1599, however, it was clear that Essex was not living up to the hype and propaganda that his expedition initially generated, and he returned in disgrace on 27 September and was placed under house arrest for abandoning his command. He continued to receive limited favour from the queen until events came to a head in February 1601 with the abortive coup discussed earlier. The Chorus's allusion thus allows us to date the composition and first performances of *Henry V* to between late March and late June 1599, when news of Essex's limited achievements in Ireland – which certainly did not warrant such an effulgent comparison – started to reach London. The implications of Shakespeare's controversial analogy between Henry and Essex have often informed historicist criticism of *Henry V* from the mid-twentieth century onwards, as will be examined further in later chapters. The Essex context also affects other areas of scholarship on the play. For example, Gurr identifies how *The Mansion of Magnanimitie* (1599) by Richard Crompton (c. 1529–99), a potential source for *Henry V*, recounted a series of historical English victories to provide lessons for the present and concludes with the defeat of the Spanish at Cadiz in 1596 led by Essex.[6] Like Hayward's *History*, Crompton's work included a dedication to the earl encouraging future successes.

There have been two key areas of contention concerning the date and context of *Henry V*. The first relates to the venue in which the play opened. The Chorus's apologetic, metadramatic references to the physical space in which the play is about to be performed – the 'wooden O' of the playhouse itself – have long invited popular speculation as to whether *Henry V* was the first play performed at the Globe theatre on the Thames's south bank, to which Shakespeare's playing company relocated from the Curtain in Shoreditch in 1599. Indeed, it was this line of argument that was pursued in 1997 when *Henry V* was chosen to be the first play staged at the new Globe theatre that now occupies London's Bankside. Dover Wilson notes that it was even once conjectured popularly that Shakespeare himself had played the part of the Chorus.[7] As Gurr observes, the Chorus could actually be apologizing for the inadequacy of the inferior old playhouse that would soon be surpassed by the new Globe.[8] If the March–June window for the first performance is correct, and going on documentary evidence regarding when construction of the Globe began (late February at the earliest), then it seems unlikely that the Globe would be ready before July or August. Given Essex's ignominious conduct by this point and bearing in mind the controversy surrounding historical analogies in Hayward's *History* during the spring, it seems highly unlikely that Shakespeare's company would have chosen to open their new playhouse with a play that alluded to the declining earl.[9]

As Steve Sohmer argues at length in *Shakespeare's Mystery Play* (1999), drawing in part on astronomical and calendrical evidence, the Globe was more likely to have opened with *Julius Caesar*, which a Swiss tourist, Thomas Platter (1574–1628), records having seen there on 15 September 1599.

Periodically, the theory is also raised that the Chorus's 'General' is not actually Essex at all, but rather the reference is to Charles Blount, Lord Mountjoy (1563–1606), Essex's successor in Ireland, who landed there in February 1600 and defeated Tyrone at Kinsale the following year.[10] The implication of such an argument is that the reference would be inappropriate until Blount's victory at Kinsale, thus dating *Henry V* to 1601. The identification is questionable, however, as Blount was never really held in the same popular esteem as Essex, to the degree evoked by the Chorus. It is also unlikely that Shakespeare would have dwelt upon the French herald's title, as in 3.6.136–7, if it preserved an onomastic echo of his intended Elizabethan hero. Proponents of the Blount argument also propose that the Chorus's speeches were written by someone other than Shakespeare, possibly following publication of the Quarto version in 1600, though this view is undermined by the fact that the Chorus appears to draw on the same historical sources, in the same manner, as the main body of Shakespeare's play.

SOURCES

The principal sources for the political material in *Henry V* were the chronicle histories of Edward Hall (c. 1498–1547) and Raphael Holinshed (d. 1580) that first appeared in 1548 and 1577, respectively, though Shakespeare mainly used the revised 1587 edition of Holinshed. In addition to the chronicles, Shakespeare drew upon the *Famous Victories* for more comic scenes, including the presentation of the Dauphin's tennis balls, Pistol's encounter with the French soldier Le Fer and Henry's wooing of Katherine. The most comprehensive resource extracting and examining the relevant passages is volume four of Geoffrey Bullough's *Narrative and Dramatic Sources of Shakespeare* (1962). The logic behind detailed source study has always been that through examination of how Shakespeare both manipulates and deviates from his sources one might obtain a better impression of the artist at work, perhaps even a greater sense of authorial intention, just as one might from watching a famous painter mix their colours and prepare their palette. Both Bullough and Taylor reveal the extent to which Shakespeare at times paraphrases Holinshed incredibly closely, as in the Archbishop of Canterbury's Salic law speech (1.2.35–101, 130–5) and in the report of how many French and English soldiers were killed at Agincourt (4.8.74–104).[11] Equally as significant are those things that Shakespeare elects to omit or downplay. There is no mention of Lollardy in the play, no hint of the madness of the French king Charles VI (1368–1422) that the historical Henry exploited so successfully, no reference to the importance of English archery at Agincourt and little more than a mumbled hint (in 2.2.155–7) that Richard, Earl of Cambridge's title to the throne lay behind his treason. One of the most contentious episodes in both the chronicle sources and Shakespeare's play is the scene where Henry orders his soldiers to kill their prisoners (4.6.35–7). Holinshed remains ambivalent about the precise motivation to kill the prisoners and in the play this is made manifest as Shakespeare distributes different perspectives on the order between several characters. Henry gives the order as a result of hearing that the French have regrouped ('But hark, what new alarum is this same? / The French have reinforced their scattered men' (4.6.35–6)), whereas the English captain Gower interprets the incident after the event as Henry's revenge for the French attack on the baggage train (4.7.5–10). Shakespeare's plural treatment of the most controversial scene in the entire play constructs the episode from the outset as an object of interpretation and debate. In doing so, Shakespeare sowed the seeds of the extensive critical controversy surrounding the episode, particularly from the twentieth century onwards, and what is interesting for purposes of the present study is the way in which there is a form of continuity between Shakespeare's interpretation of events and the multiple positions that are taken up by later critics. Studies of Shakespeare's manipulation of sources demonstrate that the playwright pays particular attention to three key issues he encounters in the chronicles: Henry's title to the French throne and the argument justifying conquest; the human cost of the war; and Henry's conduct both towards soldiers and civilians during the campaign in France. Again, all three issues are central to the play's modern critical tradition.

Over the last 25 years Shakespeare source study has moved beyond a simple identification of ingredients, and the most productive form of such criticism now remains sensitive to how selection of source inflects the kind of play Shakespeare sought to create, as is exemplified by David Norbrook's essay '*Macbeth* and the Politics of Historiography' (1987).[12] Norbrook's comments on Shakespeare's use of chronicles have particular resonance for *Henry V*:

■ The particular political complexion of Shakespeare's plays can perhaps be determined by analyzing the confrontation between radical sources and the pressures imposed on the public stage by convention and censorship. The result is not bland 'impartiality' but a tension, varying from play to play, between sources and dramatic reworking.[13] □

Developing a similar line of argument, Annabel Patterson in *Reading Holinshed's Chronicles* (1994) confronts those earlier critics whose view of Shakespeare's chronicle sources is epitomized by Michael Tomlinson when he writes that Hall and Holinshed were 'not really concerned with ideas' but that they merely offered the playwright an unambiguous, univocal vision of history.[14] Patterson reveals that Shakespeare's key source-text, Holinshed, not only pursues a 'collaborative agenda' but was consciously conceived as a multivocal, dialogic project in which the reader or 'user' was also a participant. Holinshed conceives his chronicle in such a way, Patterson continues

> ■ because he wished to register how extraordinarily complicated, even dangerous, life had become in post-Reformation England, when every change of regime initiated a change in the official religion, and hence in the meaning and value of acts and allegiances.[15] □

This particularly applied for treatment of Henry V's reign where historians, and writers who used them in their own literary compositions, faced the challenge of transforming the Lollard Sir John Oldcastle from the heretic of medieval Catholic orthodoxy into a proto-Protestant hero and martyr.[16] Early modern historians were forced to confront the inherently partisan, textual nature of historiography, and, as many New Historicist critics have gone on to observe, the textuality of history-making is also registered consciously within Shakespeare's plays themselves.

Shakespeare's manipulation of his sources was certainly not limited to the chronicles, and Gurr demonstrates that Canterbury's fable of the bees' commonwealth, used in 1.2.187–204 to illustrate to Henry the virtues of a correctly ordered state, was taken from the *Institutio Principis Christiani* ('Education of a Christian Prince') by the early sixteenth-century humanist Desiderius Erasmus (c. 1467–1536).[17] There is real irony, however, in the manner in which Erasmus's text is deployed. Canterbury uses the apian model while advocating war, but Erasmus's original supports a wholly pacifist line of argument, maintaining that the king bee never leaves the hive and has smaller wings and no sting, because it does not need them; thus princes should always stay within their realm. Erasmus then criticizes the futility of empire-building since foreign possessions are always ultimately lost in the long term and result in great loss of human life. As Gurr highlights, Shakespeare was certainly cognizant of contemporary pacifist arguments and of the extensive debate on notions of 'just war', and this only serves to support more recent *Henry V* criticism arguing that the justice of war remains one of the play's central themes (see Chapter 8).

There has also been considerable debate on the degree to which Shakespeare works from sources in *Henry V* and questions raised about the relationship between the conscious imitation of documentary materials and the use of literary conventions and contemporary dramatic working practices. The most frequently discussed passage of the play relating to this topic is the episode of Henry's disguised visit to his soldiers on the night before Agincourt (4.1). Neither Hall nor Holinshed refers to an incognito nocturnal visit. Bullough maintains that Shakespeare drew here on an incident described in the *Annals* by Roman historian Tacitus (c. 56–117 AD), where the commander Germanicus (15 BC–19 AD), walks round his camp on the night before a major battle.[18] Tacitus's histories were especially popular during the 1590s and their frank interrogation of the limits of leadership and pragmatic view of political processes were especially popular with those in the Essex circle. The *Annals* were available to Shakespeare in a translation by Richard Grenewey published in 1598. Taylor argues, however, that a closer analogue of Henry's visit is found in *Seven Books of the Iliads of Homer* by George Chapman (c. 1559–1634) which was also published in 1598 and dedicated to Essex, 'the most honoured now living instance of the Achilleian virtues'.[19] The section of Chapman's *Homer* describing Agamemnon's nocturnal walk among his army as they camp outside the walls of Troy bears a number of close verbal parallels with the Chorus to, and first scene of, Shakespeare's Act four.[20] Both attributions have been rejected by the editor of the most recent Arden Shakespeare *Henry V*, T. W. Craik, who argues for a far more organic, performance-oriented genesis of the episode. He advances the rather reductive idea that Shakespeare uses the 'disguised king' device to address the far wider issue of how to integrate the comic element into the core historical narrative, possibly by working backwards from the comic antics of the leek-eating incident in 5.1 which is set up the night before Agincourt, during Henry's encounter with Williams, and executed using the comic foil of Fluellen.[21]

Craik appears to base his reasoning upon conclusions drawn by Anne Barton in her essay 'The King Disguised: Shakespeare's *Henry V* and the Comical History' (1975). Barton draws attention to a number of instances in contemporary historical romances staged between 1587 and 1600, such as George Peele's *Edward I* (c. 1591) and Thomas Heywood's *Edward IV* (1599), in which royal figures disguise themselves and interact with their subjects for reasons that are 'fundamentally exploratory and quixotic'.[22] Such episodes evoke in turn a popular folkloric motif whereby a commoner meets and interacts with a disguised monarch as a fantasy or wish-fulfilment of inter-class social harmony unburdened by the trappings of royal ceremony, and in each of the contemporary dramatic iterations of the motif both commoner and king are enriched by the experience. But Henry's encounters with his men are far less idealistic than those seen in contemporary historical romances, and even though the quarrel with Williams reaches a comic conclusion in 5.1, the scene merely reaffirms his inferior status as a subject and does not begin to address the concerns he expressed about the king's cause.[23] Shakespeare's use and inversion of the 'disguised king' motif ultimately demonstrates the price that Henry has to pay for his success as a king, how he has to subordinate himself as an individual to his royal office.[24] Barton refers here to the idea of 'the King's Two Bodies', a legal fiction developed in the mid-sixteenth century (though based on medieval constitutional theory) that sought to distinguish between the physical 'body natural' of a monarch and their undying 'body politic', the office and identity they inherit as king or queen. The evocation of the historical romance dramatic tradition is a further example, argues Barton, of how Shakespeare goes about interrogating the nature of kingship itself. Barton's greatest contribution to the critical debate about sources is that she questions our reliance upon Shakespeare's documentary sources and draws attention back to the competitive, reactive social world of the Elizabethan playhouses and the cultural environment in which Shakespeare lived and worked.[25] In doing so, Barton also anticipates the direction of later historicist criticism that seeks to de-prioritize the idea of a purely text-based tradition from which authors draw when composing their works.

TEXTUAL CONTROVERSIES

Inexorably connected with the two preceding sections, the issue of the relative merits of the Quarto and Folio texts has attracted extensive critical attention, particularly during the later twentieth century. Until relatively recently, the focus has been predominantly on the version of *Henry V* in the First Folio (abbreviated here as F1) that has been used since the early eighteenth century as the basis for all printed editions of the play. The rationale for this has always been that this simply offers the most authoritative record of Shakespeare's intentions as is declared by the editors of F1, John Heminges (1560–1630) and Henry Condell (1576–1627), whose prefatory and editorial materials (including the table of contents organized by genres) have proved to be some of the most influential pieces of Shakespearean criticism. In their dedication 'To the Great Variety of Readers' they profess to having corrected earlier 'divers[e] stolen and surreptitious copies' of Shakespeare's plays maintaining that 'those are now offered to your view cured and perfect of their limbs, and all the rest absolute in their numbers, as he conceived them'.[26] This did not prevent F1 as a whole from attracting criticism from Shakespeare's early editors. Alexander Pope lamented that Shakespeare's very first editors were actors rather than scholars and scorned Heminges and Condell for the host of perceived errors they introduced to the play texts. Pope concludes that

■ there can be no question but had Shakespear published his works himself (especially in his latter time, and after his retreat from the stage) we should not only be certain which are genuine; but should find in those that are, the errors lessened by some thousands.[27] □

Pope does later concede that the Folio offers an 'extremely improved' version of *Henry V* to that found in the Quarto.

The textual history of *Henry V* is arranged in three stages. It appears to have started with a manuscript closely based on an authorial draft that formed the basis for F1. A Quarto text of *Henry V* (Q1) was then printed in 1600 as *The Cronicle History of Henry the fift, With his battell fought at Agin Court in France. Togither with Auntient Pistoll*. Subsequent Quarto versions were reprinted from Q1 in 1602 and 1619 (falsely dated 1608). Q1 was a much shorter text and omits over half the number of lines found in F1, including all of the Chorus's speeches; scenes 1.1, 3.1 (including the famous 'Once more unto the breach' speech), 4.2; and some of the more negative passages describing, for example, Henry's responsibility for Falstaff's death, the fate awaiting Harfleur's citizens should they not submit to Henry and Burgundy's vision of France's desolation following the English conquest. F1 was then printed in 1623 and restored all of the missing materials, including – perhaps most noticeably – the Chorus. It is this version of the text with which modern audiences and readers will be most familiar. The key debates surrounding the play text(s) and relative merits of Q1 and F1 all concern the relation and perceived hierarchy of authority between the three stages of composition and editing. Textual controversy surrounding *Henry V* emerges in the early twentieth century as an aspect of what became known as the 'New Bibliography' movement, which emphasized the need to address the technical aspects of early modern printing, handwriting and composition with much greater rigour and sophistication than before. In Shakespeare studies the New Bibliographers sought in particular to distinguish 'good' quartos (those produced from an authorial manuscript provided by the author or playing company) from the 'bad' (shortened, pirated editions produced without the authority of Shakespeare's company for use in provincial touring). As A. W. Pollard (1859–1944), E. K. Chambers (1866–1954) and others concluded, Q1 should be assigned to the latter group.[28]

One of the most significant modern statements on the Quarto versus Folio issue is Gary Taylor's 'The Text of *Henry V*: Three Studies' (1979), a series of bibliographic analyses of *Henry V* demonstrating the editing principles underlying the Oxford Shakespeare *Complete Works*, which are also conveniently distilled into a more user-friendly version in Taylor's introduction to his individual *Henry V* edition. Taylor verified the priority of F1 by demolishing the idea that Q1 is an earlier version of the text and confirmed the conclusions of earlier (New) bibliographers that Q1 is 'the result of a reconstruction by memory of the play as performed – as performed, moreover, in a severely abridged and adapted text, such as might have been used by a troupe of actors touring the provinces'.[29] Taylor assumes that many of the cuts in Q1 are made for performance to a less learned audience such as one might expect to find in the provinces.[30] As has long been noted, the particular accuracy of reconstruction in speeches by Gower and Exeter suggests that the actors playing these parts were responsible for assembling Q1 from memory. Taylor goes on to reconstruct casting assignments for the play, calculating how different roles would be doubled by actors in a reduced touring troupe. He concludes that Q1 omits the Chorus because, due to shared scenes and timing of exits and entrances, it could not be played by an actor of any of the other roles and thus compromised doubling possibilities in a smaller company.[31] Taylor's 1982 edition is more charitable than his earlier study towards Q1's utility and potential as he concedes that it 'represents a transcript of the text of Shakespeare's play by two men whose living depended on their memories, and who had acted in *Henry V* within a year or so of its first performance'.[32]

The predominantly negative view of Q1 expressed by Taylor and others has been challenged more recently by several editors committed to removing the perceived hierarchy between different versions of the play and to drawing attention to the 'plural form' of the earliest versions of Shakespeare's works.[33] Graham Holderness and Bryan Loughrey's short introduction to their 1993 edition of Q1 repudiates Taylor's arguments and maintains instead – returning to the rather elementary polarized terms used by Pollard – that it really is 'an extremely good play'.[34] As with Taylor's reading of Q1, everything hinges on the issue of authority and how one chooses to define or constitute an authoritative Shakespeare text in a critical environment where authorial holographs are now almost wholly lost. Holderness and Loughrey reject the idea that Q1 represents a memorial reconstruction preferring to read the text as an accurate record of an authorized, purposively abridged text used in provincial performance. They also begin to gesture towards the impact that such an abstract and brief rendition of Henry's history would have had on initial audiences and assert that Q1 offers a far more comic version of the king due to the great shortening of long speeches and serious materials. Like the *Famous Victories*, Q1 presents a more festive, comic-romance version of history presented through 'continual interrelations and transactions of meaning between "serious" and "comic" scenes, unpunctuated by any epic distancing'.[35]

Gurr develops the idea that Q1 offers us a unique insight into how one of Shakespeare's plays was originally performed in his New Cambridge Shakespeare editions of both Q1 (2000) and the Folio-based version of *Henry V* (2005). Gurr's view is that Q1 is based on an authorial manuscript sold to Shakespeare's playing company, the Lord Chamberlain's servants, in 1599, which was only later printed as F1, and that it represents a radical revision of raw material found in the initial play manuscript that was made to confront the many challenges of performing Shakespeare's play, both in London and the provinces in 1599–1600.[36] The great speed with which Q1 makes it to press, Gurr argues, suggests that it is an official, rather than pirated, transaction based on a fully authorized transcription.[37] F1 gives us a version of *Henry V* that Shakespeare originally wrote, whereas Q1 gives us what his company made of it, whether for staging or for its first readers.[38] Q1 provides a greater insight into a version of the play closer to that staged by Shakespeare and his company than any form seen by modern audiences. For this reason, and because it offers a test-case for examining what happens between a play's first draft and its first appearance on stage, Q1 is therefore far more valuable than has been argued previously. Of greatest interest here is the way in which Q1 suggests how Shakespeare's company dealt with practical staging problems and political ambiguities implicit in the original manuscript that have come through to F1 and thence into the wider world of critical controversy. The script editors of the Lord Chamberlain's servants might therefore be seen as the very first critics of *Henry V*, and, as this Guide testifies, they were certainly not the last to find themselves preoccupied with inconsistencies and ambiguities raised by the Folio text. For example, the omission in Q1 of the Chorus to, and opening speech of, Act three ('Once more unto the breach') appears to resolve the potentially negative implications, seen in F1, generated by discrepancies between what the Chorus praises, what we hear from Henry's rousing speech and the implied failure of the siege and assault that necessitates the threats to Harfleur's governor in 3.3.[39] Q1 shifts immediately to a far less aggressive confrontation with the governor and omits suggestion that any breach in Harfleur's walls is presently closed up with English dead bodies. The rewriters were also therefore able to minimize treatment of Harfleur so as to foreground the Agincourt battle.[40]

Gurr's considered analysis of Q1 rehabilitates any notions we may have of the pejorative associations of 'bad' quartos and forces us to contextualize, relativize or, at the very least, historicize the prevailing view that the print-based F1 text represents the ideal, authorized Shakespearean version of *Henry V*. Gurr also draws attention to the level of autonomy that existed between Shakespeare and 'his' company and the wide-ranging implications of the fact that Shakespeare seems to have been conscious that he 'was writing for himself, well aware that his own version would not be staged'.[41] The playwright's awareness that the company could alter his texts clearly informs Hamlet's instructions to the players (*Hamlet*, 3.2.38–43). Echoing Gurr in his defence of Quarto editions, and discussing details of the text and audience of Q1 at length, Lukas Erne in *Shakespeare as Literary Dramatist* (2003) argues that the traditional consensus view that Shakespeare wrote only for the stage with little care for posterity in print requires qualification. The very length of Shakespeare's plays, maintains Erne, signals that he evidently had one eye on print-based interaction and a reading audience, rather than simply penning excessive filler material that he knew would be jettisoned during his company's revisions.[42] Perhaps the greatest implication of Gurr's renewed attention to Q1 is the suggestion that the familiar Folio-based text was unlikely to have been heard at the Globe prior to 1623, and probably not until the eighteenth century.[43] Gurr thus challenges the popular vision of the play superbly captured at the start of Laurence Olivier's 1944 movie adaptation of *Henry V* that imagines the Chorus addressing London playgoers on a sunny afternoon at the Globe and gesturing to the playhouse walls surrounding him upon mention of 'this wooden O'. For all of its use in suggesting the intended context for performance in 1599, any form of Chorus drawing parallels between Essex and the returning Henry looks likely to have been absent from initial stagings.

To date there has been very little recent criticism that attempts to yoke together the textual and contextual aspects and examine the implications of re-prioritizing Q1 for our understanding of the date and initial circumstances of the play's first performance. Patterson's essay 'Back by Popular Demand: The Two Versions of *Henry V*' (1989) thus remains one of the best examples of how practical and aesthetic questions of textual ontology relate to contemporary political concerns. Patterson contextualizes different stages of the process, whereby editors and bibliographers associated the perceived textual deficiencies of 'bad' quartos (including Q1) with a wider moral illegitimacy or inadequacy, and ultimately censured their illiterate, inchoate reproduction on more class-conscious grounds.[44] Rather than treating the text as something cut by the playing company for doubling and touring, Patterson identifies Shakespeare's own hand in Q1's abridgement. Shakespeare's motives are primarily political and a response to increased governmental control over works on English history during the 1580s and 90s, including the Hayward controversy that was still ongoing at the time he composed *Henry V*. The Folio-based version of *Henry V* offered an immensely thoughtful meditation both on what it meant to be a popular, well-supported public figure and on relations between sovereign and aristocratic power, in the immediate instance, that of Essex. It would, says Patterson,

> ■ contribute to an argument for a pragmatic reconciliation between general and empress, pragmatic in the sense that 'history', by refusing to settle their rivalry, provided no basis for decisively altering the current allocations of power and lines of authority.[45] □

However, such argument ran counter to the prevailing 'official surveillance' of historical materials. As Sidney stated in the *Defence of Poesy* (c. 1580–1), historians were largely bound methodologically to reproducing the 'bare "was"' of actual events – both positive and negative – though this did not always make for good propaganda or state-sanctioned historiography.[46] In preparing Q1 in 1600, Shakespeare was thus forced to downplay the Essex-related significance of *Henry V* by omitting all hints of topical allusion and any ambiguity engendered through the plural perspective of the Chorus. Q1 thus presented, Patterson writes, 'an *almost* unproblematic view of a highly popular monarch whose most obvious modern analogy was Elizabeth herself' (Patterson's italics).[47] The reduced text offered yet another way to praise the queen obliquely and contribute to what has become known as the cult of Elizabeth. Q1 is therefore held up to be closer to the unequivocal, patriotic vision of Henry imagined by twentieth-century historicists such as E. M. W. Tillyard, and critics have indeed yet to take up the challenge of finding subversion in Q1.[48]

Henry V is also infamous among editors and scholars for containing the most debated of all Shakespearean textual cruces.[49] In F1, the Hostess, Mistress Quickly, describes the manner of Falstaff's death with the seemingly nonsensical lines: 'For his nose was as sharp as a pen, and a Table of green fields' (2.3.15–16). The eighteenth-century editor Lewis Theobald offered the eminently sensible emendatory conjecture that the lines should read 'and a babbled of green fields'.[50] The word 'a' in this line was a common form for 'he' in Shakespeare's day (and used thus in 3.6.40) and it therefore means that Falstaff babbles about green fields on his deathbed. The lines have attracted a disproportionately high number of responses, given its relative importance in the play. Candido and Forker identify 45 separate items relating to these lines published between 1928 and 1977, 12 of them in 1956 alone, following a piece by the critic Leslie Hotson (1897–1992) in the *Times Literary Supplement* for 6 April the same year rejecting Theobald's emendation.[51] Critics have been divided essentially between those who accept Theobald's reading and those who strive to maintain something close to the F1 original through various means of orthographic, bibliographic, palaeographic and metaphoric explanation. Some have proposed that 'Table' can mean 'picture', and thus Falstaff's skin had a deathly green colour. Others have suggested 'talkd' or 'fabld' in place of the incongruous 'Table'. All modern editors adopt Theobald's emendation, largely saving future generations of readers of *Henry V* from the sort of pedantic preoccupation with Shakespearean minutiae that threatens to give textual scholarship a bad name. As Candido and Forker observe, 'not all of the babbling is Falstaff's'.[52] We will continue to consider some of the earliest critical and editorial responses to *Henry V* in the next chapter.

CHAPTER TWO

The Seventeenth and Eighteenth Centuries: Neoclassicism and Early Editions

There is very little evidence of how Shakespeare's first audiences responded to *Henry V*. The title page to the 1600 Quarto declares that it was 'sundry times played by the Right honorable the Lord Chamberlain his servants', and an entry in the Revels accounts mentions a single performance at court by the King's Majesty's Players on 7 January 1605. In the prologue to his revised *Every Man in His Humour* (1616; first performed 1598), Ben Jonson (1572–1637) makes a dismissive allusion to how Shakespeare's own Chorus professedly 'wafts you o'er the seas' (suggested in *Henry V*, 5.0.6–9), and *The Noble Gentleman* (c. 1624–5) by John Fletcher (1579–1625) includes a parody of Canterbury's Salic law speech.[1] Early commentators are otherwise silent on the play and there is no record of it being staged between 1605 and 1738, which is perhaps somewhat surprising, given the Stuarts' penchant for the kinds of masques and pageantry to which it has actually been compared by later critics and directors. Emma Smith suggests that the play's immediate topicality limited its potential for success on the early stage.[2] The play also failed to align with the prevailing aesthetic tastes of the later seventeenth and early eighteenth centuries. The Stuarts and their loyalist supporters had long been influenced by the manners and the intellectual and literary traditions of the French court, and this only increased after the exile of Charles Stuart (1630–85), the future Charles II, in France during the Interregnum (1649–60). Following the Restoration of the monarchy and Charles's accession in 1660, English culture was further suffused with French influences, and the native critical tradition soon came to be dominated by a body of theory that has become known as neoclassicism. The neoclassical critical principles were derived from a selective reading of the Greek philosopher Aristotle (384–322 BC) and Roman poet Horace (65–8 BC) via the extensive debates on classical literary theory found in the writings of sixteenth-century Italian humanists. Neoclassical theory characterized art as an adherence to a system of rules established by the ancients. Creativity was therefore predicated upon an imitation of classical authors and their rules, together with an observance of decorum so as to preserve decency in accord with the manners of contemporary polite society.[3] Of particular importance was the stipulation that dramatists adhered to the three unities of time, place and action in order to sustain the credibility and seemliness of their representation.

Shakespeare's plays frequently fail to adhere to the unities, and a play like *Henry V* caused distinct difficulties when read using neoclassical criteria, as there was no Greek or Roman tradition of historical drama with which to draw comparisons for imitation. The play's episodic quality and its manipulation of time and space, engineered in part through the Chorus, repeatedly attracted particular scorn. The situation was not helped by Jonson's prefatory comment in the 1623 Folio that Shakespeare 'hadst small Latin, and less Greek', which generated well over a century's worth of speculation about the playwright's knowledge of the classics, or lack thereof. The seventeenth and eighteenth centuries saw a series of attempts at rescuing Shakespeare from the tyranny of misapplied and misguided critical and editorial criteria. *Henry V* serves as a useful indicator of exactly how willing successive critics in this period are to detach Shakespeare from increasingly outdated critical doctrines, containing, as it does, so many obvious abuses of the neoclassical rules. John Dryden, the poet and essayist often dubbed the 'father of English criticism', provides several early statements relating to the Restoration reception of *Henry V*.

JOHN DRYDEN

In his essay *Of Dramatic Poesy* (1668), Dryden set out to offer a vindication of English plays through juxtaposing the best of the native dramatic tradition with the works and aesthetic principles of classical and contemporary French literature. Dryden casts his discussion in the form of a debate, held between four interlocutors representing three of his noble contemporaries and himself. The debate typifies the 'Ancients versus Moderns' contention that inflects Shakespeare criticism until well into the eighteenth century and which consequently compromises many responses to *Henry V*. Shakespeare's histories, indeed, attract particular disparagement from one of Dryden's speakers:

■ If you consider the historical plays of Shakespeare, they are rather so many chronicles of kings, or the business many times of thirty or forty years, cramped into a representation of two hours and a half, which is not to imitate or paint nature, but rather to draw her in miniature, to take her in little, to look upon her through the wrong end of a perspective, and receive her images not only much less, but infinitely more imperfect than the life: this, instead of making a play delightful, renders it ridiculous.[4] □

Dryden's critique of English historical drama picks up on the very terms used in *Henry V* by the Chorus (4.0.49–53) to pre-empt attacks upon the play's lack of verisimilitude:

■ What is more ridiculous than to represent an army with a drum and five men behind it; all which, the hero of the other side is to drive in before him, or to see a duel fought, and one slain with two or three thrusts of the foil, which we know are so blunted, that we might give a man an hour to kill another in good earnest with them.[5] □

The Chorus's apologies, which appear to address a similar line of argument earlier advanced in Sidney's *Defence of Poesy*, provide neoclassical critics with the ideal vocabulary and opportunity through which to criticize Shakespeare's abuse of the rules.[6] Dryden uses the histories as a negative native example when viewed alongside Jonson's far more unified and decorous Roman plays, though it should be noted that Neander, the interlocutor representing Dryden himself, ultimately cannot help but admit a preference for Shakespeare over Jonson.

Despite his general criticism of Shakespeare's histories, Dryden does appear to have made use of *Henry V* several years earlier while writing his poem celebrating Charles's accession in June 1660, *Astraea Redux*. The poem was one of many occasional verses produced at the Restoration, but is marked out from those of Dryden's contemporaries by its stress not on who or what King Charles *is*, but on the sort of ruler he will *become*, and it does so, argues Scott Paul Gordon in a 2002 article, through subtle allusions to *Henry V*. Like Prince Hal in the *Henry IV* plays, Charles spent much of his time prior to coming to the throne living a life of debauchery. But through subtly comparing Charles's accession with the point of wondrous transformation seen in Henry, as remarked upon by the churchmen in 1.1, Dryden and his contemporaries could imaginatively resolve the problem of the king's disreputable past.[7] As Gordon points out, *Astraea Redux* picks up many specific points of imagery employed in *Henry V*'s opening scene, particularly those relating to the king's celestial qualities, the floodlike nature of the transformation achieved upon his accession and the 'blessed' nature of the change.[8] The Bishop of Ely's comment that 'The strawberry grows underneath the nettle, / And wholesome berries thrive and ripen best/ Neighboured by fruit of baser quality' (1.1.61–3) may be evoked, Gordon suggests, in Dryden's lines 'Twas not the hasty product of a day, / But the well-ripened fruit of wise delay'.[9] Such oblique allusions to *Henry V* demonstrate the extent to which Shakespeare's language permeated Dryden's own vocabulary, though they require a certain amount of sensitivity and ingenuity on the critic's part. Jonathan Bate performs a similar form of interpretation when he traces how allusions to Henry's wild youth were later employed by caricaturists during the mid-1780s, both to denigrate and ultimately rehabilitate the equally dubious reputation of the young Prince Regent, later George IV (1762–1830).[10] Somewhat more straightforward to examine, however, are the references to *Henry V* made by some of Shakespeare's earliest editors.

EARLY EDITORIAL COMMENTARIES

Some of the earliest criticism on *Henry V* is found in the prefaces and notes to the many scholarly editions of Shakespeare's works that appear during the eighteenth century as editors, like critics and directors, are forced to evaluate and make judgements about individual aspects of the text. As Michael Dobson reveals, the eighteenth-century editors played a vital role in establishing Shakespeare's enduring canonicity during this period and provided much of the groundwork, both textual and interpretative, for all subsequent criticism in the field.[11] Once one gets past the surprising amount of bitchiness found in editorial prefaces regarding respective editors' intellectual capabilities, there is a sustained debate about the merits of Shakespeare's failure to adhere to the neoclassical rules, the implications this has for contemporary literary appreciation, and his anachronistic use of history, especially in the Roman plays.[12] In the preface to the first scholarly edition of Shakespeare's works (published 1709–10), the poet, playwright and editor Nicholas Rowe confronts the neoclassical preference for rules and unities by arguing for a greater appreciation of the aesthetic principles with which Shakespeare was actually working, and maintaining that the playwright should be viewed on his own terms. Rowe praises the history plays for providing an accurate, unmediated mirror of events, and ignores any manipulation Shakespeare may have made to the sequence or inflection of his sources though he identifies the allusion to Essex in the Chorus to Act five.[13] Rowe also identifies a difficulty experienced by many eighteenth-century commentators: the issue of how to place or describe Shakespeare's history plays generically, in part due to the absence of any similar category in classical genre theory.

■ His plays are properly to be distinguished only into comedies and tragedies. Those which are called Histories, and even some of his Comedies, are really Tragedies, with a run or mixture of Comedy amongst them.[14] ☐

Comedy is provided within *Henry V*, argues Rowe, by the verbal presence of Falstaff generated by Mistress Quickly's description of his death.[15] In his Shakespeare edition of 1747 (co-edited with Pope), William Warburton (1698–1779) similarly divided all of the plays into either comedies or tragedies, though classed all of the histories under the latter heading.[16]

A volume of criticism by the essayist and hack writer Charles Gildon was appended to Rowe's edition in 1710. Gildon's 'Remarks on the Plays of Shakespear' are valuable for their treatment of the Chorus in *Henry V*, and they use the admissions therein as evidence that Shakespeare was aware of the principles of unity he transgresses in the play. The Chorus's opening prologue is proof that Shakespeare

■ was extremely sensible of the Absurdity, which then possessed the Stage of bringing in whole kingdoms, and Lives, and various Actions in one Piece; for he apologizes for it, and desires the Audience to persuade their Imaginations to help him out and promises a Chorus to help their Imagination.[17] □

Gildon reads Chorus's declaration that 'tis your thoughts that now must deck our kings' (1.0.28) in terms directly evoking the unities:

■ He here and in the foregoing Lines expresses how preposterous it seemed to him and unnatural to huddle so many Actions, so many Places, and so many Years into one Play, one Stage and two Hours.[18] □

Gildon's rehabilitation of Shakespeare is grounded upon one of the least representative metadramatic devices that he uses in his plays but it shows a determination to allow the playwright's own words to serve in his defence. Gildon still reveals an obsession with the unities despite his attempt to restrict their application to Shakespeare. Had Shakespeare seen but one play structured according to the classical rules then he would have produced even better works, laments Gildon, ignoring the fact that *A Comedy of Errors* (1594) and *The Tempest* (1611) adhere very closely to the unities. The one part of *Henry V* to which Gildon really objects is the final wooing scene between Henry and Katherine (5.2), which he dismissively describes as 'extravagantly silly and unnatural':

■ for why he should not allow her to speak in English as well as the other French I cannot imagine since it adds no Beauty but gives a patched and pye-bald Dialogue of no Beauty or Force.[19] □

Gildon's comments are sensible enough and he is the first of several eighteenth-century critics who question the role of scenes using the French language within the play. His image of the play's piebald or many-coloured texture identifies that Shakespeare is using language – and, crucially, different languages – to create a certain effect (which Gildon believes here is unsuccessful), and initiates a linguistic line of enquiry in *Henry V* criticism that continues into modern scholarship. Shakespeare is clearly doing something with language here; exactly what that might be would remain open to question.

Pope's edition of Shakespeare appeared in 1725 (though dated 1723) and set out to improve on both Heminges and Condell's 1623 'actors' edition' and Rowe's more recent editorial labours. The latter was flawed not least because Rowe drew heavily on the 1685 Fourth Folio, the least accurate of the seventeenth-century folios. Pope sought to restore Shakespeare's text to its pre-print 'perfect' state, purged of all of the errors introduced by Heminges and Condell. He did so by extensively and at times arbitrarily correcting those passages of Shakespeare's text judged to be the earlier editors' additions, alterations and interpolations. Pope does support Rowe, however, in defending Shakespeare from anachronistic, neoclassical readings by arguing that 'to judge therefore of Shakespeare by Aristotle's rules, is like trying a man by the Laws of one Country, who acted under those of another'.[20] He maintains instead that Shakespeare ought to be viewed and judged using different criteria and a more appropriate conception of unity:

■ One may look upon his works, in comparison of those that are more finished and regular, as upon an ancient majestick piece of Gothic Architecture, compared with a neat Modern building: The latter is more elegant and glaring, but the former is more strong and more solemn.[21] □

The reference to Gothic (i.e. medieval) architecture evokes similar structural imagery used by Rowe and Gildon when comparing the relative virtues of ancient and modern literature; it also echoes the sentiments of one of the early eighteenth-century editors of Spenser, John Hughes (1677–1720), who had assisted in Rowe's 1709–10 Shakespeare edition. In his 1715 edition of Spenser, Hughes suggested that *The Faerie Queene* should be read in relation to the context in which it was produced and received, and that neoclassical comparisons to models of antiquity are as inappropriate as a parallel between Roman and Gothic architecture. Hughes proposes instead that so-called Gothic literature may be 'agreeable in its parts', a useful counter to neoclassical conceptions of unity.[22] From this point onwards the works of both Shakespeare and Spenser became key sites at which to discuss the merits of using historical context and native, post-classical conceptions of aesthetics to make sense of early modern literature. This is where later historicist criticism has its roots. Pope makes little specific mention of *Henry V* in his preface and his footnotes on the play relate largely to textual matters. It is in his notes, however, that Pope squares up to one of his rival editors, Lewis Theobald, who had earlier criticized Pope's practice of textual correction. The preface to Theobald's 1733 *Works of Shakespeare in Seven Volumes* argues for a more conservative editorial policy than Pope's, based on making sense of the given text and working to elucidate obscurities and difficult passages. As mentioned in the preceding chapter, perhaps Theobald's greatest contribution to *Henry V* scholarship is his emendation of Mistress Quickly's line about Falstaff's death, and its discursive legacy. Theobald also drew attention to Shakespeare's knowledge of the classics and defended his use of history in arguing that it was not through ignorance that the plays deviate from the actual version of events but 'through the too powerful Blaze of his Imagination; which, when once raised, made all acquired Knowledge vanish and disappear before it'.[23] Theobald thus astutely identifies, not only how historical sources are deployed imaginatively for aesthetic effects, but also the very textuality of historiography itself and the concept that modern theorists call 'emplotment'.[24] Historians do not find a ready-made narrative sequence within historical data but are compelled to impose one through the act of recording and transmitting their results. The relationship between literature and history exercised theorists of both disciplines during the early modern period and it continues to occupy the centre ground of twenty-first-century critical theory through the widespread institutionalization of New Historicism and its distillates in the modern academy, as is discussed in Chapters 7 and 8.

Further editions of Shakespeare appeared throughout the eighteenth century with each editor claiming to have improved on his predecessors. Of these, the 1744 edition by Sir Thomas Hanmer is of greatest interest to the present study, because it cuts out the entire scene where Katherine receives an English lesson from her gentlewoman Alice (3.4). The scene offers an abrupt change of tone from the preceding one in which Henry has just threatened the governor of Harfleur using brutal images of rape and carnage should the besieged citizens continue fruitlessly to hold out. Throughout 3.4, comedy is derived from bawdy wordplay that emerges during the lesson culminating with puns on the French for 'fuck' (*foutre*) and 'cunt' (*con*). Understandably, editors seeking to preserve a decorous vision of Shakespeare had great difficulties with the scene and it was likely to have been cut from eighteenth-century performances.[25] Hanmer relegates it to his notes and while discussing passages of text deemed to be spurious additions advises that

■ The promoter of the present Edition hath ventured to discard but few more upon his own judgment, the most considerable of which is that wretched piece of ribaldry in *King Henry V.* put into the mouths of the French Princess and an old Gentlewoman, improper enough as it is all in French and not intelligible to an English audience, and yet that perhaps is the best thing that can be said of it. There can be no doubt but a great deal more of that low stuff which disgraces the works of this great Author, was foisted in by the Players after his death, to please the vulgar audiences by which they subsisted.[26] □

Hanmer's sentiments were later echoed by Richard Farmer (1735–97) in his *Essay on the Learning of Shakespeare* (1767):

■ Every friend to his [Shakespeare's] memory will not easily believe that he was acquainted with the Scene between Catherine and the old Gentlewoman; or surely he would not have admitted such obscenity and nonsense.[27] □

As with Gildon's criticism of the final wooing scene, the seemingly incongruous use of the French language prompts questions regarding the scene's function within *Henry V* as a whole, questions that have only received anything approaching satisfactory answers in late twentieth-century, gender-oriented scholarship on the play. In the meantime, the most comprehensive eighteenth-century critical response to *Henry V* is found in the editorial apparatus by Samuel Johnson.

SAMUEL JOHNSON

Johnson uses *Henry V* on several occasions in his 1755 *Dictionary* to illustrate points of Shakespearean word-usage but it is in the introduction and commentary to his 1765 Shakespeare edition that we find his most extensive treatment of the play. Johnson's preface begins by acknowledging the historical distance between Shakespeare's age and his own, but then maintains that the plays' characters have a universal reference and applicability. Shakespeare creates characters and scenarios that are credible for all ages: 'his persons act and speak by the influence of those general passions and principles by which all minds are agitated, and the whole system of life is continued in motion'.[28] As part of an extended discussion about Shakespeare's ability to move contemporary readers and audiences and convince them of the credibility of the story being presented to them, Johnson returns to the issue of the unities. Unlike earlier editors, he rejects attempts to judge the history plays using neoclassical criteria that are applicable only to tragedies and comedies and proceeds to use *Henry V* to illustrate his point. Johnson confronts the very logic of the neoclassical unities maintaining that plays are in danger of losing their force and power to move if the audience perceives them to be absurd because of temporal and spatial manipulation.

■ Imitations produce pain or pleasure, not because they are mistaken for realities, but because they bring realities to mind. When the imagination is recreated by a painted landscape, the trees are not supposed capable to give us shade, or the fountains coolness; but we consider how we should be pleased with such fountains playing beside us and such woods waving over us. We are agitated in reading the history of *Henry the Fifth*, yet no man takes his book for the field of Agincourt. A dramatic exhibition is a book recited with concomitants [i.e. physical and verbal accompaniments and variations] that increase or diminish its effect.[29] □

Johnson effectively uses the experience of reading Shakespeare as a model for how to apprehend a performance. Just as we have no difficulty with accepting changes in time, place or plot-line when reading a narrative work and moving between chapters or cantos, so our imagination fills in the gaps when watching a play: '[a] play read affects the mind like a play acted'.[30] In arguing such, Johnson returns to the sentiments of *Henry V*'s Chorus who implores the audience to 'Piece out our imperfections with your thoughts' (1.0.23) and imaginatively transport the characters about the world of the play. The Chorus therefore once again becomes a crucial point at which to measure how commentators make sense of exactly what happens when we go to hear and see a play. For Johnson it is by no means an admission of defeat, as neoclassical readings might treat it, but it registers tacit anxieties about the limits of staging, as he identifies in his textual commentary to *Henry V* itself in relation to the passage immediately following the line quoted above:

■ This passage shows that Shakespeare was fully sensible of the absurdity of showing battles in the theatre, which indeed is never done but tragedy becomes farce. Nothing can be represented to the eye but by something like it and 'within a wooden O' nothing very like a battle can be exhibited.[31] □

Johnson remains troubled by the Chorus right up until the play's final scene and admits that

■ The lines given to the Chorus have many admirers; but the truth is that in them a little may be praised and much must be forgiven; nor can it be easily discovered why the intelligence given by the Chorus is more necessary in this play than in many others where it is omitted.[32] □

Johnson's discussion of how the play engages an audience, and his treatment of the Chorus here, brings to the fore a major, recurrent issue in *Henry V* criticism: the audience's role in supplementing, interpreting and evaluating the information (or 'intelligence') presented to us by the many different voices of the play. At this point Johnson does not register that the Chorus's intelligence in fact contradicts much of what we actually see staged within each scene, though he identifies an interpretative fault-line which continues to occupy modern critics.

Elsewhere in his commentary Johnson mentions Katherine's English lesson, but passes over any suggestion of impropriety in favour of using the scene to exemplify, what he disparagingly calls, the 'French spirit':

> ■ Alice compliments the Princess upon her knowledge of four words and tells her that she pronounces like the English themselves. The Princess suspects no deficiency in her instructress, nor the instructress in herself. Throughout the whole scene there may be found French servility and French vanity.[33] □

Johnson likes Henry's soliloquy in 4.1 on the night before battle, but scorns the St Crispin's day speech in the following scene and churlishly, perhaps debatably, observes that the king was wrong to assume that the feast of Crispin would forever be associated with Agincourt: 'Late events obliterate the former: the civil wars have left in this nation scarcely any tradition of more ancient history'.[34] Echoing Gildon, Johnson finds the wooing scene to be the play's weakest part and criticizes the unseemliness of Henry's workmanlike attempts to win Katherine. Ever keen to defend Shakespeare's artistry, Johnson blames the scene's failings on its subject matter:

> ■ The truth is that the poet's matter failed him in the fifth act and he was glad to fill it up with whatever he could get; and not even Shakespeare can write well without a proper subject. It is a vain endeavour for the most skilful hand to cultivate barrenness, or to paint upon vacuity.[35] □

Johnson's most consistent preoccupation in his commentary to *Henry V* is the fate of Falstaff and his Eastcheap companions and he highlights each point in the play that looks back to the jovial world of the *Henry IV* plays. Johnson spends as many lines remarking on Mistress Quickly's description of Falstaff's death as Shakespeare takes to express the event itself and he rebukes the playwright somewhat for failing to deliver on what he had promised at the end of *2 Henry IV*: 'Let meaner authors learn from this example that it is dangerous to sell the bear which is yet not hunted, to promise to the public what they have not yet written'.[36] He concludes that Shakespeare could not ultimately accommodate Falstaff's presence within the 'general design' of *Henry V*. With Pistol's exit in 5.1.82, Johnson finally bids farewell to the comic spirit of the three plays about Henry and believes that every reader regrets its departure. He would not be the last to suck every part of the comic marrow out of the Eastcheap contingent's lines in *Henry V*. The comic characters have consistently proved popular on the stage; but Johnson's commentary on *Henry V*, together with that on the *Henry IV* plays, is one of the first examples of what becomes a veritable critical obsession with Falstaff that never really abates until the later twentieth century.

Johnson's edition constitutes a turning point in eighteenth-century Shakespeare studies due to the sophistication both of his editing and his depth of insight into the plays. His prefatory statements and consistent interest in the Falstaffian elements of the play sowed the seeds for the burgeoning character-centred discussions that would become a hall-mark of nineteenth-century criticism, and may have stimulated one of the earliest Shakespearean character studies focused on a single figure, *An Essay on the Dramatic Character of Sir John Falstaff* (1777) by Maurice Morgann (1762–1802). Like many of the eighteenth-century editors, Johnson came to establish the critical agenda for later responses to *Henry V* by identifying some of the most problematic parts of the play: the role of the Chorus, the presence of comic elements in historical narrative, the significance of languages and the exercise of the audience's imaginative and evaluative faculties.

NEOCLASSICAL ADAPTATIONS

Conterminous with the editorial and interpretative labours of the eighteenth-century critics and a wholesale attempt to correct and improve Shakespeare, one finds an almost contradictory situation on the contemporary stage, where the majority of his plays were performed in heavily adapted versions, many of which were modified in line with the neoclassical aesthetic principles hotly discussed by the scholars. The rhymed verse drama *The History of Henry the Fifth* (published 1668) by Roger Boyle, Earl of Orrery, is little more than a fantasia using aspects and characters of Shakespeare's play. It deals largely with events follow-ing Agincourt and omits any form of physical representation of the battle in favour of a verbal report of the French defeat. There is no question as to the justice of Henry's cause and even the French themselves admit their villainy and hold themselves responsible for their prisoners' deaths in response to their attack on the English baggage.[37] The play then shifts to a far more amorous theme and follows Henry and a new character, Owen Tudor, as they vie for Katherine's affections. The play as a whole consists mainly of a series of verbal exchanges and descriptions of offstage events, as befit neoclassical dramatic principles, and it reaches its climax with the Treaty of Troyes (1520), the Dauphin's complaint upon being disinherited and the French capitulation to Henry. Boyle's play is of most interest here in that it serves as a dramatic counterpart to the sentiments of Dryden's *Astraea Redux* and continues to celebrate Charles's accession and reign through comparisons with his successful forebear suggested by its central theme of a rightful heir inheriting a kingdom and wooing a Katherine (as Charles had).[38] Samuel Pepys (1633–1703) saw performances of Boyle's play in 1664 and 1668 and described it as 'a most noble play—full of height and raptures of sense'.[39]

While in no sense an adaptation of Shakespeare's play per se, the 1720 farce *The Half-Pay Officers* by Charles Molloy (1706–67) continues to show the enduring appeal of *Henry V*'s comic contingent as it incorporates the characters and dialogue of Fluellen, Macmorris and a Pistol-like figure called Culverin who participates in a leek-eating scene. A far more developed adaptation of *Henry V* from this period is Aaron Hill's *King Henry the Fifth: Or, the Conquest of France, By the English: A Tragedy* (written 1721; first performed and published 1723). Like several of the contemporary editors that sought to treat Shakespeare's histories as either comedies or tragedies, ignoring the distinct existence of historical drama, Hill recasts *Henry V* as a tragedy structured according to neoclassical ideas of unity and decorum. Hill earns his place in a critical reception history of *Henry V* as his text offers a number of creative solutions to the many perceived problems with Shakespeare's play identified by the early editors. Even before penning his play, Hill had jousted in print with Pope and corresponded with fellow Shakespeareans, Gildon and John Dennis (1657–1734).[40] As Smith highlights, Hill's adaptation adheres far more closely to the unities 'by confining the action to France and opening the play at Harfleur'.[41] Hill's plot foregrounds the machinations of the three traitors: Cambridge, Scrope and Grey, and introduces the character of Harriet, Scrope's niece, as the instrument of their cause. Harriet had previously been loved and left by Henry and now seeks revenge for her abandonment through following the king to France disguised in men's clothes – like several of Shakespeare's own stage heroines – and aiding her uncle's plot. From the outset of Hill's text and the rewritten prologue, the play promises to offer more in the way of developed female roles and clearly signals that this is to be a tragedy of love more than war:

■ Hid, in the Cloud of Battle, Shakespear's Care,
Blind, with the Dust of War, overlook'd the Fair [i.e. women]:
Fond of their Fame, we shew their Influence, here,
And place them, twinkling through War's smokey Sphere.
Without their Aid, we lose Love's quickening Charms;
And sullen Virtue mopes, in sterile Arms.
Now, rightly mixed, the enlivened Passions move:
Love softens War, – and War invigorates Love.[42] □

In the same vein, Hill also adopts elements of the Katherine and Owen Tudor romance found in Boyle, though the Princess's paramour turns out to be Henry all along. Hill responds to critical questions raised by the Chorus, by cutting his role and redistributing many of his lines to other characters. Hill creatively redeploys Shakespeare's original lines throughout the play and splices them into different parts of the text, often re-assigned to new characters. The play opens, for example, before Harfleur with the traitors sharing lines from 1.1 and 2.0 regarding Henry's transformation and the mobilization to France. Elsewhere, it is Katherine who now gets to complain (to Harriet) about ceremony just as Shakespeare's Henry had in 4.1.219–72.[43] Hill confronts the vexed issue of staging Agincourt itself by having the offstage actions of battle narrated with great brevity through a song by the 'Genius of England' and removes the equally problematic final wooing scene.[44] Prior to the battle Harriet confronts Henry and, unable to enact her revenge, kills herself and with her dying breath reveals her uncle's conspiracy. Hill's use of Harriet aligns the play far more with eighteenth-century dramatic tastes and the melodramatic 'tragic frisson of the fallen women' common in the 'she-tragedies' of contemporary playwrights, including Rowe.[45] Hill clearly fashions his play as a love tragedy and further preserves a sense of decorum by excising the comic roles of Fluellen, Pistol, Nym, Bardolph and Macmorris.[46] Hill's play is still much underrated, even by his most recent biographer. In addition to the insights it brings about eighteenth-century responses to Shakespeare's work, it invites further comparison with a play *Sir John Oldcastle* – produced in the same year as *Henry V* by Anthony Munday (1553–1633), Robert Wilson (1579–1610), Michael Drayton (1563–1631) and Richard Hathway – which also foregrounds the three conspirators' role and motives, though it makes no mention of Scrope's niece. Hill's play also looks forward to later twentieth-century Shakespeare criticism and lines of enquiry regarding gender and the place of women in the histories, as he attempts to expand the very limited number of female roles in *Henry V*.

Hill's *Henry the Fifth* was restaged during the 1730s and 40s when its anti-French sentiments were as popular as ever. By this point Shakespeare's own *Henry V* was being performed again and returned to the stage, after well over a century's absence, at Convent Garden in February 1738. The play became increasingly popular as the century progressed and had particular resonance during the Seven Years' War against France (1756–63) when it was staged each year.[47] The emphatic subtitle on the playbills 'With the Conquest of the French at Agincourt' illustrates how *Henry V* began to be employed once more as a stimulus of patriotic enthusiasm.[48] The French-supported, pro-Catholic Jacobite rebellion of 1745 prompted revivals of *King John* (1595–6) and *Henry V*, and lines from the latter were also quoted in *The Peace-Makers*, a caricature attacking opponents of the first British conflict over the Falkland Islands in 1770.[49] Similarly, in response to fevered anti-French popular opinion following the 1789 revolution, *Henry V* was used to vocalize English resolve in the face of a perceived French threat in performances starring John Kemble (1757–1823) staged between 1789–92. Kemble's version made extensive cuts to many of the more controversial scenes and downplayed hints of ambiguity in the play by removing the Chorus; in doing so *Henry V* was returned to the lean, patriotic form found in the 1600 Quarto. Kemble's production and its few revivals certainly play up the elements of historical spectacle and established an influential precedent for the multiple patriotic and heroic stage interpretations seen during the nineteenth century that reflected the dominant tenor of *Henry V* criticism throughout the same period. We will consider this criticism in the next chapter.

CHAPTER THREE

The Nineteenth Century: Romantic and Victorian Interpretations

It is in the nineteenth century that we first find extended critical essays dedicated to discussing *Henry V* in detail, as opposed to fragmentary observations in editorial commentaries. The century as a whole sees the emergence of literary study as a distinct academic discipline. Increasing numbers of individual scholarly, rather than acting editions of the play are produced during this period together with versions specifically designated as school editions, in response to the eventual establishment of compulsory education in England during the 1870s and consequent growth in new audiences of younger readers. The scholarly field had developed in breadth and complexity to such an extent by the end of the nineteenth century that M. C. Bradbrook (1909–93) describes this period as 'the Industrial Revolution of Shakespeare studies'.[1] Looking back to the beginning of the century, however, one finds Shakespeare criticism dominated by some of the leading figures of German and English Romanticism and the lectures, essays and reviews of August Wilhelm von Schlegel, Samuel Taylor Coleridge (1772–1834) and William Hazlitt. The Romantic critics reacted both to their predecessors in Shakespeare studies (particularly Johnson) and to the turbulent political situation of the day, principally events surrounding the French Revolution and the rise of Napoleon Bonaparte (1769–1821). They rejected the overwhelmingly piecemeal criticism that Shakespeare had received to date and took particular exception to the eighteenth-century preoccupation with neoclassical rules and conceptions of unity. Schlegel himself was one of the first to use the term 'romantic' to describe his own oppositional relation to the neoclassicist aesthetic tradition. Adherence to artificial rules ran counter to the Romantic valorization of liberty, individual creativity and the powers of the imagination. The Romantics' reactionary spirit was not limited to merely formal taxonomic concerns. It looked to the wider political and cultural context of the Napoleonic wars and drew analogies between what Jonathan Bate calls the 'hegemonic tendencies of French neo-classical culture' and Napoleon's conflicts with, and territorial conquests of, opposing European countries.

■ It was a rejection born of indignation at the wider sense in which France was imposing its laws beyond her own borders: to speak of France's assault on 'the dramatic liberties of other nations' was implicitly to evoke the extinction of other kinds of national liberty.[2] □

The history plays were to prove particularly popular weapons on the anti-Gallic cultural battlefield of early nineteenth-century Shakespeare studies and conceptions of national pride, or at least national and political self-consciousness, are never far from the Romantics' treatment of the plays. As Coleridge writes, a primary object of Shakespeare's histories 'was to make his countrymen more patriotic; to make Englishmen proud of being Englishmen'.[3] Coleridge writes very little about *Henry V* specifically though his contemporaries Schlegel and Hazlitt provide two highly influential accounts of the play and its hero.

A. W. SCHLEGEL

Schlegel's extensive exposition and discussion of Shakespeare took the form of lectures that were first given in Vienna between 1808 and 1809 and translated into English in 1815. They are characteristic of the far more detailed, analytical methodology that would form the basis of Shakespeare criticism from this point onwards. Schlegel took issue with Johnson's fragmentary approach to Shakespeare's plays and argued instead for greater attention to be paid both to the organic unity of individual works themselves and to the unity of Shakespeare's canon as a whole. Challenging the neoclassical critics' obsession with anachronistic rules about unity and decorum, Schlegel proposed that the unity of a work of art comes from within, that organic wholeness is innate rather than imposed externally in the form of rules.

■ Form is mechanical when, through external force, it is imparted to any material merely as an accidental addition without reference to its quality; as, for example, when we give a particular shape to a soft mass that it may retain the same after its induration [hardening]. Organical form, again, is innate; it unfolds itself from within, and acquires its determination contemporaneously with the perfect development of the germ [seed].[4] □

Schlegel's organicist theories were immensely influential, not only within Shakespeare studies, but also within later literary theory. Schlegel establishes that it is the critic's role to identify the 'hidden essences' of literary works and, as Bate observes, the discovery of hidden aesthetic unity becomes institutionalized during the early twentieth century through the rise of Practical Criticism and 'New Criticism'.[5] It has also been suggested that Schlegel's preference for unity from within rather than imposed, external rules was conditioned by contemporary anti-Gallic currents and a belief that organic aesthetic unity went hand-in-hand with autonomous national identity.[6] Just as Hill, a century earlier, used Agincourt to enact a symbolic victory of English dramatic models over the dominant French cultural traditions of his day, so *Henry V* and the English histories taken together offered a means of re-conceiving and rehabilitating indigenous aesthetic traditions. Schlegel argues that all ten of Shakespeare's histories form a unified sequence and treats them repeatedly as a single historical cycle divided into individual movements. He refers to the histories as 'one' of Shakespeare's works, 'for the poet has evidently intended them as parts of a greater whole'.[7] Each individual play must therefore be viewed in relation to that which comes before and after. *Henry V* is particularly complex when discussed in this manner as it is poised between the ignominious past of Richard II's deposition and Hal's 'greener days' and – despite Henry's present military and diplomatic successes – the equally unhappy future that sees France lost and England divided, as Shakespeare had already depicted in the first tetralogy.

Schlegel discusses Henry's character with great brevity, identifying merely that Shakespeare

■ portrays him as endowed with every chivalrous and kingly virtue; open, sincere, affable, yet still disposed to innocent raillery, as a sort of reminiscence of his youth, in the intervals between his perilous but glorious achievements.[8] □

He then moves on to address how *Henry V* itself works as an aesthetic entity. Henry's reign clearly posed a problem for Shakespeare as its dominant event is the king's war with France, and war 'is much more an epic than a dramatic object'.[9] The crux of the issue is the representation of agency and the forces controlling individuals. The presence of chance or fate can never be avoided when representing war, argues Schlegel, and yet this conflicts with his earlier conception of the nature of drama, as it is 'the business of the drama to exhibit to us those determinations which, with a certain necessity, proceed from the reciprocal relations of the different individuals, their characters and passions'.[10] Because it perforce requires (through the limitations of the stage) an artificial, metonymic mode of representation, as both the Chorus and its critics recognized, the dramatic evocation of war can only be a means to an end, 'the means by which something else is accomplished, and not the last aim and substance of the whole'.[11] Schlegel makes the astute observation that it is on the night before Agincourt that Henry receives his greatest test, and perhaps faces his greatest challenge, as it is his rights and duties as king that are in question at the play's core, rather than any question of his generalship or tactical acumen. This certainly explains the choice of scenes with which Shakespeare represents the Agincourt victory. Shakespeare never depicts the fortunes of war as a 'blind deity' but prefers to 'anticipate the result from the qualities of the general, and their influence on the minds of the soldiers'.[12] Furthermore, maintains Schlegel, 'without claiming our belief for miracles' Shakespeare sometimes

■ exhibits the issue in the light of a higher volition: the consciousness of a just cause and reliance on the protection of Heaven given courage to the one party, while the presage of a curse hanging over their undertaking weighs down the other.[13] □

Shakespeare's representation of war is bound up inexorably with creating a credible conception of an individual's relationship both with metaphysical forces and positivist, temporal entities. Despite the centrality of war to the play, Schlegel identifies the importance of human qualities and, crucially, the representation of relationships between characters. One can see how Schlegel's theories on organic unity and the inter-relationship between elements within a play are particularly apposite for *Henry V*. Rather than criticizing the presence of the Eastcheap characters as indecorous distractions from the principal dramatic action, Schlegel perceives them as an integral aspect of Shakespeare's artistry that weaves together 'the general events of the war with a fullness of individual, characteristic, and even sometimes comic features'.[14] The four captains in 3.3.1–80 are seen to fulfil a similar complementary function. Before discussing specific plays, Schlegel had earlier praised this syncretizing aspect of Shakespearean characterization: 'he surpasses even himself in so combining and contrasting them, that they serve to bring out each other'; this is the 'very summit' of characterization, for an individual must be viewed in relation with the others.[15]

Schlegel's treatment of *Henry V* further demonstrates his commitment to an aesthetic based on making sense of how all of the pieces fit together when he discusses the Chorus, again confronting one of the bugbears of neoclassical criticism. He defends the Chorus by reading his speeches at face value, identifying how they foreground the importance of the audience's own imagination. They also 'unite the epic pomp and solemnity with lyrical sublimity', affording Shakespeare the means to treat matters which are not 'properly dramatic' without placing long, distracting descriptive speeches into ordinary characters' mouths.[16] Shakespeare's attempts at staging battles are thus contrasted with classical drama, where all such events are merely recounted. Schlegel's defence of the Chorus ultimately rests – as might be expected from one of the founding fathers of Romanticism – on the capacity of the imagination:

> ■ It is certainly laughable that a handful of awkward warriors in mock armour, by means of two or three swords, with which we clearly see they take especial care not to do the slightest injury to one another, should decide the fate of mighty kingdoms.[17] □

But the opposite would be much worse: actually to achieve such a vast spectacle would render the spectator 'incapable of bestowing that attention which a poetical work of art demands'.[18] Imaginative supplementation is preferred to the interruption of any intellectual or emotional engagement with the play. Such a statement is perhaps partially obscured by historical differences between Schlegel's suggestion of the so-called fourth wall of the stage and Elizabethan ideas about the relationship of actor and audience. Nevertheless, Schlegel pinpoints a question addressed by nearly every critic and director of *Henry V*: exactly how much realism do we want from the play? This was certainly a burning issue on the nineteenth-century stage. Criticism such as that of Leigh Hunt (1784–1859), who was disappointed with an 1830 production that inadequately represented Agincourt using 'a little huddle of soldiers', was met by successive directors who sought to leave less to the audience's imagination and replaced 'imaginary puissance' with spectacular, more realistic evocations of Harfleur, Agincourt and Henry's triumphal return, often using elaborate sets and a cast of many hundreds.[19] The extravagant productions of William Macready (1839), Samuel Phelps (1852), Charles Kean (1859) and Charles Calvert (1872–9) would attempt to silence critical accusations that Henry's war could not be staged convincingly.[20]

Schlegel concludes his treatment of *Henry V* with an exposition of Henry's political motives for war and of the clergy's machinations supporting the French conquest. His comment about the concluding union between Henry and Katherine identifies that political expedience clearly underlies all of the king's actions depicted throughout the play: 'It must not, therefore, be imagined that it was without the knowledge and will of the poet that a heroic drama turns out a comedy in his hands, and ends in the manner of comedy with a marriage of convenience.'[21] As later critics recognize, *Henry V*'s conclusion is just as problematic as the endings to some of Shakespeare's other comedies such as *The Taming of the Shrew* (1592) and *Measure for Measure* (1604).

Schlegel's short, yet dense, discussion of *Henry V* revisits many key areas of earlier critical debate, particularly regarding the play's epic form, its organic unity and the Chorus's function. Critics throughout the nineteenth and twentieth centuries will return to the cyclic conception of the English histories and *Henry V*'s place within a complex, unified sequence. Schlegel's comments both about the extent of Henry's personal virtue in Shakespeare's depiction of war and the concluding marriage of convenience also anticipate the more ironic readings of Henry that Hazlitt introduces into the English critical tradition.

WILLIAM HAZLITT

Character-oriented Shakespeare criticism had begun to emerge during the later eighteenth century, though it only really came to dominate English scholarship during the nineteenth century, in no small measure, due to the polemic questions raised in Hazlitt's *Characters of Shakespear's Plays* (1817). Hazlitt begins by locating himself in relation to earlier critics and the majority of his preface consists of extensive quotations about characterization taken verbatim from Pope and Schlegel. Hazlitt cites the passage from Pope's preface that praises how every character in Shakespeare 'is as much an individual, as those in life itself' and maintains that each figure could be identified from the distinctiveness of their speeches alone even if their names were omitted.[22] His own, initially rather modest, stated objective is to amplify such remarks and supplement Schlegel's extensive contemporary observations through providing more illustrative examples from the plays themselves. In his essays, journalism and reviews, Hazlitt is always at his best when on the offensive and the *Characters* preface is no exception. His target here is Johnson's 1765 edition. Johnson is criticized for being too systematic, too bound by propriety and conventions, and hampered by an unimaginative discursive style of writing. Johnson's appreciation of characterization was also limited in that it was founded on a belief that the playwright excelled in reproducing character types: '[t]hus [Johnson] says of Shakespear's characters, in contradiction to what Pope had observed, and to what every one else feels, that each character is a species, instead of being an individual'.[23] Hazlitt's criticism keeps returning to the point that Johnson's critical mode lacked imagination and an organic, sensitive quality:

> ■ He was not only without any particular fineness of organic sensibility, alive to all the 'mighty world of ear and eye', which is necessary to the painter or musician, but without that intenseness of passion, which, seeking to exaggerate whatever excites the feelings of pleasure or power in the mind,

and moulding the impressions of natural objects according to the impulses of imagination, produces a genius and a taste for poetry.[24] □

Such a pronouncement epitomizes not only Hazlitt's methodology but also the whole spirit of the Romantics' sympathetic and empathetic conception of critical engagement with Shakespearean characters.[25] Hazlitt thus also set himself apart from Schlegel who grounds his analysis of character within a greater structural and thematic matrix.

The discussion of Henry begins with repetition of a point made both by Schlegel and Hazlitt's contemporary English critic Nathan Drake (1766–1836): that the king was evidently one of Shakespeare's favourites since the playwright appears to work hard to apologize for his actions throughout the play.[26] Shakespeare's Henry is, however, entirely undeserving of this honour:

■ He was fond of war and low company: – we know little else of him. He was careless, dissolute, and ambitious; – idle, or doing mischief. In private, he seemed to have no idea of the common decencies of life, which he subjected to a kind of regal licence; in public affairs, he seemed to have no idea of any rule of right or wrong, but brute force, glossed over with a little religious hypocrisy and archiepiscopal advice.[27] □

Henry's war is entirely engineered as a distraction from his own weak title and supported by a corrupt clergy; Shakespeare does not withhold exposing this process in action. Hazlitt sees the conquest of France as a capricious exercise of Henry's power driven less by a specific material cause than by a force, cast almost as a natural law, that sees absolute monarchs bound to display and test their power 'not when it consults the rights and interests of others, but when it insults and tramples on all justice and humility'.[28]

Hazlitt's critique of Henry quickly collapses into a more general discussion of the abuses of monarchical power and he frequently appears to elide between discussion of Shakespeare's character and the historical king. Criticism of *Henry V* here is obviously conditioned by Hazlitt's staunchly anti-monarchical stance and left-wing, self-confessedly Jacobin politics; it appears to be a deliberate attempt to provoke the political and cultural establishment of his day.[29] It also provides the occasion for a topical comparison between Henry's campaign and the recent European coalition to defeat Napoleon, which culminated in the battle of Waterloo (1815).[30] For all of Hazlitt's interest in interiority and psychology seen elsewhere in the *Characters* volume (for example, in his *Hamlet* essay) from which his eminence in Shakespearean character criticism largely derives, there is relatively little textual evidence or illustration thus far to support the negative reading of Henry. There is great attention paid to what the king says and does, but what really seems to annoy Hazlitt is Henry's resistance to attempts to project any model of a mind at work. Indeed, it is the disjuncture between what Henry says and then does that epitomizes his perceived villainy, the fact that there are clearly 'hidden motives' at work but the text lacks any kind of 'I know you all' moment (found in *1 Henry IV*, 1.2.192–214) where the protagonist tells us what is really going on.

The reader of Hazlitt's contentious first three pages is made complicit in this aggressively oppositional stance through repeated use of collective first-person pronouns declaring, for example, that 'we feel little love or admiration' for Henry or that 'we only like kings according to the law'.[31] Hazlitt then tempers his attack by turning to the place of Henry within the play itself, revealing the slightly artificial nature of a methodology which implies that characters can be treated in isolation from the plays in which they are located. This is in stark contrast to Schlegel's organicist theories of character relativity that Hazlitt lauds in his preface but it anticipates the inclination towards an essentialist mode of character study (which treats characters as extra-textual entities, as if they were real people) that continues to develop throughout the nineteenth century and reaches its apogee in the work of A. C. Bradley. We like Henry in the play, Hazlitt maintains, because 'there he is a very amiable monster, a very splendid pageant'.[32] His attraction resides, we are told, in the very fact that the play reminds us of its unreality.

■ We take a very romantic, heroic, patriotic, and poetical delight in the boasts and feats of our younger Harry, as they appear on the stage and are confined to lines of ten syllables; where no blood follows the stroke that wounds our ears, where no harvest bends beneath horses' hoofs, no city flames, no little child is butchered, no dead men's bodies are found piled and festering the next morning – in the orchestra![33] □

This is as close as Hazlitt gets to addressing the vexed issue of the play's metadramatic engagement with the audience or the place of the Chorus.

Hazlitt then turns from the politics of the play to its poetry and identifies a number of pleasing passages. His tone now is far more relaxed than in the essay's first half, but here too attention soon turns to Shakespeare's use of constitutional and political metaphors. He praises Ely's account of Henry's transformation and Canterbury's model of the bees' commonwealth, the latter described (no doubt with some irony) as a 'beautiful rhetorical delineation of the effects of subordination in a commonwealth'.[34] He identifies with approval that Fluellen takes over from Falstaff as the principal comic courtier attending the king and, like Johnson, he approves of Henry's soliloquy in 4.1. Perhaps the most insightful observation in the essay's second half is Hazlitt's praise of two prose passages in *Henry V*: the encounter with Williams, and the court-ship of Katherine. As he says, 'we like them both exceedingly, though the first savours perhaps too much of the king, and the last too little of the lover'.[35] To the last, Hazlitt seems to be unable to establish a coherent, consistent, unambiguous picture of Henry in the play. It is this recognition of the play's inherent ambiguity that looks ahead well over a hundred years to the ironic, double readings of Henry that develop from the mid-twentieth century onwards. Hazlitt is aware of the king's negative qualities and of the attempts to obfuscate political machination through rhetoric and pageantry, and yet he also acknowledges the persistent attraction that Henry holds for audiences. As Richard Levin points out, Hazlitt's essay cannot be treated as an unequivocally ironic reading of Henry's failings, but it is a sensitive first enquiry into the moral and political ambivalence of the play and its hero.[36] As mentioned above, Hazlitt also paves the way for more extensive essentialist character studies that continue to play upon the critic or audience's emotional engagement with the protagonists of Shakespeare's drama. As such it is difficult to overestimate Hazlitt's level of innovation and influence in *Henry V* criticism.

As one might expect, Hazlitt's readings of Shakespeare attracted a degree of controversy and reaction, both from his contemporaries and later commentators. Reacting against Hazlitt's foregrounding of character as the source of unity in Shakespeare, the German critic and philosopher Hermann Ulrici looked back to Schlegel to treat the history plays as complex organic structures unified from within.

HERMANN ULRICI

In *Shakspeare's Dramatic Art* (1846) Ulrici spends little time addressing issues of characterization in *Henry V*. He blames a 'blind hatred' of monarchy for Hazlitt's prejudiced and ultimately unhelpful reading of Henry's character; however, he admits that the matter of Falstaff's rejection casts a shadow over an otherwise wholly heroic view of the king. Of far greater concern is the relationship of *Henry V* to the overall sequence of Shakespeare's English histories and its function relative to the narrative arc spanning the whole epic cycle of the ten plays. Echoing Schlegel, Ulrici viewed the histories as a five-act cycle: the *Henry VI* trilogy (1591–2) and *Henry IV* plays constitute two acts while *Henry V* is the third; *King John* and *Henry VIII* (1613) stand, respectively, as prologue and epilogue.[37] Awareness of *Henry V*'s place in a greater historical sequence obviously has serious implications for how we react to positive and negative aspects of the play. Henry possesses, so Ulrici argues, an undisputed claim, moral integrity and his nobles' support, but 'the intrinsic rottenness of his historical position is still discernible'.[38] The organic degenerative metaphor ('rottenness') is indicative of Ulrici's appropriation of Schlegel's terminology and critical perspective. *Henry V* ends well but the Chorus immediately informs us of how newly won French possessions become a source of misery for the Lancastrians. As in many, if not all, of the histories, Shakespeare presents a false ending as he is forced to fit the 'natural' material of historical events into the artificial mould of a five-act, two-hour play, or units thereof. *Henry V's* conclusion thus demonstrates the inexorable connection of war and peace because our knowledge of the impending tragedy of the fall of Henry VI and the Yorkists' rise overshadows our appreciation of the peaceful ending.[39] Placing *Henry V* within a cyclical vision of English history removes the need to judge whether the conclusion is good or bad, celebratory or ironic, as it removes the mistaken idea that the histories can be divided between tragedy and comedy, as the eighteenth-century commentators proposed.[40] Ulrici develops this argument in the expanded 1876 edition of his study and suggests that *Henry V* may only originally have been staged in cycles with the other histories.[41] A cyclical conception of the histories therefore provides us with a formal means of compre-hending Shakespearean genre and of identifying what makes historical drama distinct from tragedy or comedy.

Ulrici maintains that Shakespeare's representation of war in the his-tories further supports the argument that they constitute a unified epic cycle, as war best demonstrates the organic nature of historical process. Wars may be initiated by rulers, 'but in truth, a national war, such as we have here [in *Henry V*] depicted, is *never*, simply speaking, made, but is an organic growth, like every other historical phenomenon' (Ulrici's italics).[42] Shakespeare captures this organic, epic spirit of the age through bringing together as many different elements of the social order as he can: kings, nobles, commoners, national regions, foreign enemies. Later critics will echo Ulrici's observations on Shakespeare's totalizing national and international perspective(s) in *Henry V*, though increasingly articu-late their conception of the play's diverse components in terms of lin-guistic differences. War also reveals the presence of a greater cosmic order, argues Ulrici, since every war 'is essentially a judgment of God'. The play therefore creates a sense of religious awe:

■ It elevates our reverence of God, to see a handful of tired and famished Englishmen, animated by their own and their king's heroism, and in full resignation to the will of God, attacking and routing three or four times as numerous an army of well-fed and well-equipped Frenchmen.[43] □

The play, especially through its depiction of war, thus aims to represent the 'moral purification and amendment of man'.[44] This too connects with Ulrici's theories on the organic nature of history, as he argues that Shakespeare shows how war is linked to the essence of history itself: as a means of judgement, justice and advancement for the human race.[45]

In discussing the histories as a whole, Ulrici recognizes that Shakespeare chose to concentrate on a one-hundred-year period that formed a boundary between what Tom McAlindon characterizes as 'the age of feudalism, chivalry, and monasticism, and the age of royal absolutism, burgher wealth, and scientific enquiry'.[46] Shakespeare, argues Ulrici, then creates a form which 'encompassed, foregrounded, and brought into an organic, artistic unity the colliding forces and contradictions of the time'.[47] Ulrici identifies a conception of cyclical history in Shakespeare by reading the plays through the lens of the dialectical understanding of how historical events cannot escape the pattern of thesis, antithesis and synthesis proposed by the philosopher Georg Hegel (1770–1831). Human and political failings produce crises and conflict which in turn generate change and progress. *Henry V* fits into this model insofar as it represents the last positive moment within the tumultuous dialectic that leads to the Tudor accession and synthesis of Lancaster and York. Ulrici's interest in relating *Henry V* to a wider enquiry into the nature of historical process anticipates many twentieth-century concerns regarding the relative presence of order and disorder in the histories and he draws upon the same Hegelian explanatory model as the Marxist critic Paul N. Siegel, who examines how Shakespeare chooses to concentrate on fault-lines and points of crisis in English and Roman history.[48] Ulrici also demonstrates how we can discuss *Henry V* in relation to historiography from philosophical and aesthetic, as well as the more common historicist and topical perspectives.

G. G. GERVINUS

G. G. Gervinus's *Shakespeare Commentaries* (English translation 1863) offers yet another illustration of the systematic analytic criticism that characterizes nineteenth-century German scholarship on *Henry V*, behind which – for all of Hazlitt's pioneering observations – English critics lagged at least until the middle of the century. Gervinus's comments on Shakespeare's histories contribute productively to the overall picture of *Henry V*'s critical reception when he begins to explore their patriotic dimension and utility. The histories are clearly the product of an age of national stability and pride:

■ How eloquently in Richard II, in Henry V and VI, not alone does the patriotic spirit of the poet speak, but also the self-conceit of a people who have again learned to know themselves in the midst of successful events. [...] The whole age influenced the creation and the spirit of these historical pieces, and these again had a corresponding influence upon the patriotic spirit of the people.[49] □

Gervinus gestures here towards the importance of a contextualized interpretation of the play and actually articulates a version of what the twentieth-century New Historicist Stephen Greenblatt calls 'social energy', a reciprocal process whereby artistic works both feed upon and perpetuate a particular vision of society, in this case, one that is unashamedly patriotic and buoyed by post-Armada fervour.[50] There was also a particularly partisan motive behind Shakespeare's presentation of his hero, suggests Gervinus:

■ It is to me more than probable, that a jealous patriotic feeling actuated our poet in the entire representation of his Prince Henry: the intention, namely of exhibiting by the side of his brilliant contemporary Henry IV of France [1553–1610], a Henry upon the English throne equal to him in greatness and originality.[51] □

Gervinus begins by confronting a contentious topical political issue and sets out to read Shakespeare's histories by questioning, 'in what relation the claims of the hereditary right of the incapable, however good, who endanger throne and fatherland, stand to the claims of the merit of the capable, however bad, if they save and maintain the state'.[52] But Gervinus's take on the right versus might dichotomy is overwhelmingly conservative and his reading of *Henry V* reveals an unproblematic hero-king supported by his family, nobles, churchmen, the commons and the different regional groups that make up his army. Henry's claim to France is just, his visit with his troops on the eve of battle entirely successful, and through his modesty and humility in attributing the Agincourt victory to God, he makes full atonement for his father's sins.[53] Not for the last time in a pro-Henry, patriotic reading, reverence for sacred authority is held up as one of the king's defining attributes:

■ The poet works with the same idea, with which Aeschylus [525–456 BC] wrote his warlike pieces, *the Persians* and the *Seven before Thebes*: that terrible is the warrior who fears God, and that on the other hand the blossom of pride ripens into the fruit of evil and the harvest of tears.[54] □

What is particularly interesting about Gervinus's commentary throughout is that despite his initial declaration that the English histories engage more with the public sphere and 'thoughts political and national' than with the 'internal' history of individuals (i.e. morality and psychology), his treatment of *Henry V* wholly centres on the king's character.[55] As he admits, 'the whole interest of our piece is in the development of the ethical character of the hero', and he proceeds to chart the fortunes of Henry's 'many-sided' personality, now that he has arrived in his 'vocation' as king.[56] For all of the play's potentially epic canvas and its engagement with 'thoughts political and national', Henry and his motives have by this point become an irresistible focus for critical attention.

Gervinus's commentary is of most use for present purposes in that it offers a good illustration of an unequivocally positive, patriotic reading of *Henry V* and exhibits some of the key features of such a standpoint: the evocation of a jingoistic, post-Armada England; the obligation to explain and justify every nuance of the king's qualities and abilities; and the appeal to religious authority to support Henry's actions. Gervinus also suggests that the patriotic and ethical dimensions of *Henry V* could be of equal or greater significance than its aesthetic or linguistic qualities, but that this need not be viewed as a negative or detracting point.[57] In this regard, critical judgements on the relative merits of the play's pageantry and poetry reflected similar debates found in contemporary reviews of nineteenth-century stagings of *Henry V*. Gervinus's tentative attempts to locate *Henry V* in relation to the patriotic spirit and energy of the Elizabethan age appear quite limited, however, when compared to the pioneering historicist scholarship of the critic Richard Simpson.

RICHARD SIMPSON

Simpson plays an important role in *Henry V*'s reception history, as he is the first critic to offer an extended account of how the play relates to the politics of the 1590s. His essay 'The Politics of Shakspere's Historical Plays' appeared in 1874 alongside his 'The Political Use of the Stage in Shakspere's Time' and together they blaze a historicist trail that would not be followed in earnest in *Henry V* scholarship until the 1940s. Simpson's method is to trace how, where and why Shakespeare deviates from his sources and then go on to identify echoes of the play's preoccupations in early modern texts and documents. Shakespeare rarely refers to facts about his own era directly, but he nevertheless (argues Simpson) participates in contemporary political discussion. Simpson reads *Henry V* as an unequivocally pro-Essex play exhibiting principles to which the earl is judged to have been committed. Taking a slightly idealistic view of Essex, Simpson maintains that the earl sought a greater political union between all parties and nations advocating 'equal justice to all, a general toleration in religion, and an abolition of the privileges of one sect and of the penalties attached to the other'.[58] Henry himself, it is argued, matched such a syncretic vision. Shakespeare's play therefore models the kind of proactive stance required of an ideal ruler and depicts war 'not as an agony of brutal passions, but as an agent of civilization'.[59] For Simpson, Henry's war is unquestionably just and he goes on to suggest that Shakespeare deliberately set out to refute the ideas of Cardinal William Allen (1532–94) advanced a decade earlier concerning the iniquity of Catholics fighting in an unjust war.[60] Simpson's notion of a just war is unmistakably inflected by the patriotic sentiments of contemporary Victorian readings of *Henry V*, and he admires Essex's hawkish stance and the vision of war as a civilizing agent: 'Quiet times give the reins to the strong oppressor, and the intolerant bigot. War with its dangers is the school of tolerance'.[61]

Simpson is especially keen to identify those points in the play where Shakespeare is scornful or satirical towards the early modern church. In his treatment of *Henry IV* he had already suggested that Shakespeare may have leant more towards Catholic than Protestant sympathies in presenting Falstaff as a satire on Puritan self-righteousness, just as the original Oldcastle, the Lollard heretic, was lampooned in earlier Catholic satires.[62] Shakespeare's negative representation of churchmen as Machiavellian intriguers continues throughout the histories, says Simpson, as evinced by the manipulative clergy in *Henry V*'s first act.[63] Simpson's historicist criticism is remarkably original for this period and he is the first critic to suggest that Shakespeare adopts an oppositional stance to Elizabethan political and religious orthodoxy and to outline how the plays may be viewed as subversive.[64] He makes a valuable contribution to Shakespeare studies as a whole, through his nuanced understanding of how a text not simply reflects its historical context or sits against a contextual backdrop, but actively participates in an ongoing political dialogue.

EDWARD DOWDEN

Dowden's *Shakspere: A Critical Study of his Mind and Art* (1875) was one of the most influential nineteenth-century studies on Shakespeare. The book went through 12 British editions before 1901 and is a pre-eminent example of the robust, methodical approach that typifies Victorian Shakespeare scholarship.[65] Dowden's aim is to

■ connect the study of Shakspere's works with an inquiry after the person-ality of the writer, and to observe, as far as is possible, in its several stages the growth of his intellect and character from youth to full maturity.[66] □

The histories, he believes, offer the best opportunity for pursuing this investigation as they not only reveal a great deal about how Shakespeare relates to his age, but also demonstrate how through his study of history the playwright builds up his own 'moral nature' and 'fortifies himself for the conduct of life'.[67] Henry V, it is maintained, provides a key role model for the playwright in this process, as Dowden believes that 'we know what Shakspere would have tried to become himself if there had not been a side of his character which acknowledged closer affinity with Hamlet than with Henry'.[68] A dominant theme of Dowden's work is his subject's instructive potential and he wastes no time highlighting that the histories constitute 'a school of discipline' for the reader in the 'finite issues of failure and success in the achieving of practical ends', rather than in the more sublime spiritual and essential qualities found in the tragedies.[69] Such discipline is still framed in moral terms and, like Ulrici and Gervinus, he identifies a providential, retributive vision of history: that evil actions ultimately invite divine censure.

Dowden also views the plays as a connected sequence that traces how one may succeed or fail in attaining 'a practical mastery of the world', and Henry represents the zenith up to which all of the histories' characters are leading: 'the man framed for the most noble and joyous mastery of things'.[70] Henry thus answers a question Dowden poses earlier: '[b]y what means shall a man attain the noblest practical success in the objective world?'[71] Throughout his treatment of the play – which is really a treatment of the king alone – Dowden returns to Henry's practical virtues:

■ His courage, his integrity, his unfaltering justice, his hearty English warmth, his modesty, his love of plainness rather than of pageantry, his joyous temper, his business-like English piety.[72] □

The emphasis here is all on external qualities and a behaviourist conception of character demonstrated through Henry's actions. For Dowden, Henry is like the fact-fixated Gradgrind in the novel *Hard Times* (1854) by Charles Dickens (1812–70); his interest and genius lies solely in the 'discovery of the noblest facts' and it is through his mastery of such facts that he is able to know the world and remain loyal to truth and reality.[73] Dowden's Henry is uninterested in unreality and pretence and is guided wholly by a commitment to the facts of life that keeps him free of egotism and duplicity.[74] The king is cast as a rather sentimental character, acutely 'knowable' and familiar and the embodiment of homeliness, heartiness and piety. The picture of Henry that emerges is actually quite simplistic, perhaps even reductive, and there is little indication of complexity of character. Instead, Dowden turns Henry into an exemplar of good conduct, a working model of desired practical qualities. His interpretation of the king's nocturnal visit in 4.1, for example, is set out as an illustration of how one should act:

■ He is not, like his father, exhausted and outworn by the careful construction of a life. If an hour of depression comes upon him, he yet is strong, because he can look through his depression to a strength and virtue outside of and beyond himself. Joy may ebb with him or rise, as it will; the current of his inmost being is fed by a source that springs from the hard rock of life, and is no tidal flow. He accepts his weakness and weariness as part of the surrender of ease and strength and self which he makes on behalf of England.[75] □

Dowden seems uninterested in any form of problematic internal qualities; his Henry is a muscular Christian hero of the slap-on-the-back and brisk-handshake variety. There is no hint of veiling or duplicity on Henry's part of the sort that Hazlitt identified, or any reference to anything else in *Henry V* other than those elements that impact upon Shakespeare's delineation of the king. Dowden illustrates how it is possible to talk about Henry as a hero as much in personal and practical as in public and patriotic terms, and also how one can make elaborate observations about his character without ever really probing the surface, nor feeling any necessity to do so. Dowden's principal contribution to *Henry V* scholarship is his endorsement of a Henry that represents not simply a mirror for kings (as Schlegel suggested) but a didactic model or set of facts aimed at teaching practical lessons to the reader and audience.

The spirited, rousing, personal impact of *Henry V* remains a central theme in criticism throughout the mid- to late nineteenth century and there is certainly no shortage of critical assessments of the play during this period that stress an unambiguous and unapologetically patriotic line.

HEROIC HENRYS

Writing in 1841, Thomas Carlyle (1795–1881) cannot help but make passing mention of *Henry V* in his study *On Heroes, Hero-Worship and the Heroic in History*. He holds up the play as Shakespeare's greatest attempt to capture the epic, heroic mode:

■ There is a noble Patriotism in it, – far other than the 'indifference' you sometimes hear ascribed to Shakespeare. A true English heart breathes, calm and strong, through the whole business; not boisterous, protrusive; all the better for that. There is a sound in it like the ring of steel.[76] □

The publisher Charles Knight (1791–1873) similarly identifies an energizing quality to the play in the 'critical notice' to *Henry V* reprinted in his *Studies of Shakspere* (1849):

■ There are periods in the history of every people when their nationality, lifting them up into a frenzy of enthusiasm, is one of the sublimest exhibitions of the practical poetry of social life. In the times of Shakspere such an aspect of the English mind was not unfrequently presented. Neither in our own times have such manifestations of the mighty heart been wanting. But there have been, and there may again be, periods of real danger when the national spirit shows itself drooping and languishing. It is under such circumstances that the heart-stirring power of such a play as *Henry V* is to be tested.[77] □

Knight's comments resonate with a similar concern for the practical dimension of the play and its poetry to that seen in Dowden's work, but also presage the way in which *Henry V* becomes employed both in the early twentieth century and again during the Second World War – by critics and directors – to galvanize the 'national spirit' in a time of crisis.

In his essay 'On Character-Development in Shakspere as Illustrated by *Macbeth* and *Henry V*', which was originally presented as a paper to the New Shakspere Society in January 1886, the critic R. G. Moulton juxtaposes the contrasting methods of characterization employed in the two plays. While *Macbeth* (1605) reveals 'real growth and development in the character itself, brought about by the succession of the incidents', *Henry V* does not himself develop as a character; it is merely our view of him that expands as the play progresses.[78] In this regard Henry's character is never seen to advance during the course of the play. He is a 'complete character' from his very first appearance and any sense of crisis or complication arises purely through the testing of heroic achievement.[79] Henry illustrates therefore a development in the presentation of a character. Moulton's critique treats Henry in the same way that we might view a modern comic-book hero: he is essentially without weakness and cannot fail, and it is only our knowledge of his character and abilities that develops as the narrative unfolds. Moulton proposes that the English nation, as much as Henry himself, is the hero of the play. Henry is less a character than an embodiment of a national spirit. Moulton does not waste the opportunity to draw comparisons with a more recent national hero and identifies in Henry an image of the Duke of Wellington (1769–1852), the victor of Waterloo.[80]

Such comparisons prove irresistible for another great Victorian critic, the poet Algernon Charles Swinburne (1837–1909), who first measures Henry up against the Prussian expansionist King Frederick the Great (1712–86), then evokes a more contemporary allusion to British power in India, which had been established in the eighteenth century by Robert Clive (1725–74), consolidated by Warren Hastings (1732–1818), and reinforced in the later nineteenth century by the British Raj, the period of direct British rule which began in 1858 in response to the Indian Mutiny (1857–9). Swinburne professes that Shakespeare's 'typical English hero or historic protagonist is a man of their type who founded and built up

THE NINETEENTH CENTURY 55

the empire of England in India; a hero after the future pattern of Hastings and of Clive'.[81] He also touches upon a point that frequently re-emerges in *Henry V* criticism, and one earlier hinted at by Gervinus: that Shakespeare's artistry suffers during his attempts to create a convincing, attractive patriotic hero. As Swinburne says of the three plays in which Henry appears: 'of all Shakespeare's plays they are the most rhetorical; there is more talk than song in them, less poetry than oratory, more finish than form, less movement than incident'.[82] Such sentiments accord with Dowden's identification of a set of practical facts in *Henry V* and Moulton's comments on how Henry's heroism is represented at the cost of character development and complexity. At this stage such comments are observations rather than censure and, with the exception of Hazlitt's early pronouncements, the view of *Henry V* and its hero in nineteenth-century criticism is predominantly positive. However, one can begin to identify the development of a more sustained negative critical tradition in the work of the literary scholar and classicist William Watkiss Lloyd.

WILLIAM WATKISS LLOYD

Lloyd's discussion of *Henry V* in his *Critical Essays on the Plays of Shakespeare* (1875) begins by revisiting earlier claims that the play only makes sense when read in sequence with the previous histories. Not only does the moral of the action in *Henry V* have implications for the story of Henry VI, in that we know that Henry's victory is merely provisional, but the play also requires us to consider 'anterior' elements from *Henry IV*, relating both to Falstaff and to Henry IV's dying advice that Hal 'busy giddy minds/ With foreign quarrels (*2 Henry IV* 4.3.342–3), together with the Bishop of Carlisle's prophetic warning about England's future from *Richard II* (4.1.125–40).[83] All of the anterior points Lloyd identifies make no suggestion that the king's actions in *Henry V* are to be viewed heroically and, indeed, threaten to compromise a positive interpretation of the play at any time:

■ In the mind of the spectator of the present play, as in that of the king, there is therefore the latent sense, the half-suspended consciousness, that a back account of original misdoing may be at any time, and must at last be brought forward.[84] □

Betraying a trace of the essentialist mode in criticizing Henry as if he were directly responsible for what he says and does in the play, Lloyd then berates the king for too easily accepting the clergy's advocacy of his claim to France. Lloyd draws parallels between episodes in Canterbury's recitation of French history in 1.2 and the actions of the first and second Lancastrians. The history is full of usurpations and contested claims and Louis IX's desire to secure his claim to France (mentioned in 1.2.77–85) is compared to that of Henry V himself, though Shakespeare would have found this matter in his source Holinshed, which is quoted almost verbatim here.[85] It is the religious hypocrisy of the play to which Lloyd particularly objects and he baulks at Henry's frequent references to God, seeing them as sanctimonious more than sincere. Lloyd also expands upon Hazlitt's criticism of 'brute force, glossed over with a little religious hypocrisy and archiepiscopal advice':

■ Side by side with the blaze of heroism throughout the play, we have lively allusion to the havoc and atrocities of war, and side by side also appeals to God; and it is shame and pity if we cannot see the native blackness of ambition all the more distinctly, when the very practice and figure of mangled peace and desolated society lies bleeding before us, and wrangling princes trample upon humanity to resent a mock and found ill-gotten power, and cover all with the cloak of half-faced piety and spurious religion.[86] □

Unlike Hazlitt, however, Lloyd finds the soliloquy on the night before Agincourt particularly unimpressive, scorning any suggestion that Henry is truly penitent and seeing the speech as comprised entirely of the king's disappointment at his subject's ingratitude and a personal complaint about the hardship of his own situation.[87] This is a far cry from the positive practical lesson that Dowden identified in the scene. Lloyd is equally as cynical about the Chorus's function, challenging the view that it represents Shakespeare's own voice and seeing it instead as the mouthpiece of unthinking public opinion:

■ He embodies the spirit of the crowd that rush well-dressed to any bustle of external parade, and are ever ready to mistake success for right and splendour for glory, gold chains for judgment and a uniform for a hero.[88] □

Lloyd's observations certainly open up the debate concerning exactly whose side the Chorus is on. He also makes the insightful point that the Chorus is less an apologist (as earlier critics suggested) than it is an emphatic device that draws attention to the link between the fifteenth-century story and the sixteenth-century performance.[89] Lloyd again anticipates later critical preoccupations and the work of Harold C. Goddard and Robert Ornstein who treat the Chorus as a form of alienation device designed to arrest an uncomplicated or unambiguous appreciation of *Henry V* (see Chapter 6).

Such an unequivocally critical view and accompanying aggressive stance had been practically unheard of since Hazlitt's lone attack in 1817.

But for all of Lloyd's difference of perspective, there are limits to the extent to which simply lambasting a character's failings can be considered productive criticism, and there is little attempt to address Shakespeare's construction and deployment of such a character. Lloyd is an important indicator, however, that there are ample grounds for a balanced debate about Henry's virtues and failings (though he restricts himself solely to the latter), a debate that would develop in complexity throughout the twentieth century and beyond. One should not, however, misrepresent or over-simplify the play's nineteenth-century critical landscape. The achievements of the earlier generations of German scholars that established a vocabulary for discussing the play's structure and relation to the other histories would also be recognized by subsequent critics, such as Tillyard, interested in cyclic, organicist readings of *Henry V*. As subsequent chapters of this Guide will reveal, concerns about the relative merits both of *Henry V*'s hero and of the play's structure and integrity remain at the core of twentieth-century criticism.

CHAPTER FOUR

The Early Twentieth Century: What Makes a Good King?

Literary criticism of the early twentieth century continues to refine the rigorous, analytic methodologies for interpretation and criticism developed during the later nineteenth century and the discipline becomes more firmly rooted within a professional, institutional academic setting. Victorian critics such as Dowden and Moulton had already marked out themselves and their mode of enquiry from the more subjective, reflective commentary typical of earlier generations of men of letters such as Johnson and Hazlitt. But later-nineteenth- and early twentieth-century critics of *Henry V* were just as interested as their forebears in examining and accounting for Shakespeare's construction of Henry's character and ensured that any investigation of the play's structure, genre and tone was centred on, and rarely distanced from, a critique of the king himself. As we have seen, it would be wrong to suggest that every nineteenth-century critic was unreservedly positive about *Henry V* or to look to the spectacular Victorian theatrical productions as a direct and wholly repre-sentative indicator of a contemporary scholarly consensus. However, one does continue to find reiterations of a heroic, patriotic view of Henry throughout the first quarter of the twentieth century up to and during the period of the First World War.

HENRY GOES TO WAR (1)

At the very start of the twentieth century the Boer Wars fought between Britain and the South African republics of the Orange Free State and Transvaal provided another opportunity for commentators and directors to use *Henry V* as an imaginative resource for articulating and arousing popular patriotism. Lewis Waller's 1900–1 production at the Lyceum Theatre, London, was one of the last great spectacular envisionings of the play. A reviewer for *The Stratford Herald* highlighted its application to contemporary martial endeavours, invoking the name of Lord Robert Baden-Powell (1857–1941), famously remembered for founding the

Scouting movement, who successfully defended the town of Mafeking in modern-day South Africa against the Boers for nine months between 1899 and 1900.

> ■ Even in the matter of cheery good humour and resource Henry and his handful of starved English before Agincourt seemed to share the same spirit across five centuries with Baden-Powell and the defenders of Mafeking.[1] □

Such sentiments had already been proposed by the eminent literary scholar Sir Sidney Lee who wrote a short souvenir pamphlet to accompany Waller's production in which he suggested a topical emendation to the Chorus's line about Essex's return in 5.0.31:

> ■ We feel instinctively that the change of a simple word ('Afric' for 'Ireland') would carry a step further Shakespeare's method of vivifying the past by associating it with the present, and would give this sentence an application even more immediate to our own contemporary history.[2] □

Lee thus identifies a continuity between Shakespeare's political use of history and the contemporary allusive appropriations of the play's heroic fervour. His specific reference to there being an instinctive reflex to draw such a productive comparison between past and present is particularly interesting as it articulates a response found throughout *Henry V*'s reception history: that the play inevitably transcends the fifteenth-century historical moment of its narrative matter and the sixteenth-century moment of its composition and performance to invite contemporary comparison and application. Perhaps this is a result of the Chorus's prompting as he asserts the play's reliance upon an audience's contemporary understanding of warfare – be it with swords, muskets, machine-guns or tanks – to piece out the imperfections of Shakespeare's text. The play, continues Lee, cannot help but rouse, 'in every man, woman and child of English birth and breeding, who is endowed in normal measure with the healthy instinct of patriotism', a national spirit shared with that of the original Elizabethan audiences.[3] Lee's notion of the correct response to the play might be criticized in that it evokes one's passions more than it engages one's rational and critical faculties, though this may be entirely forgivable in a publication aimed at a predominantly non-academic audience. Lee continues in a similar vein in his book *Shakespeare and the Modern Stage* (1906) though he proceeds to qualify his ideas on the constructive (rather than simply reactive) function of patriotism: 'Shakespearean drama enjoins those who love their country wisely to neglect no advantage that nature offers in the way of resisting unjust demands upon it'.[4] Through demonstrating how national glory is both won and lost, and exhibiting its generally transient and brittle state, the history plays offer a lesson in the mechanics of patriotism to be applied in the present.

In the introduction to his 1908 edition of *Henry V* Lee reads the play as a study of an exemplary English character, subordinating any element of formal or topical potential interest to his *idée fixe* with Henry in a manner that demonstrates the full extent to which critics can go to turn a complex, multivocal dramatic work into a one-dimensional biographcal study.

> ■ Shakespeare's *Henry V* is as far as possible removed from what is generally understood by drama. It is without intrigue or entanglement; it propounds no problems of psychology; its definite motive is neither comic nor tragic; women play in it the slenderest part; it lacks plot in any customary sense. In truth, the piece is epic narrative, or rather heroic biography, adapted to the purposes of the stage. The historical episodes – political debate, sieges, encampments, battles, diplomatic negotiations – with which the scenes deal, are knit together by no more complex bond than the chronological succession of events, the presence in each of the same dramatis personae and the predominance in each of the same character – the English King, in whose mouth the dramatist sets nearly a third of all the lines of the play. A few of the minor personages excite genuine interest, and there are some attractive scenes of comic relief, but these have no organic connection with the central thread of the play. Shakespeare's efforts were mainly concentrated on the portraiture of 'this star of England', King Henry, whom he deliberately chose out of the page of history as the fittest representative of the best distinctive type of English character.[5] □

Rather than trying to integrate each individual aspect into an organic whole, Lee sees Henry as the sole unifying device in the play. Lee's treatment of the play hereafter remains fixated teleologically upon what Henry will ultimately achieve and become by the final act. Lee heaps effulgent praise on Henry's martial character but is aware that the skills and attributes becoming of an effective soldier do not always mean that he would make a particularly friendly or sympathetic figure. Lee is one of the first of many to identify a necessary utilitarian quality in his hero, realizing that Henry's effectiveness (as Shakespeare presents it) is the result of both inculcating affection and exercising ruthlessness: '[h]e conducts war with such humanity as is practicable'. Lee concludes his remarks by celebrating Henry's unequivocal status as a national hero:

> ■ Alone in Shakespeare's gallery of English monarchs does Henry's portrait evoke at once a joyous sense of satisfaction in the high potentialities of human character and a sense of pride among Englishmen that a man of his mettle is of English race.[6] □

Earlier commentators such as Gervinus, Dowden and Swinburne wrote about how *Henry V* relates to often rather abstract notions of nationalism, but more than any critic before him, Lee identifies an unmistakably English brand of patriotism at the play's heart.

Lee's praise is echoed in Felix E. Schelling's study of eary modern historical drama, *The English Chronicle Play* (1902). *Henry V* unequivocally displays how 'the paragon of chivalry expands into the hero king' and the play achieves an epic, rather than a dramatic unity through its focus upon the king's personality.[7] Developing a line suggested earlier by Gervinus, Schelling maintains that the English chronicle play form – with *Henry V* as one of its finest exemplars – emerges almost organically in response to a collective upsurge in patriotic sentiment following the defeat of the Armada on 29 July 1588.[8] Offering an elementary form of historicist reasoning, Schelling sees Shakespeare and his contemporaries responding as much to social energies and national spirit as to formal and generic traditions. Schelling's thesis is initially persuasive, though it frequently imposes an intuitively constructed sense of popular consciousness and lacks the evidential basis employed by the Victorian historicist Simpson. It should be noted also that Pugliatti has dispelled the notion that there was a spontaneous, collective celebratory sprit immediately following the famous naval battle and revealed that the outcome was initially quite confused.[9] Even once victory was assured and proclaimed, a threat of further invasion remained until the end of the sixteenth century, including in the year of *Henry V*'s first performance. Interestingly, Schelling begins his discussion of *Henry V* with the very revealing admission that he sets out to challenge what he perceives is already by this point the orthodox contemporary view that Henry is nothing more than a hypocrite.[10] One assumes that Schelling alludes to the pervasive nature of Hazlitt's censorious comments for as we have seen, although anti-Henry sentiment emerges in several late-nineteenth-century discussions of the play, such as Lloyd's hostile response discussed in Chapter 3, there is very little that approaches the level of criticism levelled at Henry from the 1920s onwards. One exceptional example might be the brief remarks of George Bernard Shaw (1856–1950) who, in reviewing an 1896 performance of *1 Henry IV*, objected to Shakespeare's presentation of such a 'Jingo hero' and 'able young Philistine', concluding that the character's popularity 'is like that of a prizefighter' for whom nobody feels sorry.[11] Schelling's comment and overall defensive stance both support the wider thesis of his book that chronicle plays develop out of a spirit of popular patriotism and positivity and reveal an awareness that Henry *could* attract criticism and controversy, even if the representation of his actions could be entirely accounted for and defended. One critic who does begin to criticize Henry in earnest, particularly for his hypocrisy and ruthlessness, is A. C. Bradley.

A. C. BRADLEY

Bradley is often referred to as the last of the great Victorian critics, not merely in terms of chronology, but because of his extraordinary attention to character analysis and the mode of Shakespeare study that has its roots even further back with Morgann and Hazlitt. But Bradley may be considered more productively in the light of early twentieth-century criticism since his treatment of Henry as a calculating, ruthless pragmatist marks a departure from earlier eulogistic accounts and looks ahead to the imminent proliferation of critical, ironic readings. In his lecture 'The Rejection of Falstaff', first given at Oxford in 1902 (published 1909), Bradley sets out to explore the motives behind Henry's rejection at the end of *2 Henry IV* and the implications this has for our understanding of both characters in the *Henry IV* plays and *Henry V*. Bradley's treatment of *Henry V* is inexorably bound up with his discussion of the two earlier plays but his essay is useful here as it sees Falstaff's rejection as symptomatic of Henry's character traits that continue into the later play. We should perhaps not be surprised at Henry's hypocrisy when he casts off his old friend as he had earlier explained the rationale for affiliating with base company in his first 'I know you all' soliloquy in *1 Henry IV* 1.2.192–214. Bradley's dilemma, however, is that both Falstaff and Henry are attractive characters and yet how do we account for Shakespeare's decision to excise the one and present the other as a hypocrite? The difficulty arises, says Bradley, from our surprise at Henry's conduct which in turn is the result both of our unwillingness to conceive that Shakespeare should deceive us about his characters and the fact that, particularly in the histories, we are always attempting to read Shakespeare as a 'partisan'.[12] We are inclined, almost instinctively, to see Shakespeare as being incontrovertibly on the side of his heroes and protagonists, yet this is misguided:

> ■ He shows us that Richard II was unworthy to be king, and we at once conclude that he thought Bolingbroke's usurpation justified; whereas he shows merely, what under the conditions was bound to exist, an inextricable tangle of right and unright.[13] □

Rather than constructing an unproblematic Shakespeare, Bradley rightly identifies that ambivalence and potential (mis)interpretation on the audience's part are vital aspects of the playwright's artistry. Similarly, in *Henry V*, Shakespeare invites us to view the king as a national hero and popular favourite possessed of enthusiasm, modesty, charm and piety. But such attributes are not presented merely for their own sake: '[h]aving these and other fine qualities, and being without certain dangerous tendencies which mark the tragic heroes, he is, perhaps, the most *efficient* character drawn by Shakespeare' (Bradley's italics).[14] For Bradley this is the key to Henry's character and actions. Despite the king's attractive facets he possesses 'a readiness to use other people as means to his own ends'.[15]

Learned early modern audiences would certainly have been aware that this aspect of Henry lies at the heart of the kind of *realpolitik* expounded upon and advocated by Niccolò Machiavelli (1469–1527) in *The Prince* (1513), an influential treatise on effective (or 'efficient', to use Bradley's word) methods of rule. Machiavelli identified that successful rulers could not be bound to polarized values of morality and immorality, good and evil, but should combine charisma, pragmatism, ruthlessness and duplicity for political expedience as situations dictated. Being a 'good' king politically did not automatically equate with a moral conception of goodness, and many later twentieth-century critics including Stephen Greenblatt, Jonathan Dollimore and Alan Sinfield expand upon the difficult implications of this point as it applies to *Henry V*. For the time being, despite recognizing the significance of Henry's pragmatism, Bradley still finds it difficult to understand why Shakespeare should invite the audience's resentment of the prince that carries on well into *Henry V* through references to the Eastcheap contingent. He believes that we are actually led by the end of *2 Henry IV* to turn from Falstaff for ourselves, since Shakespeare could surely never have intended to end a play on a 'disagreeable' note.[16] Again the later history of Shakespeare criticism amply demonstrates that irresolution and lack of closure are common in many of the plays and – far from being something to be avoided or explained away – they can provide the starting point for insightful critical analysis. Difficulties arise once more in that, so Bradley is convinced, it is almost impossible for us not to find delight and amusement in Falstaff and to forgive his lies.[17] In doing so, Bradley manufactures one of the chief obstacles that he believes Shakespeare himself presents. This is yet another example both of the enduring critical obsession with Falstaff and of the implications this fixation has for objective appreciation of *Henry IV* and *Henry V*.

As the language of my own text in the preceding paragraph may reflect, Bradley's expository method centres on a belief that his view is identical to ours as audiences, readers and critics. Like Hazlitt, he uses collective first-person pronouns to voice 'our' shared responses to the plays and ventriloquize how we react to Henry, as seen in his phrasing of his essay's remit: 'What do we feel, and what are we meant to feel, as we witness this rejection? And what does our feeling imply as to the characters of Falstaff and the new King?'[18] Such a method implies perforce that there is a unitary, correct form of response to Shakespeare with which we – the everyman audience – are expected to accord. Equally as problematic for modern readers is Bradley's essentialist conception of character and contrivance of interiority and thought-processes for Falstaff and Henry. Typical of Bradley's method of filling in explanatory blanks by recreating characters' unvoiced thoughts is his extrapolation on the lines in *2 Henry IV* (5.5.75–9) about how Falstaff deludes himself that the new king must only be *seen* to reject him, believing that he would be sent for by Henry before nightfall. Further layers of delusion might be traced in the supposition that Falstaff really knew that he would not be sent for but feigns such to fool Master Shallow who accompanies the knight from Gloucestershire in the final act.[19] The essentialist approach also supports Bradley's wider arguments about Henry's pragmatism and the inherent difficulty with rejecting Falstaff. Henry's conduct is blamed on a familial trait:

■ The truth is, that the members of the family of Henry IV have love for one another, but they cannot spare love for any one outside their family, which stands firmly united, defending its royal position against attack and instinctively isolating itself from outside influence.[20] □

In a similar vein, Bradley suggests that Shakespeare clearly loses control of his character after writing Falstaff's part: '[h]e created so extraordinary a being, and fixed him so firmly on his intellectual throne, that when he sought to dethrone him he could not'.[21] Falstaff is thus left on his own to lumber his way beyond the play texts in the imaginations of critics and audiences.

Bradley's pro-Falstaff – and, by implication, anti-Henry – stance was widely criticized, largely due to its methodology. In a 1914 article on Falstaff, the American critic E. E. Stoll (1874–1959) poured scorn on Bradley for his Romantic mode of sympathizing intensely with Shakespeare's characters and criticized his consequent reasoning as being amateurish, unscholarly and intuitive.[22] Stoll's own discussion of *Henry V* in *Poets and Playwrights* (1930) is hardly more advanced and seems rather lightweight by modern scholarly standards, consisting of vague platitudes about the portrait of human life offered in the play and subjective pronouncements about Henry's 'practical', 'sportsmanlike' and 'manly' character.[23] Dover Wilson later challenges Bradley directly in *The Fortunes of Falstaff* (1943) arguing that the knight plays the part of a Vice figure who is clearly intended from the outset of the Henriad to be abandoned without condemnation either in *2 Henry IV* or – Dover Wilson maintains – during *Henry V*.[24] The loss of the clown, Will Kempe (c. 1560–c. 1603), from Shakespeare's company in 1599 appears to have led to the former option.

Despite his evident methodological failings, Bradley is important to include in this Guide, not only because his comments on Henry's conduct in rejecting Falstaff predicate a more cynical reading of *Henry V* but also because they begin to stress the potentially negative aspects of what makes Henry a successful, effective king. Ultimately, Bradley earns his place in any Shakespearean reception history since so many critics on *Henry V* throughout the twentieth century write in reaction to the Bradleian mode of character essentialism, as we shall see below.

HENRY GOES TO WAR (2)

Following the outbreak of the First World War in 1914 *Henry V* assumed a new form of topical relevance. With mass conscription across Europe and appallingly high levels of casualties and losses, Shakespeare's play about fighting in France inevitably evoked an even darker conception than ever before of the visceral immediacy of war. Critics and commentators quickly found that *Henry V* could be employed to speak about the war and they used Shakespeare's 'happy few' to reflect upon the many millions fighting between 1914 and 1918 over much of the same geographical territory that Henry had won during the fifteenth century. The connection between medieval and modern combatants was poignantly evoked in a short story called 'The Bowmen' written by Arthur Machen (1863–1947) for the London *Evening News* in September 1914 in which the ghosts of fallen English archers from Agincourt appear upon the battlefields and assist their countrymen by shooting German soldiers with invisible arrows. The story quickly transformed into popular myth with many soldiers claiming to have actually seen Henry's archers during combat.[25] Within the early twentieth-century context, fighting in France no longer entailed fighting against the French. Warfare in the play was now treated more in the abstract and it was personal and national integrity that attracted greater attention than the anti-Gallic literalism of eighteenth- and nineteenth-century *Henry V* criticism and adaptations. In wartime productions of the play, notions of realism shifted from 'the antiquarian search for correct heraldic devices or Elizabethan staging methods into an emotional realm of wartime experiences, of separation, fear, bereavement, comradeship'.[26]

Midway through the First World War, the year 1916 saw extensive celebrations for the tercentenary of Shakespeare's death. The wartime context heightened the patriotic spirit of the occasion and *Henry V* played a predictably key part in consolidating national fervour. Passages from the play were marshalled to celebrate the war and denigrate the enemy (and their Shakespeare scholarship) in Francis Colmer's *Shakespeare in Time of War* (1916).[27] In the *Shakespeare Tercentenary Observance in the Schools and Other Institutions* pamphlet produced the same year, 'Notes on Shakespeare the Patriot' by Sir Israel Gollancz (1863–1930) singles out Henry as a particularly appropriate contemporary model: 'Shakespeare gives us, in the person of the King, his ideal Patriot-Englishman, and the play rings out to-day as a trumpet-call to all'.[28] Throughout the war, *Henry V* remained popular for school productions and speech days.

J. A. R. Marriott's *English History in Shakespeare* (written in 1916, published in 1918) provides a good example of a wartime appropriation of the histories, especially *Henry V*. Several of the Victorian critics had written about the energizing quality of the plays; Marriott in turn highlights their particular value in wartime and beyond:

■ The study of the Chronicle Plays may well serve to steel our hearts to the efforts and sacrifices which are still undoubtedly ahead of us in the war, and to atune our minds to an earnest consideration of the domestic problems which will await solution on the return of peace.[29] □

Marriott aims to draw out the political moral of the histories not merely as solace for the present but – and perhaps more importantly – as a lesson for the future. Like Dowden, he reads the histories for their presentation of models of active heroism and identifies that Henry V constitutes the ideal heroic character of all the plays. He then works through many of the commonplaces of a patriotic reading of Henry, determined to preserve 'one of the few remaining heroes of my boyhood'.[30] The title of Marriott's most relevant chapter, 'King Henry the Fifth: The Spirit of England in Victory', indicates his aggressively pro-Henry line. The play gives Shakespeare the chance to depict 'the ideal Christian knight; a ruler who was at once popular and successful; a man whom we may both love and admire'.[31] Returning to an earlier object of contention, Marriott believes that Henry's inherent brilliance in fact necessitates the Chorus's apologies for the inadequacy of the medium through which the hero is presented; the climax of Shakespeare's studies in English kingship requires the innovation of the Chorus.[32] Marriott praises Henry's merciful, pious and dignified conduct, and admires his simplicity and familiarity. Henry remains 'the model for all time of patriotic poetry', infused with 'the glow which comes, and can only come from a passionate love of country and of kind'.[33]

Marriott's chapter offers a representative example of how patriotic readings of *Henry V* typically both foreground certain aspects (Henry's virtuous qualities, particularly his piety) and negotiate or omit others (such as the killing of prisoners or the justice of the cause). On the latter point Marriott preserves a positive interpretation of Henry's decision to go to war by claiming that Shakespeare uses the opening act to offer an anticlerical critique. Any suggestion of guilt is shifted to the clergy, as Canterbury himself encourages: 'The sin on my head, dread sovereign' (1.2.97).[34] Elsewhere Marriott draws on medieval and early modern historical sources to support Shakespeare's heroic depiction of Henry.

As we will see, post-war critics were to become far less willing to negotiate problematic or (to use Bradley's term) 'disagreeable' aspects of the play. The first significant post-war response, by the journalist and academic Gerald Gould, remains to date one of the most vehemently negative critiques of the play and its hero, and certainly informs a vast amount of subsequent *Henry V* criticism.

GERALD GOULD

Located in an issue of *The English Review* for 1919 alongside items on military discipline and demobilization is Gould's modestly titled landmark essay 'A New Reading of *Henry V*'. Gould makes one of the most important contributions to twentieth-century *Henry V* scholarship and his work intersects with many of the themes and preoccupations already discussed, particularly relating to Henry's character and the treatment of Falstaff. It also breaks a lot of new ground in presenting a more cynical, yet sophisticated reading of the play. Gould's opening lines proclaim that *Henry V* is the most 'persistently and thoroughly misunderstood' of Shakespeare's plays, the reason being that critics thus far have failed to respond to its deeply ironic nature.[35] In doing so, he confronts both the pro- and anti-Henry line taken in previous studies. Dismissing critics such as Marriott who read *Henry V* at face value as patriotic, Gould demands a more nuanced interpretation of the king's perceived heroism and reformulates exactly how this should be done.

> ■ That Shakespeare was a patriot there is neither reason nor excuse for denying. What must be denied is that *Henry V* is patriotic. Precisely because Shakespeare *was* patriotic, he must have felt revolted by Henry's brutal and degrading 'militarism'. (Gould's italics)[36] □

Gould also challenges Hazlitt's and Bradley's responses to Henry. Those of the former were founded on a belief that, since Shakespeare apparently favoured Henry, the play fails because he actually turns out to be such a despicable individual. Bradley too did not conceive that Shakespeare could somehow offer a criticism of the king in *Henry V* and maintained that a correct, positive reading must be sought at all costs.[37] Gould's interpretation is indeed new in that he raises the question as to whether we are ever supposed to like or identify with Henry. Unlike many earlier critics who either apparently forget that Henry's character was based on an historical figure or elide (like Hazlitt) the historical and dramatic Henrys, Gould remains mindful of the playwright's role in shaping his text and its characters. Henry may be a 'bad', unattractive, problematic character, but that is exactly how Shakespeare intended him to be read. Henry's 'disagreeable' aspects that Bradley identifies and the contradictions in *Henry V* that Gould proceeds to detail are all part of Shakespeare's consciously ironic presentation. Therefore, says Gould, '*Henry V* is a satire on monarchical government, on imperialism, on the baser kinds of "patriotism", and on war'.[38] Henry's characteristic hypocrisy, selfishness and cold pragmatism appear consistently across all three plays in which he features and it is these attributes that Gould identifies as illustrative of Shakespeare's conception of militarism. Echoing Bradley's comments on both efficient leadership and the self-centredness of the Bolingbroke line, Gould argues that

> ■ in such 'militarism' as Henry's [Shakespeare] saw an outstanding example of what cold successfulness means in the political and international sphere, and this impression was fortified by his reading of the characters of Henry's father and brother. In devoting the play of *Henry V*, which is both a complete play in itself and the conclusion of a trilogy, to a satire on 'militarism', he was providing a central and conclusive example of a constant theme.[39] □

The infamous rejection scene at the end of *2 Henry IV* can be explained by realizing that Shakespeare hated Henry and his family but loved Falstaff. It can be understood by reading it quite literally: we are *supposed* to feel revulsion, distaste; it is meant to be a disagreeable ending. Shakespeare thus sacrifices Falstaff to cast Henry as a ruthless, cold-hearted 'prig'.

Gould goes on to address two key areas of concern that remain, even today, at the forefront of *Henry V* criticism: the contrivance of Henry's dynastic claim to France and subsequent justification of war, and his brutality while campaigning. Gould begins by questioning whether dynastic wars can ever be justified given that 'they cost the blood of the common people who have nothing to do with dynasties', and remains mindful that this is not an anachronistic observation but a matter that also preoccupied early modern writers including Erasmus and Sir Thomas More (1478–1535).[40] Shakespeare's intention to satirize Henry's cause is clear from the opening scene featuring the scheming churchmen, and Gould argues that the whole of the first act consciously seeks to confuse the motivations and causes for war, encompassing as it does domestic policy, ecclesiastical self-interest, dynastic justice, peer expectation (see Exeter's comments in 1.2.122–4) and vengeance for the Dauphin's mockery. Complications continue in that Henry had already made demands on the French prior to the events of the play, to which the Dauphin's embassy and tennis-balls respond, and before Canterbury has revealed details of Henry's claim to France derived from his great-grandfather Edward III (1.1.87–90). Gould carefully maps out how references in the play to Anglo-French diplomacy (including in 2.4 and the Chorus to Act three) continually confuse a specific claim to 'certain' possessions in France and a more general claim to the French throne itself.[41] This is not, says Gould, mere carelessness on Shakespeare's part; contradiction and absurdity are a calculated means of stressing the insincerity of Henry's character that further undermines the authority of his claims.[42] Henry's brutality invites similar censure and Gould's essay shines a light on many of the unpleasant, unheroic parts of the play that are largely ignored by previous critics. It is difficult to admire Henry following the violent demands made to Harfleur's governor in 3.3.81–123 that target women, children and the elderly. Gould again identifies that confusion and contradiction are Shakespeare's principal means of generating irony, forcing us to adopt an interrogative stance towards the play. Such is the case in the episode with Williams and Bates on the night before Agincourt where Henry attempts to obscure the issue of the campaign's justice by referring to the soldiers' sins committed before the war.[43] The motives behind the killing of prisoners are equally as confused (as discussed earlier in this Guide): is it done out of angry vengeance or as a precaution against another French assault? Finally, Gould points out the resemblance between the inglorious profiteering of Pistol, Nym and Bardolph and Henry's own acquisitive motives for going to France; territorial conquest is simply theft writ large.[44]

At the very end of his essay Gould cannot resist returning to Falstaff and seeing *Henry V* as an extended confirmation of the king's character traits epitomized in the rejection scene in *2 Henry IV*. He draws a slightly over-wrought, chiasmic comparison between the scene in *Henry V* depicting the conspirators' exposure (2.2) and the scene in which Falstaff's death is described (2.3):

■ [These scenes] comprise the unmasking of the treachery of Cambridge, Scroop, and Grey, *with enormous stress laid on the sin of ingratitude towards a former comrade* – and the death of Falstaff, *the victim of the King's ingratitude towards a former comrade.* (Gould's italics)[45] □

Again we are encouraged to draw an ironic comparison, and Gould establishes the Henry–Falstaff axis – the antithesis between 'cold success and sinful humanity' – as the central theme of the Henriad. Gould's concluding statement that the king has proved 'a false friend', and his implication that this is Shakespeare's final moral judgement upon Henry, can seem rather anticlimactic given the essay's larger, more radical claims.[46] However, it is Gould's argument that Shakespeare actively invites interrogation of Henry's 'cold success' that really stands out here. Gould without a doubt advances the sophistication of *Henry V* scholarship through his nuanced appreciation of the difference between delineating perceived failings of the play and its hero and recognizing that Shakespeare has already built in an ironic critique. His attention to points of ambiguity and contradiction anticipates the methods of many later treatments of *Henry V* that appear during the 1950s–70s and he lays solid foundations for subsequent critics who seek to find more than a crude pageant play and pasteboard patriotic hero and who remain keen to recognize the complexity and intelligence of Shakespeare's work. Although Gould dwells upon Falstaff in part of the essay, he also opens up whole new areas of *Henry V* to interpretation and identifies many of the problematic, contradictory passages that still invite extensive criticism: the churchmen's machinations and justification of war; the violence of the Harfleur parley; Henry's unsatisfactory response to Williams's concerns; and the parodic relation of the Eastcheap contingent to the principal protagonists. All of these are revisited in later chapters of this Guide.

It is difficult not to place Gould's essay in context and view it alongside the more widespread popular cynicism towards combat and militarism that emerges post-1918 when more people than ever before had obtained firsthand experience of warfare in its most visceral form and discovered that it would not be a great and glorious thing to die for one's country. *Henry V* criticism of the 1920s and 30s continued to focus upon the king's character and relationship with Falstaff and there is no shortage of positive, patriotic readings. But there were also increasing numbers of commentators who followed Gould's lead in subjecting *Henry V*, and Shakespeare's attitude to its hero, to more politically alert scrutiny. *Henry V* character criticism itself continued to move on from simple identification of desirable and undesirable attributes to the more complex issue of the problematic relationship between Henry's humanity and his royal office. Two of the best critical treatments of this theme are the contrasting essays by John Palmer and Una Ellis Fermor, both of which appeared in 1945.

HENRY AS KING AND MAN: JOHN PALMER AND UNA ELLIS-FERMOR

Palmer's posthumously published *Political Characters of Shakespeare* sets out to elucidate how the playwright explores the relationship between the human and political aspect of several characters from the English and Roman histories. Shakespeare is cast as a latter-day Plutarch (46–127 AD) interested in rulers' private lives more than their public actions, and Palmer maintains that the plays demonstrate that 'his main concern was not so much with the politics as with the men who made them'.[47] Palmer begins by accepting that for many Henry will always appear as the conventional Christian hero but recognizes that this should only be the starting point for further analysis: to what end does Shakespeare present such a figure and how does the writer really regard his creation? Shakespeare's method, says Palmer, is more balanced:

> ■ He took his hero for better or for worse. He says in effect: 'Here is your mirror of all Christian kings. No one can deny that he cuts a very splendid figure. You may like him or not; that is not my affair. I have imagined for you such a man and he is just the sort of man who would behave as this man behaved and achieve what he achieved'.[48] □

Once Henry has become king, however, he begins to dwindle as a man while his status as a hero enlarges. *Henry V* becomes a character study of how the (merely) human individual struggles to 'come to terms with the swelling monarch'.[49] The Chorus signals the momentousness of this task from the outset; it is less an apology than an indication that Shakespeare is shifting up a gear.[50] Palmer argues that the entire play shows the struggle between Henry as king and Henry as man, and that the two are symbiotically connected:

> ■ Apotheosis of the king proceeds hand in hand with disturbingly intimate revelations of the man. They are warp and woof in a tapestry from which a central figure of heraldic simplicity is, on a closer view, discerned as a fallibly human creature.[51] □

Shakespeare therefore builds into the play a series of moments where the king interacts with elements that draw out his more human aspect, the most significant of which is his nocturnal visit to his troops in 4.1. The scene offers a chance to recover Henry 'the man' from beneath his role as politician and military leader. Shakespeare's depiction of Henry is entirely positive here, Palmer maintains; it represents the difficult balance of priorities achieved in his character:

> ■ He is not deliberately anatomising a moral humbug or plumbing the depths of self-deception to which a successful politician may be driven. He is presenting in all simplicity a political hero – the things that a political hero, when he is Henry of Monmouth, quite inevitably does and says.[52] □

Palmer reads the soliloquy (4.1.218–72) that follows the conversation with Williams and Bates as Henry's first sincere utterance, not only in *Henry V* but in all three plays in which he appears.[53] He concludes by reiterating that Shakespeare intended neither censure nor commendation of Henry but rather recognizes 'what sort of man succeeds in public life and in Henry he presents us with just that sort of man'.[54] For Palmer *Henry V* presents quite a balanced interplay between king and man, allowing both facets of Henry magnificent occasions to express their respective virtues and limitations. Palmer is still convinced that Shakespeare's interest lies in evoking the human beneath the public office but he repeatedly avoids making polarized value judgements about Henry's character, recognizing that effective leadership requires actions of questionable moral worth.

Whereas Palmer believes that the play depicts a balance, or at very least a tangible relationship between human and political character, Ellis-Fermor draws an illuminating contrast between the presentation of these aspects in *Henry V* which complements, yet ultimately challenges, Palmer's reading.[55] In her book *The Frontiers of Drama*, Ellis-Fermor returns to the issue of *Henry V*'s relation to the entire sequence of the English histories and argues that their unity derives not from a patriotic national spirit, as Schelling and others maintained, but from the 'central and continuous image' of the ideal statesman-king.[56] Like Dowden, Ellis-Fermor sees Henry as the culmination of a figure developed throughout the course of the histories, the 'summation of his idea of a king, of the man who should fit at every point the demands laid upon him by public office'.[57] While Henry IV exhibits many of the attributes befitting the ideal Tudor conception of kingship he is fatally flawed by his weak title to the crown, the result of the usurpation shown in *Richard II*. Henry IV vocalizes this frustration to his son in their final meeting:

■ God knows, my son,
By what bypaths and indirect crook'd ways
I met this crown □

(*2 Henry IV*, 4.3.312–14)

Implicit also here, says Ellis-Fermor, is the recognition that Henry V epitomizes the perfect combination of both the right and ability to rule, something that none of Shakespeare's other English kings are shown to possess throughout the two tetralogies. Shakespeare has finally 'resolved his demands upon such a figure into certain clearly defined qualifications and summed them all in Henry V, with his unflawed, hereditary title and his assured possession of all kingly attributes'.[58] For Ellis-Fermor, Henry represents the perfect king:

■ With his broad-based popularity, his genuine love of public service for its own sake, his strong sense of responsibility, and his equally clear sense of its relation to privilege, his shrewd statesman's brain, successfully masked as that of a simple soldier, he stands where, perhaps, no king in drama has stood before or after him. Church and state, commoners and noblemen, soldiers and civilians, he knows them all, with a knowledge rooted in the taverns of Eastcheap, and holds them in his hand, too practised, popular, and secure to make a show of mastery.[59] □

Even more than this, Henry appears to embody the sense of cosmic order and harmony expressed at length in Ulysses's famous speech on 'degree' (1.3.74–137) in Shakespeare's *Troilus and Cressida* (1602), an order that relies, in its temporal manifestation, upon 'the figure of the perfect public man'.[60] Tillyard in The *Elizabethan World Picture* (1943) makes frequent recourse to this speech when setting out his vision of a universal cosmic order to which all of Shakespeare's contemporaries apparently subscribed, and as we shall see in the next chapter such a notion of a monolithic world view heavily inflects Tillyard's reading of Shakespeare's histories.

Earlier generations of critics tended to leave things on a positive, celebratory note when viewing Henry as the culmination of Shakespeare's treatment of kingship. But Ellis-Fermor proceeds to suggest that in setting out the ideal statesman-king Shakespeare presents Henry as being simultaneously both 'more and less than a man'. Everything about Henry that we see in the play is the expression of a public figure, the embodiment of his office, the royal body politic:

■ Henry V has indeed transformed himself into a public figure; the most forbidding thing about him is the completeness with which this has been done. He is solid and flawless. There is no attribute in him that is not part of this figure, no desire, no interest, no habit even that is not harmonized with it. He is never off the platform; even when, alone in a moment of weariness and intense anxiety, he sees with absolute clearness the futility of privilege and the burden of responsibility, he still argues his case in general terms, a king's life weighed against a peasant's, peasant against king.[61] □

Ellis-Fermor goes further in arguing that it is fruitless to look for any sense of personality or character of Henry behind that of the king. Henry as an individual is 'utterly eliminated' and it is more appropriate to think of him in terms of a function than as a character; he is a 'dead man walking'.[62] Henry therefore represents the logical extension of a principle extensively explored and debated during Elizabeth's reign, that monarchs must subordinate any sense of private desire, motivation and subjectivity to the demands of their office and the greater public good. This theme is at the heart of Sidney's *Arcadia* (first published 1590) and features in many of the entertainments and masques presented to Elizabeth. *Henry V,* suggests Ellis-Fermor, also contributes to this discourse and the play should be read as a conscious response on Shakespeare's part to the dichotomy between king and man. After presenting Henry as the perfect statesman-king Shakespeare begins to recoil from such a figure and realizes its limitations. The histories therefore constitute an 'experiment' or an 'exploration' into this idealized figure but Shakespeare ultimately rejects his findings and, once *Henry V* was written, turns instead to more inward, personal, private conceptions of virtue and character, as exemplified in the likes of Hamlet or Brutus. Ellis-Fermor thus attempts to account for Shakespeare's shift away from English historical drama and, like several later critics such as Tillyard, tries to rationalize why *Henry V* should be the last of the Elizabethan histories:

> ■ It would seem, then, that in the very act of completing the [statesman-king] figure, Shakespeare became aware of a certain insufficiency, and that dissatisfaction was already implicit in his treatment of Henry V, the culminating study of the series. What was there implicit is revealed by degrees in his treatment in the later plays of similar characters, or characters similarly placed.[63] □

Ellis-Fermor has moved beyond discussing Henry in simple binary terms as a good or bad king, man or character and, like Bradley and Palmer, acknowledges the aesthetic challenges presented by the attempt to portray an effective king as a rounded, human individual.

Ellis-Fermor's interpretations are echoed later by Derek A. Traversi in the 1957 revision to his *Approach to Shakespeare* (first published 1938) as he offers, not so much a defence of Henry, as a recognition of a political reality that 'the administration of justice, upon which depends order within the kingdom and success in its foreign wars, demands from the monarch an impersonality which borders on the inhuman'.[64] Rather than seeing this as a contradiction or a problem to be resolved, Traversi accepts that a certain level of inhumanity is necessary for effective rule. Palmer, Ellis-Fermor and Traversi all recognize that when Henry assumed the office of king he adopted a particular role – complete with unique costume and props – that both mirrors and is mirrored by the part played by the actor taking on the title role in Shakespeare's drama. The self-referential, metadramatic nature of *Henry V* would be re-examined in the 1970s and 80s by Greenblatt and others, as discussed in Chapter 7 of this Guide.

The period covered in this chapter represents an important stage in the development of *Henry V* criticism. It marks the point at which critical evaluations of the play progress beyond reductive character assessments of whether Henry is or is not a good king and into far more complex treatments of both the degree to which Shakespeare himself encourages a critique of the king and the difficulties of dramatizing the thoughts and actions of an effective ruler. As we have seen, critics in this period become far more attuned to identifying the play's multivocal, multivalent properties and the fact that it stages a struggle between competing versions of Henry. They are equally sensitive to how Shakespeare assumes something of a neutral stance in order to achieve a credible degree of political realism in *Henry V*, and they elaborate on the sentiments of

Henry's soliloquy in 4.1 to explore how Shakespeare continues to interrogate what makes a good king, and what distinguishes a king from the common sort. The critical focus on this principal political theme seems to have kept scholarly eyes firmly upon the bigger picture and larger explanatory structures. As a result there are hardly any extended close readings of *Henry V* of a kind that works such as *Macbeth* and the *Henry IV* plays attracted during the early to mid-twentieth century.[65] The studies discussed in this chapter are still unavoidably Henry-centred and there are few treatments that concentrate, for example, on the play's unity or structure without collapsing into an appreciation of the central character's pivotal role. Yet again *Henry V* appears to make most sense when viewed in relation to the other histories, particularly the second tetralogy, and we have examined a number of critics who discuss Henry as king in relation to the events of the *Henry IV* plays, particularly the rejection of Falstaff. As we shall see in the next chapter, many of the ways in which *Henry V* was discussed and employed during the First World War are revisited during the Second World War. As the works of Tillyard, Lily B. Campbell and Dover Wilson demonstrate, politics ceases to be simply an identified theme in *Henry V*. Instead, there is increasing sophistication in the way that critics discuss the play's function within its initial historical context and explore how it both reflects and enacts political ideology, not only in the 1590s, but during the 1940s as well.

CHAPTER FIVE

The Mid-Twentieth Century: History, War and Epic

Despite the negative readings of *Henry V* and its hero that emerged after the First World War, and productions of this period presenting a more pacifist line, the play's patriotic potential once again influenced both critical and dramatic responses following the outbreak of the Second World War in 1939. Adding greater complexity to the more rudimentary jingoistic identifications made in earlier treatments of *Henry V*, criticism of the 1940s began to explore the different ways in which the play engages with the historical contexts of both its composition and subsequent re-staging, and to consider how Shakespeare experiments with a form best suited to the representation of war: the dramatic epic. The period covered in this chapter saw the establishment of the critical perspective and methodology latterly termed historicism, which still, in modified guises, forms the basis of much modern-day criticism. Before discussing the chief practitioners of this approach, and some of the questions it raises, a distinction should be drawn between interpretations of this period that sought to *apply* the play to the wartime context and those that offered extended literary analysis locating *Henry V* in relation to its original historical milieu. It is with this first form of interpretation that we will begin here.

HENRY GOES TO WAR (3)

Perhaps the most famous and most influential appropriation of *Henry V* of the Second World War was Laurence Olivier's film version that was released in November 1944. Detailed discussion of its history and reception lie beyond the scope of this Guide, but the film presents a treatment of *Henry V* that is closely aligned with themes and concerns raised both throughout the play's earlier reception and in critical responses of the 1940s.[1] The film is unashamedly patriotic and draws an immediate allusion to contemporary events through its dedication to 'the Commandos and Airborne Troops of Great Britain, the spirit of whose ancestors it has been humbly attempted to recapture in some ensuing scenes'.[2] It appeared within six months of the D-Day landings in Normandy and there is an implicit invitation to identify Henry's victories in France with the historical moment of the ongoing campaign. However, in order to achieve the kind of rousing, patriotic effect that more than one critic has called 'Churchillian' (alluding to Britain's Prime Minister at the time of the Second World War Sir Winston Churchill (1874–1965)), over 1700 lines had to be cut from the play, in part to allow greater emphasis to be placed on the visual spectacle of the Agincourt battle, but also to efface any sense of contradiction or subversion from the original text. As the Lord Chamberlain's servants found when making the revisions that resulted in the 1600 Quarto (discussed in Chapter 1), the full Folio-based text does not lend itself readily to uncomplicated propaganda. The Olivier film cut all scenes suggesting that England was under threat either from Scotland or within, scenes that presented the enemy as a noble or worthy adversary, and any material that cast a shadow over Henry's character and conduct such as the Harfleur parley, Bardolph's hanging and the killing of prisoners. Olivier also avoided any depiction of bloodshed at Agincourt, heightening the film's mythic, rather than realistic, quality.[3] Unlike the Quarto version and many previous stagings, Olivier's film preserved the Chorus despite the fact that for the first time ever the play could indeed depict 'the very casques / That did affright the air at Agincourt' (1.0.13–14) and was no longer reliant purely on ragged foils augmented by audience imagination. The film's presentation of the first act makes a very good case for retaining the Chorus through actually playing up the metatheatrical dimension by representing an Elizabethan staging of *Henry V*. In doing so it draws attention to the original theatrical moment of the play – or an imagined recreation thereof – and reminds the cinema audience of the detachment between the three key historical moments that the play is about: 1415, 1599/1600 and (implicitly) 1944. The Chorus therefore never allow us fully to lose a sense of how the story of the historical Henry may be applied within different contexts.

Also appearing in 1944, though written during the early 1940s, G. Wilson Knight's long essay 'The Olive and the Sword' attempted in its own way to use Shakespeare as a patriotic, inspirational resource and aimed 'to show what reserves for the refuelling of national confidence exist in Shakespeare's poetry'.[4] Making frequent recourse to urgent and dramatic imagery, Wilson Knight describes the war in dragon-slaying terms, casting Britain as St George – using unmistakably *English* symbolism – and identifying in Shakespeare's works a recurrent interest in narratives 'deeply concerned with the royal soul of England' that presented Christian chivalry in similarly heroic terms.[5] In particular, Shakespeare represents both the embodiment of a unified national identity and the means to reconstitute national unity based on a shared cultural identification. As Graham Holderness writes, the essay is 'more propaganda than scholarship, since the starting-point of the argument is very explicitly not "literature" but the contemporary situation', but it offers a good example of the relative ease with which *Henry V* and its hero could be readily rehabilitated and pressed into national service, and of the resilience of pro-Henry responses.[6] After drawing comparisons between Richard III and Adolf Hitler (1889–1945) and characterizing Hotspur's martial swaggering as 'fascist', Wilson Knight identifies *Henry V* as the summation of the English histories' attempts to model the ideal combination of 'righteousness with power' and 'strong action with religious humility'.[7] It is the gravity of Shakespeare's attempt to Christianize military conquest that therefore necessitates the Chorus's opening apology and casts the play to follow in epic terms.[8]

Wilson Knight then works through the play quoting extended passages demonstrating, without irony, Shakespeare's emphasis on a nation unified for war. Canterbury's speech on the bees' commonwealth, the common enterprise of the regional captains, and the providential exposure of treachery prior to the conquest, all contribute to the image of embattled, though hardy national unity. More problematic episodes such as the Harfleur parley and Henry's conversation with Williams are downplayed. Henry's pious attribution of the Agincourt victory to God (4.7.83–4) apparently further characterizes the king as a 'model of English general-ship'. Wilson Knight's conception of the play's celebratory conclusion draws upon Burgundy's speech about national concord rather than the Chorus's closing mention of Henry VI and the loss of France. His treatment of *Henry V* thus revisits, and to a degree answers, questions raised in his essay's introduction relating to the nation's Christian duty to fight and the need for a national symbolic vocabulary drawn from Shakespeare with which to both inspire and sanction heroic action.

The essay's own history exemplifies how both *Henry V* and its criti-cism could be put to wartime service. Prior to its publication in 1944 it was performed as a three-act play called *This Sceptred Isle* at the West-minster Theatre, London, in July 1941.[9] The play consisted of dramatic scenes that later formed the basis for the lengthy quotations in the essay (and included Wilson Knight himself reading Henry's part) and was interspersed with the actor Henry Ainley (1879–1945) delivering the patriotic commentary relating to each play. Wilson Knight's essay also foregrounds many of the preoccupations found in Tillyard's scholarship produced at around the same time. In particular, there is a similar desire to read the history plays as an extended lesson in the evils of national and social disorder and the corresponding merits of order and unity.[10] For Wilson Knight, Shakespeare's ideological power resides in his ability to structure his plays around narrative patterns and symbols associated with the maintenance of order. There is little detail given at this stage as to how order might be achieved as a political reality and it is wielded more as a desired metaphysical principle that is best represented, if not reified, by the symbol of the crown: 'The Crown symbolises the nation's soul-life, which is also the greater self of each subject'.[11] The chain of analogies that Wilson Knight identifies between metaphysical order, monarchy, national unity and the epic canvas of Shakespeare's histories would also form a vital part of Tillyard's argument in his seminal study of the plays.

E. M. W. TILLYARD

It is difficult to underestimate the significance of Tillyard's *Shakespeare's History Plays* (1944) and virtually impossible now to analyse the histories without acknowledging or at least negotiating the pervasive influence both of his historicist methodology and his elaborate thesis on the providential vision of history identified in the two tetralogies. Shifting away from purely aestheticist readings and the character-centred studies found in Victorian and early twentieth-century Shakespeare scholarship, Tillyard set out to demonstrate how the history plays can be interpreted as political writings.[12] With the exception of Richard Simpson's pioneering essays of 1874, *Henry V* criticism up until the 1940s made little extended attempt to examine the historical context of the play's production and initial reception or to discuss the play in relation to early modern conceptions of the world and state. Tillyard, however, sought to make sense of the play (and all of the histories) by reconstructing a detailed picture of the Elizabethan world view and then considering how Shakespeare drew upon the dominant ideas and traditions of his day. While acknowledging a debt to the historicist scholarship of Edwin Greenlaw, who had earlier explored how works by Spenser and Sidney reflected Elizabethan political standpoints and preoccupations, Tillyard eschews simply reading Shakespeare's histories as naive historical allegories.[13] Tillyard's far more ambitious – and contentious – historicist method saw him contrive an idealized historical background detailing how and why Elizabethans viewed the political and natural world, and their place within it, as a framework for reading literary texts. Such a methodology entailed a huge amount of contextual spadework before attention even turned to the histories themselves and Tillyard set out much of this historical and intellectual reconstructive exposition in a separate book, *The Elizabethan World Picture*, which was conceived in concert with *Shakespeare's History Plays*.[14] (He distils much of this material into the first half of the latter book.) Tillyard reconstructed a world view heavily indebted to medieval and classical cosmological models that presented the universe as a hierarchical system or chain of being with God and the spirits above, followed by mankind and then the animal and plant kingdoms below. The political state was a microcosm of this hierarchy: divinely ordained order in the cosmos corresponded to a monarch's divinely sanctioned rule over the body politic of his kingdom. Maintenance of this hierarchy and the preservation of order in the state was therefore the 'natural' condition of the universe, with any disruption to this model having cosmic (rather than merely temporal) implications.

Tillyard then uses this idea of divinely ordained political order to read Shakespeare's histories, identifying a complex, unified programme of providential history connecting the two tetralogies and presenting them as an extended morality sequence with England itself as the recurrent protagonist.[15] Richard II's deposition represented a violation of universal order which then provoked the divine judgement and punishment exacted upon England through the rebellions of Henry IV's reign, the Wars of the Roses and the rise of the villainous 'scourge of God' Richard III, before Henry Tudor – evidently with divine authority – delivered the kingdom from evil and restored order. Such a model contrives divine approval of the Tudor accession and, by extension, the ruling dynasty under which, and for whom (argues Tillyard), Shakespeare writes: 'The Elizabethan political order, the Golden Age brought in by the Tudors, is nothing apart from the cosmic order of which it is a part'.[16] The providential historical model also complements Tudor interest in the political utility of historiography (mentioned in the Introduction) and the dynasty's own use of contrived genealogy to legitimize its accession, another aspect of what has become known as the Tudor Myth. Tillyard constructs an essentialist, extra-textual picture of Elizabethan conceptions of order through drawing heavily upon the similarly providential version of events recorded in Hall's chronicle together with later Elizabethan works such as *The Mirror for Magistrates* (first published 1559), the homily *Against Disobedience and Wilful Rebellion* (1574) and many other literary sources endorsing the virtue of order and degree. The history plays, argues Tillyard, thus present a vision of Tudor orthodoxy, an approved aetiology of the contemporary political situation as supported by the workings of a providential system with which all of Shakespeare's audiences would have been familiar.

■ In the total sequence of his plays dealing with the subject matter of Hall he expressed successfully a universally held and still comprehensible scheme of history: a scheme fundamentally religious, by which events evolve under a law of justice and under the ruling of God's Providence, and of which Elizabeth's England was the acknowledged outcome.[17] □

So what does Tillyard say about *Henry V*? As indicated above, and like many of the play's nineteenth-century critics, Tillyard can only really treat *Henry V* in relation to Shakespeare's earlier histories, but it is this relative or comparative perspective that makes his discussion rather anticlimactic given the momentum of the book's argument thus far. Having earlier staged the rise and reign of the great villain of his providential sequence, Richard III, Shakespeare was compelled to concentrate on Richard's antithesis, the 'copy-book paragon of kingly virtue', Henry V.[18] Tillyard's overall treatment of *Henry V* casts Shakespeare as simply going through the motions in writing a play about a political hero that must somehow represent 'the symbol of some great political principle'.[19] The difficulty arises, as do the play's limitations, says Tillyard, in that Shakespeare could not readily find such a principle that Henry might represent. He was thus forced to concentrate on Henry as man, rather than as king.[20] Further problems arise as Shakespeare deviates from the characterization of Hal in the *Henry IV* plays, though he still wrestles with showing the ideal relationship between human nature and royal office, such difficulties leading to 'a great falling off in quality' in the later play.[21] Having earlier gone to great lengths to recover the contemporary political and intellectual background to the histories, Tillyard offers a merely perfunctory account of how Shakespeare, in composing his depiction of Henry's reign, fulfilled his double obligation to the chronicle sources and to Elizabethan audience expectations. There is surprisingly little integration of Tillyard's section on *Henry V* with the wider thesis about order and disorder, and instead he seems content to enumerate the play's structural shortcomings: its perceived failure to engage consistently with the cosmic lore of the other histories, the rhetorical 'flatness' and 'unevenness' of the verse, the haphazard employment of comic characters and the hurried exaggerations of the final wooing scene.[22] The majority of these points we have encountered before, often in much earlier, neoclassical criticism. By the end of the play, argues Tillyard, Shakespeare had moved beyond the public concerns of the histories' epic canvas, exhausted what he had to say on such matters and looked ahead to dramatizing the more private, inner dilemmas of his tragic heroes such as Hamlet or Brutus.[23]

Taken on its own, Tillyard's brief treatment of *Henry V* says relatively little that is new or illuminating. The play's place within a historical cycle has been discussed before, as have anxieties about its structure, sources and relation to the tragedies. When viewed in relation to the other wartime responses to *Henry V*, we can certainly identify shared areas of interest. Like Wilson Knight, Tillyard saw the figure of the monarch as integral to social and cosmic order, and his elucidation of the Elizabethan world picture shows the historical 'working' behind such a view. It might also be argued that Tillyard's desire to find an immutable universal structure for conceiving order in the world grows out of the period of conflict and disorder in which he wrote. Despite the absence of a heroic or jingoistic Henry in Tillyard's study or of any mention of the contemporary situation, there is still recourse to a conservative vision of political order, of which the king is an unimpeachable representative, and it is Henry's place in this system rather than his individual actions that are of greatest importance to Tillyard. As Holderness contends:

> ■ The play about the nature of 'England' is more important than the play about the military victories of a warrior-king. Tillyard's business was not with winning the war but with reconstituting the national culture in expectation of an Allied victory.[24] □

Regardless of the merits of Tillyard's specific treatment of *Henry V*, an introduction to his overall methodology and thesis is necessary here as it explains the origins of the historicist critical paradigm which has come to dominate modern Shakespeare studies, and because it aids our understanding of the approaches adopted by the numerous subsequent critics that have discussed the play by confronting and challenging Tillyard's conclusions. The degree to which *Henry V* fits into a providential pattern of order and disorder remains a recurrent critical preoccupation, and, whether one agrees with it or not, Tillyard's thesis has assumed the status of the orthodox or 'traditional' interpretation of the histories as a whole, the terms of which critics of the twentieth and twenty-first centuries are forced to address.[25]

In his 1985 article charting 40 years of responses to Tillyard, Robin Headlam Wells observes how criticism on the political background to the histories produced during the 1950s and 60s continues to be shaped by 'the conceptual premise of a controlling scheme of retributive justice' that runs throughout the sequence of plays.[26] But as the post-Tillyard reception history of *Henry V* reveals, there are many different lines of questioning with which to challenge the method and thesis of *Shakespeare's History Plays*. Is it right, for example, to foreground *Henry V*'s political dimension but play down the significance of formal or theatrical concerns (i.e. why does Shakespeare write a play not a treatise or homily)? How easy or desirable is it to reconstruct fully Shakespeare's engagement with contemporary political thought? Was he as uncritical of Hall as Tillyard himself seems to be?[27] Does not a 'world picture' posit too singular or monolithic an idea of Shakespeare's audience, a static relationship between literature and history bought into by every Elizabethan? If the histories are, essentially, state-sanctioned instruments devoid of subversion aimed at promoting order, how (as John Drakakis asks) does such coercion translate to the real world, to an actual system of rules-governing behaviour?[28] As we shall see in subsequent chapters, there has been no shortage of critics taking up such questions.

Later critics have also offered alternative explanatory patterns to Tillyard's model. John Wilders's *The Lost Garden* (1978), for example, proposes that the histories consistently evoke an Edenic context and the fall of a political ideal conceived of as a lost paradise.[29] For present purposes, however, the focus remains on one of Tillyard's immediate contemporaries who was similarly committed to reading *Henry V* in relation to early modern historical events and concepts.

LILY B. CAMPBELL

Wartime transportation difficulties meant that the American scholar Lily B. Campbell was unable to consult Tillyard's study while writing her own book *Shakespeare's Histories: Mirrors of Elizabethan Policy* (1947), but there is nevertheless great similarity in their historicist approaches to the plays. Like Tillyard, Campbell saw Shakespeare not simply as a playwright interested in particular political themes, as critics such as Marriott and Palmer suggested, but as the producer of political works that were actively engaged in contemporary debates. Campbell's method entailed establishing a detailed picture of contemporary issues that formed the ideological backdrop to the plays in order to identify how the histories reflect the 'dominant political pattern' of Elizabethan political philosophy.[30] As her subtitle suggests, the book centres on how the plays 'reflect' their historical context and before turning to *Henry V* itself she grapples with the issue of whether Shakespeare, as an artist, can ever offer a direct, unmediated perspective on contemporary concerns:

■ That Shakespeare's approach to any contemporary problem of politics or religion must, because he was an artist, have been an indirect approach cannot be disputed if taken to mean only that Shakespeare did not use his plays as polemical tracts. But the use of the word *indirect* ignores the fact that, as I shall try to show in succeeding chapters, the chief function of history was considered to be that of acting as a political mirror. The idea of holding the mirror up to nature (or politics) pervaded the whole conception of art during the Elizabethan period, but to identify the conception of the mirror with indirection seems to me inaccurate.[31] □

The first half of Campbell's study therefore examines early modern conceptions of exactly how history could be used as a didactic and instrumental resource: how history could provide lessons for the present through obliquely drawing comparisons between fifteenth- and sixteenth-century events and concerns. As she writes: '[e]ach of the Shakespeare histories serves a special purpose in elucidating a political problem of Elizabeth's day and in bringing to bear upon this problem the accepted political philosophy of the Tudors'.[32] Again, like Tillyard, Campbell sees the histories as reflections of Tudor orthodoxy, as the 'right' answers to pressing political problems. She too is interested in the history plays' cyclical structure, not just as a formal unity, but as a 'political pattern' of sin and punishment and the working out of a scheme of divine vengeance following Richard II's deposition. Campbell, however, does not use the providential pattern as the governing structure of her book and there is far more autonomy between chapters in her treatment of each play's political background than in Tillyard's study.

Whereas the earlier history plays reflected Elizabethan concerns with discordant matters such as rebellion and succession, *Henry V* (writes Campbell) depicts the English triumphant in a righteous cause. The central issue is war and the progress of a warrior-hero and thus 'the play becomes in form and content epic'.[33] It therefore follows that the principal political issues with which Shakespeare engages in the play should relate to war. While at times Campbell's chapter on *Henry V* serves most valuably as a discursive source study, she is quick to eschew any kind of reductive allegorical reading of the play that would draw uncomplicated analogies between Henry's campaign and Essex's expeditions to France and Ireland. She focuses instead on three areas of contention reflected in *Henry V*: just war, military procedure and contemporary debates on the relative merits of ancient and modern military authorities. Campbell's treatment of the latter two issues identifies the extent of Shakespeare's debt to the numerous military treatises produced in increasing numbers from the 1560s onwards, comparing Henry's conduct to that prescribed by contemporary manuals. Campbell also finds a parody of the Elizabethan battle of military books in the scene with the regional captains at Harfleur, and locates Fluellen's eagerness to discourse on 'the disciplines of the war' (3.3.39) in relation to the increasingly dated school of opinion that favoured classical military strategy above contemporary tactics for gunpowder weapons.[34] The comedy of Fluellen thus derives both from his pedantry and his outmoded perspective on military matters.

Commentary on Shakespeare's use of such sources is nowadays relegated more to the footnote or introduction of scholarly editions, but the problem into which Campbell goes in the most depth, and one that has remained on the critical agenda, is that of the justification of war. During Elizabeth's reign the English were never forced to fight on native soil and (for the most part) enjoyed relative peace. English forces were, however, fighting in Scotland, Ireland, France and the Netherlands, and successive invasion scares during the 1580s and 90s kept military matters at the forefront of the Elizabethan audience's minds. Campbell argues that *Henry V* engages with Elizabethan debates about justifying war that developed out of growing hostilities in Continental Europe and the moral questions raised by the prospect of Christians fighting against Christians.

She points to the numerous sermons and treatises produced in this period that sought to endorse war fought for a just cause in the public and national interest that was initiated following due counsel and deliberation. As in modern-day conflicts, the justice of wars fought overseas raised problematic questions requiring careful scrutiny of the aggressor's motivations, and Campbell identifies an Elizabethan precedent for the first act of *Henry V* in Leicester's extensive consultation with Archbishop Whitgift prior to the earl's military intervention in the Netherlands in 1585.[35] Henry's speech in 1.2.13–32 on the importance of just cause and Canterbury's subsequent, confident affirmation of the king's claim is interpreted, with little difficulty, as evidence that Shakespeare has presented due process in justifying war using the terms of contemporary treatises on the subject.[36] Campbell also revisits the related problem, earlier mentioned by Simpson, of an individual soldier's responsibility for the justice of the cause in which they fight, as is raised in Henry's debate with Williams. Cardinal Allen had written in 1587 arguing that the English war in the Netherlands was unjust on the basis that it was not fought to defend English subjects and that since Elizabeth was excommunicated in 1570 – and thus deprived of the ability to invoke divinely sanctioned just cause – her soldiers owed a greater obligation to God than to their monarch.[37] Campbell reads the Williams episode as a direct response to the terms of Allen's argument, charting how it supports the Tudor position that the king has a responsibility to ensure the justice of their cause and the subject has a duty to obey their king. Williams's fears about a subject's soul should the cause be wrong are addressed in Henry's speech that distinguishes between the licensed actions of a soldier and the private sins, such as contrived murder, rape and robbery (4.1.141–77), committed during war. War, as God's vengeance, says Henry, will punish the perpetrators of such deeds:

■ Then if they die unprovided, no more is the King guilty of their damnation than he was before guilty of those impieties for the which they are now visited. Every subject's duty is the King's, but every subject's soul is his own. □

(4.1.166–70)

This, for Campbell, satisfies Williams and neutralizes the problematic question, as is confirmed in the reply to Henry's speech: ''Tis certain, every man that dies ill, the ill upon his own head. The King is not to answer it' (4.1.178–9). But for Williams to be (in Campbell's words) a 'good pupil' and have learned 'the lesson that Shakespeare through King Henry took so much time and pains to teach', one has both to pass over the fact that Henry has skilfully moved the argument away from disputing the justice of his cause and then to ignore the subsequent exchange about the king's unwillingness to be ransomed that nearly brings things to blows.[38] Campbell concludes this part of her chapter by demonstrating that the best way for Shakespeare to support the notion that the king's cause was indeed just was to stress how Henry repeatedly assigns credit for his victory to God, echoing again the sentiments found in Elizabethan military manuals that war was the scourge of God.[39]

Campbell's book offers a valuable illustration of the extent to which *Henry V* engages with several prominent themes, ideas and standpoints found in recurrent political debates of the later Elizabethan period. The brand of historicism it advances is at its best when it views historical context as an active ingredient of the play itself, rather than as a benign, passive background or a source of contemporary analogies serving to unlock problematic scenes or characters. The attempt to take things a step further and maintain that Shakespeare always knew and took the correct side of a political argument assumes that he – and we – can identify what might be understood as the 'accepted political philosophy of the Tudors', and that such a monolithic concept existed in the first place. As later 'new' historicists argue, equivocality and ambiguity are substantive features of both literary texts and political discourse, and indeed the linguistic and metaphoric resources that they share lead us to question whether we should even distinguish the one from the other. The idea that literature might reflect history is also problematic and as early modern mirror lore itself maintained, a reflection offered both similarity and difference, and mirrors could present both a likeness of how things are and a projection of how things should be. Mirrors can also be angled to reflect different things and any form of historicism always risks simply cherry-picking a subjective selection of the most appropriate contextual materials. Campbell's Whitgift allusion mentioned earlier offers a case in point. Historical events of 1585 may well offer an Elizabethan precedent for a play of 1599 but what form does the association between text and context actually take? Would Shakespeare have been aware of this event or does its significance only become clear with historical hindsight? Might not the sermon about just war given by Lancelot Andrewes (1555–1626) on the eve of Essex's Irish expedition in March 1599 offer a more useful or influential precedent?[40] Campbell's treatment of *Henry V* remains important, however, as it illustrates that one needs to try to understand the justification of Henry's war, perhaps one of the most topical and consistently problematic themes in the play for modern commentators, by placing it within the historical context of the period in which Shakespeare wrote. This then still begs the question: are there limitations to what we can consider as relevant, applicable contextual materials? New Historicism of the 1980s onwards takes up this issue in earnest, as we shall see in Chapter 7.

Shakespeare's representation of war, and the need to address accusations that *Henry V* sensationalizes a war of aggression, also had a significant impact on two highly influential critical editions produced in the mid-twentieth century: Dover Wilson's Cambridge edition (1947) and J. H. Walter's edition for the Arden Shakespeare (1954).

JOHN DOVER WILSON

The introduction to Dover Wilson's edition fuses the concern to apply *Henry V* to the present day, expressed by several of the critics discussed so far in this chapter, to the perennial, character-centred debate about Henry's positive and negative qualities. Dover Wilson presents an unambiguously pro-Henry interpretation that celebrates the play's power to stir his twentieth-century contemporaries, before addressing the arguments of its detractors, such as Hazlitt:

> ■ *Henry V* is a play which men of action have been wont silently to admire, and literary men, at any rate during the last hundred and thirty years, volubly to contemn. But even critics learn something from times like the present; or at least one humble member of the tribe imagines he has done so.[41] □

Characterizing himself as one of the literary 'tribe' who is nevertheless able to appreciate the perspective of the man of action, he identifies how the play thrives upon its topicality both in 1599, with reference to the Essex expedition, and in the 1940s, drawing a now-customary comparison between Henry's speech before Agincourt and the famous speech given by Sir Winston Churchill following the Battle of Britain in which he claimed that 'Never in the field of human conflict was so much owed by so many to so few'.[42] Using the play's relevance and inspirational potential for his own contemporaries as a touchstone, he quickly dismisses the Tillyardian views that *Henry V* is merely a perfunctory conclusion to Shakespeare's historical sequence and that it frustrated early audience expectations raised by patriotic works such as *King John* or *Richard II*. Dover Wilson's implicit purpose throughout his introduction is to recover a positive reading of the play and its hero by confronting and negotiating a series of perceived critical misunderstandings about both the form and content of *Henry V*. Indeed, the introduction actually adopts a structure that loosely mirrors, and consequently addresses, an itemization of the play's faults made by the critic Mark Van Doren (1894–1972) in the brief treatment of *Henry V* found in his 1939 book, *Shakespeare*.[43] Van Doren had detailed how in *Henry V* 'the heroic idea splinters into a thousand starry fragments' through the doubts expressed by the Chorus, the 'puerile' appeal to audience patriotism and the sense of gaiety that replaces high passion.[44] Dover Wilson addresses each of these points and begins by defending Shakespeare's use of the Chorus (in a similar manner to Wilson Knight) through maintaining that the sublimity of subject matter necessitated innovation in dramatic presentation.

> ■ If the greatest story in English history, as he and his contemporaries thought it, was ill-suited for normal dramatic treatment, then a new form of drama must be invented. Theme and hero clearly called for epic; and the problem was how to use the theatre for this purpose.[45] □

The Chorus served as a means of connecting a series of heroic episodes, of bringing together different locations, events and voices, and of heightening the 'epical tone' through the metatheatrical alternation between narrative description and dramatic representation.[46] Shakespeare felt no compulsion to excuse the temporal and spatial manipulations found in *Antony and Cleopatra*, but *Henry V*, argues Dover Wilson, went beyond any ordinary historical theme, forcing the playwright to use the same kind of choric negotiations with his audience that John Milton employs in *Paradise Lost* (1674).[47]

Shakespeare's heroic subject matter nonetheless generated problems of 'spirit' as well as of 'form', and Dover Wilson is fully aware of the pro- / anti-Henry debate centred on the king's justification for war and conduct in battle.[48] Specific points of the debate are avoided, but he identifies that both the play's admirers and detractors recognize Shakespeare's interest in representing worldly success, and goes on to stress that this constitutes a strength, not a limitation, of *Henry V*.[49] Whereas Shakespeare's treatment of war may have caused problems for earlier generations of critics, for Dover Wilson it provides the starting point for re-evaluating the play as he seeks to avoid reductively identifying the heroic theme with unsophisticated jingoism or patriotic sentimentality. Shakespeare's contemporaries offer a productive way of understanding heroic poetry, and Dover Wilson reminds us that Sidney in the *Defence of Poesy* designates 'heroical' poetry – by which he meant both epic and romance – as the greatest of all literary genres for its ability to inculcate virtue while simultaneously delighting the reader.[50] *Henry V* can therefore be treated in far more depth than a simple drum-and-trumpet show. As Dover Wilson goes on to argue, the play not only celebrates heroic virtue but also explores its very nature. However, before proceeding any further in rehabilitating the heroic Henry, Dover Wilson feels compelled to confront Hazlitt's infamous, biting characterization of the king's rule as 'brute force, glossed over with a little religious hypocrisy and archiepiscopal advice'. Addressing the letter if not the spirit of Hazlitt's attack, Dover Wilson looks to the play's first act and meticulously demonstrates how Shakespeare manipulates his sources to emphasize that Henry is certainly *not* simply a puppet of the churchmen and the ensuing war a cynical attempt to ward off royal attention from domestic fiscal policy.[51] Canterbury's promise of financial aid for war and his demonstration of Henry's title in the Salic law speech should therefore be treated as separate concerns. If anything, writes Dover Wilson, it is Henry who uses the churchmen, though whether that constitutes an adequate defence or rebuttal to Hazlitt's point is debatable. Shakespeare uses the Salic law speech to appeal to contemporary rhetorical tastes: 'Being constitutionally litigious, Elizabethans loved a good pleader, while it flattered their national pride to hear it *proved* that France belonged to them' (Dover Wilson's italics).[52] It is significant to note here how Dover Wilson diverts Hazlitt's wide-ranging attack on Henry's character into the terms of the debate on just war. Rather deftly, though perhaps not entirely convincingly, he is then able to recover a vision of the heroic Henry by again alluding to the play's enduring topicality:

■ When the Henry of the play, therefore, affirms that he puts forth his 'rightful hand in a well-hallowed cause' [1.2.293], he is speaking the simple truth. The war against France is a righteous war; and seemed as much so to Shakespeare's public as the war against the Nazis seems to us. Once this is realized, a fog of suspicion and detraction is lifted from the play; the mirror held up in 1599 shines bright once more; and we are at liberty to find a hero's face reflected within it.[53] □

Attention then turns to understanding exactly what kind of conception of heroism Shakespeare works with in the play. For Dover Wilson, Shakespeare's greatest concern is to present, not just a great conqueror in the mould of Tamburlaine, but a balanced, believable human hero. For the first two acts Henry certainly adopts the pose of the conquering hero and distanced public figure, but for Dover Wilson the taking of Harfleur marks a turning point, both for Henry and the audience.

■ For no sooner does the governor yield than we become conscious that Henry's fierce intimidation is a mere device to bring an end to the siege, on the part of a commander anxious, because of sickness among his troops, to hurry on to Calais; while in the brief order, 'Use mercy to them all', given to Exeter whom he leaves in temporary command of the town, we have the first glimpse of a real man behind the traditional heroic mask.[54] □

From this point onwards we get to see more of Henry as a man, rather than simply as a heroic king, and this informs his nocturnal visit to his troops (Dover Wilson sidesteps the difficult Williams episode), the speech about ceremony (4.1.219–72), the St Crispin's Day speech before Agincourt and the general levity found in the final wooing scene.

The 'gaiety' derided by Van Doren therefore actually functions to bring Henry to life, to give him humanity and depth of character. Harfleur also represents a turning point for the audience as it is the first time that we get to see the horrors of war: the dehumanization required for effective soldiery encouraged in the 'Once more unto the breach' speech, the great losses that 'close the wall up with our English dead' and the threatened violence facing non-combatants should the siege persist. In Dover Wilson's view, *Henry V* depicts war both as a heroic vocation and as 'the greatest of human evils', and Shakespeare's artistry manifests in his ability to present the one after the other.[55] The dual perspective on war serves not to produce an ironic undercutting, as Gould and Palmer argue, but to give a more realistic picture of heroism that emphasizes sacrifice, agony and loss as well as glory and success. Dover Wilson thus re-conceives how we understand the play's representation of heroism: it is heroism shown *despite* the horrors of war. *Henry V*, he suggests, embodies what would become known as the Dunkirk spirit; it is an epic of fortitude and endurance akin also to the tenth-century Anglo-Saxon poem *The Battle of Maldon*.[56] Shakespeare's desire to present the violent realities of war also explains the killing of prisoners, which Dover Wilson defends on the basis that it demonstrates Henry's decisive, active qualities and the pragmatic need to serve his army's best interests.[57] He adds a comment in a footnote that anticipates later commentators' bitter criticism of the episode: 'The truth is, commanders in the field often have dreadful decisions forced upon them, which civilians condemn because they shut their eyes to, or are ignorant of, the still more dreadful alternatives'.[58] Dover Wilson offers a valuable refinement of how we can view *Henry V* as heroic and his suggestive comments on how the play may be read as a form of dramatic epic were developed in Walter's introduction to his 1954 Arden edition.

J. H. WALTER

Like Dover Wilson, Walter adopts a defensive position throughout and again begins by considering the play's 'epical' form, observing that the Chorus not only stresses the gravity of the work to follow but also provides the means by which it can adhere to the unity of action through the recounting of details omitted from dramatic presentation.[59] Walter takes up Sidney's conception that the heroic mode was best suited to moral instruction and the depiction of exemplary models for imitation. Walter bases his entire interpretation of *Henry V* on a belief that Shakespeare's governing aim was to write an epic about the ideal Christian prince, and identifies a wide range of parallels between the play and early modern authorities on monarchical statecraft, particularly

Erasmus's *The Education of a Christian Prince* (1516).[60] Walter then uses the figure of the ideal Christian prince to negotiate many of the play's problematic episodes. He places great significance on the religious conversion that appears to take place upon Henry's coronation, as noted by the churchmen in 1.1.25–69. The reformation that they observe in him is not, writes Walter, simply a hasty narrative attempt to distinguish Hal from Henry but the culmination of a process through which the king learnt lessons of kingship throughout the *Henry IV* plays.[61] Henry's religious credentials, as affirmed by Canterbury and Ely in the opening scene, therefore establish him as a true Christian monarch and thus position him beyond reproach when he calls upon the archbishop for advice as he asserts his claim to France. Walter again uses his unfaltering projection of Shakespeare's intention to support a pro-Henry interpretation:

■ To portray Henry as the dupe of two scheming prelates, or as a crafty politician skilfully concealing his aims with the aid of an unscrupulous archbishop, is not consistent with claiming at the same time that he is the ideal king; indeed it is destructive to the moral epic purpose of the play.[62] □

As one can see, Walter assumes that his own claim about the king is identical with Shakespeare's.

Confidence in Shakespeare's vision of an ideal king also informs Walter's interpretation of the Harfleur parley, Williams episode and killing-of-prisoners scene. He takes pains at each instance to defend the king's conduct, detailing how each episode further reveals his adherence to a model of compassionate Christian kingship, as Henry carefully considers the implications for his troop's bodily and spiritual health of each military action. Returning to a favourite topic of earlier criticism, Walter also uses the epic model to defend Shakespeare's decision to present the rejection and subsequent death of Falstaff. As with the death of Aeneas's lover Dido in *The Aeneid* (29–19 BC) by Virgil (70–19 BC), so Falstaff's demise is seen as a necessary step in the hero's development:

■ The play gains in epic strength and dignity from Falstaff's death, even as the *Aeneid* gains from Dido's death, not only because both accounts are written from the heart with a beauty and power that have moved men's hearts in after time, but because Dido and Falstaff are sacrifices to a larger morality they both ignore.[63] □

Walter defends the play's final scene by interpreting it as the fulfilment of a Christian prince's duty both to consolidate his conquest and to secure peace through marriage. Victory at Agincourt was not enough to establish Henry's title to France and it was only after further campaigning that he signed the Treaty of Troyes in 1520, the brokerage for which takes

place offstage during the wooing scene. It is only through the possessions won by the treaty, argues Walter, that Henry truly becomes the
'complete Christian monarch'.[64] The idea that Shakespeare attempts to
present a dramatic vision of the complete hero is vitally important for
Walter's reading of the play and he uses it to counter earlier criticism
about the perceived flatness or limitation of Henry's character:

■ The virtuous man has no obvious strife within the soul, his faith is simple
and direct, he has no frailties to suffer in exposure. It is just this rectitude
and uprightness, this stoicism, this unswerving obedience to the Divine Will
that links both Aeneas and Henry, and has laid them both open to charges
of priggishness and inhumanity.[65] □

Thus, the absence of complication or internal contradiction is actually a
vindication of Henry's heroic integrity, though one is again left to
question the extent to which Walter has downplayed legitimate areas of
interpretative difficulty or controversy.

Throughout this chapter we have seen how critics have gone about
confronting some of the difficult questions that *Henry V* raises about
both the mechanics and the morality of staging war, be it in the 1590s
or the 1940s. Critical concerns voiced by eighteenth- and nineteenth-
century scholars about the Chorus and the relation of the history plays
to comedy and tragedy are given renewed impetus by those critics discussed above, interested in reconsidering the question of genre, who
attempt to understand *Henry V* in epic terms. The traditional, martial
subject matter of epic continues to prove even more controversial and
we have seen the fundamentally defensive postures adopted by critics
and editors seeking to preserve a positive, heroic vision of the king. At
times practitioners of such methods could be criticized as being too partial or selective in their choice of discursive materials, though it is not
the place of a reception history to prescribe the approaches that should
be taken to texts. It is nevertheless interesting to observe something of
a continuity between the earliest responses to *Henry V* and those discussed in this chapter, for the picture of the play that emerges from the
latter, which elects to downplay or defuse potentially controversial
episodes, starts to look more like the stripped-down Quarto than the
intractably problematic Folio.

Many of the ideas, questions and methodologies discussed here look
ahead to the dominant concerns of the remaining chapters of this Guide.
It is nowadays very easy to attack the Old Historicism of Tillyard and
others, but in Chapter 7 we will return to historicist analysis of *Henry V*
and consider whether the New Historicism of the 1980s onwards offers
any significant advance in critical sophistication. The issue of just war

raised by Campbell and others also continues to have resonance through to *Henry V* criticism of the present day, as is discussed in my final chapter. Before moving that far ahead, attention must be turned to the increasing number of critics writing on *Henry V* during the 1950s–70s, who, while not entirely dismissing historicist methods, remain sensitive to the play's formal and aesthetic qualities and recognize that questioning, ambivalence and complexity are a conscious part of Shakespeare's design.

CHAPTER SIX

The Mid- to Late Twentieth Century: Ambivalence and Play

Critics from the second half of the twentieth century onwards increasingly confront and challenge the binary hero/villain, eulogy/satire interpretations of *Henry V* by exploring how Shakespeare actively cultivates a sense of uncertainty, inconsistency and ambivalence in his presentation of the hero and his actions. Whereas earlier criticism adopted opposed positions in a debate between positive and negative readings, one now finds more widespread acknowledgement that the play itself offers an ongoing interrogation of both the king's character and the validity of his actions in declaring and waging war. As the critics discussed in this chapter argue, contradiction and a sense of struggle between political and ethical conceptions of good conduct are not only features of *Henry V*'s critical tradition but also an intentional part of Shakespeare's original design for the play itself. The identification of points of contradiction, irony and ambivalence in a work, together with a conscious eschewal of historical and biographical contextualization, were central principles of the so-called New Criticism that developed in the United States during the 1930s and which remained prevalent until the 1960s. The critics presented in this chapter are all indebted to some degree to the New Critics' attention to irony and ambivalence and also provide the basis for much of the subsequent criticism on *Henry V* as they propound, with increasing sophistication, the essential notion of a 'multiple' reading of the play. They identify different techniques through which Shakespeare, as the playwright John Arden puts it, offers both an 'official' version of Henry and his war and a more subversive, ironic 'secret' version, or indeed how he incorporates 'a secret play within the official one'.[1] Two of the most influential mid-century statements on Shakespearian ambivalence are those by A. P. Rossiter and Harold C. Goddard.

A. P. ROSSITER

In his lecture 'Ambivalence: The Dialectic of the Histories', delivered at the Shakespeare Summer School at Stratford-upon-Avon in 1951 to coincide with Anthony Quayle's production of the second tetralogy, Rossiter identifies the characteristic 'doubleness' of the histories: how national greatness and triumph are repeatedly undercut by individual melancholy, frustration and tragedy.[2] There is, he argues, an explanatory pattern to the histories that he terms 'retributive reaction' that is seen, for example, at the end of *Henry V* in the Chorus's closing reference to the *Henry VI* plays and the loss of France, a dispiriting reminder that practically 70 years of civil dissension lie between Agincourt and the curative victory at Bosworth.[3] Rossiter posits such a pattern as an alternative to the order-oriented historical model found in Hall and his Old Historicist interpreters, particularly Tillyard. Such an approach risks reductivism and over-simplification, as is evident in historicist interpretations of Falstaff: 'any ideological view which makes *Henry IV* into a princely morality reduces Falstaff to little more than a symbol of all the fat and idle temptations which royalty rejects'.[4] The effect of such a reading is to neglect the 'comic criticism' that Falstaff supplies.[5] Rather than trying to fit every element of the histories into a single political explanatory framework, one might remain sensitive to the aesthetic potential of parody and parallelism, to the capacity of the Eastcheap contingent – so often the focus of critical attention – to provide a 'farcical travesty' of more stately, public scenes.[6] It is this potential for parody embedded within perceived ideological orthodoxy that leads Rossiter to a greater appreciation of how a work can present two mutually opposed, though equally valid interpretations. For Rossiter, the essence of aesthetic ambivalence is that

■ two opposed value-judgements are subsumed, and that both are valid (i.e. for that work of art or the mind producing it). The whole is only fully experienced when both opposites are held and included in a 'two-eyed' view; and all 'one-eyed' simplifications are not only falsifications; they amount to a denial of some part of the mystery of things.[7] □

Within Shakespeare's histories, ambivalence manifests as dramatic irony that causes

■ an exact juxtaposition of opposites in the mind of the audience: opposites, in that the 'true' for one hearer (the stage Persona) must exclude the 'true' for other hearers, who take the same words in a far extended sense, of which the hearing Persona is known to be unaware.[8] □

Rossiter then proceeds to offer illustrations of dramatic irony in the *Henry IV* plays. He reminds us of what we might lose from a play when attempting to treat it as a historical document or a statement of political orthodoxy. Comedy and parody in the histories play a vital role as alienation devices that question conceptions of ceremony and order.

> ■ Throughout the Histories it is in the implications of the Comic that shrewd realistic thinking about men in politics – in office – in war – in plot – is exposed: realistic apprehension outrunning the medieval frame. Because the Tudor myth system of Order, Degree, etc. was too rigid, too black-and-white, too doctrinaire and narrowly moral for Shakespeare's mind: it falsified his fuller experience of men. Consequently, while employing it as FRAME, he had to undermine it, to qualify it with equivocations: to vex its applications with sly or subtle ambiguities: to cast doubts on it ultimate human validity, even in situations where its principles seemed most completely applicable.[9] □

Curiously, however, Rossiter fails almost entirely to see how useful his critique is for opening up a new discursive field for *Henry V* as he reads it simply as a 'propaganda-play on National Unity: heavily orchestrated for the brass'.[10] If comedy, play and parody are the means of generating dramatic ambivalence and irony, then through his decision to kill off Falstaff in *Henry V* Shakespeare largely removes the possibility of a 'two-eyed', dialectical reading of the play. Later critics question whether comedy is the only obvious obverse or inversion of the kingly, heroic and patriotic aspects of *Henry V*, but Rossiter's overall emphasis on Shakespeare's studied ambivalence has huge discursive potential. Despite his own limited view of *Henry V*, Rossiter's lecture, which was published in 1954 and again in 1961, offers an immensely useful interpretive framework for reconsidering the debate about the king's character and actions, and all of the pro- and anti-Henry readings that have long formed a central component of the play's critical history.

HAROLD C. GODDARD

Rossiter's immediate contemporary, Goddard, was far more willing to identify ambivalence and irony in *Henry V* and discusses the play at length in *The Meaning of Shakespeare*, which was first published in 1951. Goddard begins by considering some of the criticisms commonly levelled at *Henry V*: that it is more history than drama; that its subject matter is simply too much for Shakespeare; and that it fails as a play due to its overbearing patriotism.[11] According to many earlier critics, the Chorus's role is to apologize for such perceived shortcomings. But who, asks Goddard, is the Chorus? The Chorus's reference to 'our bending author' (Epilogue, 2) clearly distinguishes the speaker from Shakespeare himself. He therefore appears to be a confection of History itself ('filling in the gaps in the story by making abridgments'), the stage manager (offering apologies for the stage) and the voice of public opinion.[12] For Goddard the last of these is the most significant as it marks the potential distance between historical fact and popular perception. The Chorus allows Shakespeare to articulate both simultaneously:

■ Through the Choruses, the playwright gives us the popular idea of his hero. In the play, the poet tells the truth about him. We are free to accept whichever of the two we prefer. God does not indicate what we shall think of his world or of the men and women he has created. He puts them before us. But he does not compel us to see them as they are. Neither does Shakespeare.[13] □

Goddard thus uses the Chorus to introduce the possibility of a 'two-eyed' (to use Rossiter's term) reading of *Henry V* and he proceeds to work through the play chronologically, providing an eloquent critical description of events that remains sensitive to the possibility of inconsistency and irony, and to the tension between what we are told and what we are shown. Goddard is particularly alert to verbal ironies, drawing out echoes of the Lancastrian usurpation in Canterbury's speech on French genealogy (as Lloyd had back in 1875), tracing imagery employed in pursuing the English claim, and highlighting how in the metaphor of the bees' commonwealth the archbishop purposively introduces a martial element into their otherwise harmonious social model (1.2.193–6).[14] Goddard's close reading identifies further irony at the start of Act two and compares the argument over the title to the Boar's Head tavern to the claim to France presented in the preceding scene. The Eastcheap contingent are no longer viewed simply as comic relief but cast as an additional commentary on the king's actions: 'Shakespeare can never be trusted not to comment on his main plot in his underplot'.[15] Rossiter's interpretation of the comic characters as interrogative foils in the *Henry IV* plays thus applies just as much to *Henry V*.

Goddard's method throughout is to draw out detailed verbal analogies that are often missed when trying to force Henry into an unequivocally positive or negative mould, and which are passed over by the Chorus's version of events. The Chorus is silent, for example, on Richard, Earl of Cambridge's claim to the English throne, via his brother-in-law Edmund Mortimer, whom Richard II designated heir, preferring instead to attribute his treason to greed alone. Goddard goes on to compare the hypocrisy that is anatomized and scorned at the traitors' exposure to that of Henry: 'The picture Henry draws of the traitors as they seemed is an almost perfect picture of the ideal king so many have found in Henry himself'.[16] Further parallels are drawn between Bardolph's church-robbing and Henry's ecclesiastically supported French conquests; between Williams and

Bates's attempts to attribute responsibility for war to the king (4.1.129–40) and Henry's earlier warning to Canterbury about the latter's culpability in encouraging war (1.2.13–32); and between the king's nocturnal prayer (4.1.277–93) and that of Hamlet's uncle Claudius, since both of them seek atonement for a throne founded on murder.[17] Addressing the frequent criticism made by earlier commentators, Goddard identifies the wholly ironic intention of the final wooing scene, given that its implications and ultimate end product (the future Henry VI and the acquisition of France) are verbally undermined by the prophetic closing Chorus.[18]

Goddard is particularly interested in those parts of the play where an audience's perception or memory of events is markedly different from what we are actually shown. Nowhere is this more the case than in the representation of Agincourt:

■ Anyone fresh from a reading of it thinks the fourth act of this play gives the picture of a dashing hero leading his little army with indomitable courage, physical and moral, to victory over a foe overwhelmingly superior in numbers. But if asked for the evidence of Henry's part in the battle he searches the text in vain. He has carried over his impression from the Choruses, from Henry's 'tiger' speech to his soldiers, from previous indirect knowledge of the hero-king from history or secondhand accounts of this very play, or if he has seen it on the stage, from the unwarranted interpolations of some stage director. [...] Shakespeare has portrayed many battles and shown many military leaders in combat, but not King Henry V in the Battle of Agincourt.

The magician makes us see things that are not there. Shakespeare does something similar to the imagination of the man who finds the heroism of Henry in the five scenes devoted to this battle, which, in the interest of the facts, may be summarized as follows:

1. Pistol captures a French gentleman.
2. The French lament their everlasting shame at being worsted by slaves.
3. Henry weeps at the deaths of York and Suffolk and orders every soldier to kill his prisoners.
4. Fluellen compares Henry with Alexander and his rejection of Falstaff to the murder of Cleitus. Henry, entering angry, swears that every French prisoner, present and future, shall have his throat cut. The battle is over. The King prays to God to keep him honest and breaks his word of honor to Williams.
5. Henry offers Williams money by way of satisfaction, which Williams rejects. Word is brought that 10,000 French are slain and 29 English. Henry gives the victory to God.[19] □

Goddard's often-quoted summary of Shakespeare's Agincourt helps us both to recognize the extent to which the playwright persistently undercuts the presentation of heroism here and to appreciate the inherent doubleness of his attitude to the battle itself, how the 'two-eyed' view of events is always present even if we do not realize that we may be watching, as it were, with only one eye. Goddard also intimates, though he does not fully develop the point, that Shakespeare was more interested in the moral rather than the military aspects of Agincourt, in what the battle reveals about Henry as a man rather than as a king.[20] Goddard's critique is important for *Henry V*'s critical tradition because it follows the same spirit as Rossiter's treatment of ambivalence but does for the play exactly what Rossiter fails to do. It highlights the potential for an ironic, 'two-eyed' interpretation and, furthermore, recognizes the obstacles to such a reading presented by the play itself, including Henry's Machiavellian attempts to appear as all things to all men.[21] The answer, Goddard indicates throughout, is to remain sensitive to the aggregate of detailed verbal ironies and to treat the comic scenes as an additional – rather than a diversionary – commentary on the main plot. If we regard Henry like the golden casket in *The Merchant of Venice* (1596–7), writes Goddard, 'fairer to a superficial view than to a more searching perception, [...] instantly the play becomes pervaded with an irony that imparts intense dramatic value to practically every one of its main scenes'.[22]

The reference to 'dramatic value' here is significant as it draws attention not only to the king's own play-acting and verbal duplicity that we have encountered before and will examine in more detail in the next chapter, but also to *Henry V*'s artistry and dramatic form. It is these aspects of Shakespeare's play that are the central concern of another pair of critics whose studies complement each other: S. C. Sen Gupta and Robert Ornstein.

S. C. SEN GUPTA

Sen Gupta begins his book *Shakespeare's Historical Plays* (1964) by reacting against the influence of historicist critics such as Tillyard and Campbell, claiming that 'it is necessary to redress the balance, to reaffirm the purely poetical value of historical drama and to treat the ten plays from *King John* to *Henry VIII* as works of art and not as political and didactic treatises'.[23] The historicist inclination to view the plays as moralities risks reducing characters simply to types or political standpoints. There is also potential inconsistency in the political lessons that are advanced throughout the histories: *King John* celebrates national resistance against a foreign foe whereas there is great scorn voiced in the opening scenes of *1 Henry VI* when the French are reported as doing exactly the same thing.[24] Sen Gupta later questions the extent to which Henry V's life represents a desirable didactic model: '[i]t could as well be read as a morality on the wrong type of kingship, which begins with a riotous youth and ends with foreign conquest that succeeds for a short period but is followed by disastrous after-effects'.[25] Rather than reading

Henry V as a work of history that happens to be in dramatic form, Sen Gupta focuses on how Shakespeare makes changes to his historical subject matter for aesthetic purposes, arguing that the playwright's construction of plot and characters were his primary concern.

> ■ The ideas projected by Shakespeare's 'histories' may be said to be moral, but only in the sense that all thinking about life, or all application of ideas to life, is moral. But the principal characteristic of such ideology is that it cannot be detached from the life portrayed in the dramas, from the movement of plot and evolution of character.[26] □

Sen Gupta's emphasis on Shakespeare's interest in character construction also leads him to challenge Rossiter's essay on ambivalence. In a play in which ideological lessons and standpoints are to be viewed with caution, ambivalence for its own sake seems rather redundant. Sen Gupta eschews any notion that Shakespeare delights in equivocation and remains committed to identifying a unified aesthetic design in the history plays. Although Shakespeare may appear to stage alternative interpretations of incident and character, there remains a unitary basis for interpretation, the recovery of which, Sen Gupta implies, is every critic's aim: '[a]lthough different views are presented, Shakespeare delves beneath the doubleness of opposed value-judgments to a core of meaning which is revealed through this opposition but is not identical with it'.[27]

Sen Gupta's reading of *Henry V* itself pursues an essentialist line, like that of Bradley, which seeks to explain the apparent contradictions in Henry's character, identified by other critics as an intentional ambivalence encouraged by Shakespeare, by treating them as character traits of a 'man of action who is uncritical about his own assumptions'.[28] Henry is 'clever, alert, and able to take firm and quick decisions, but his mind is singularly unanalytical'.[29] He fails to enquire into Canterbury's motives for promoting war or to ponder the fragility of the case. He never considers the deeper implications of Cambridge's treachery nor ever really examines, even in his prayer on the night before Agincourt, the justice of inheriting his father's usurped office but merely asks forgiveness for what occurred.[30] It could of course be argued that none of Shakespeare's kings display the kind of depth of self-scrutiny that Sen Gupta describes, as they are bound by historical and narrative propriety. Would not an analytical Henry seem more like a detached critical observer, akin to a historian, than a subjective protagonist of historical events in which he is implicated and involved? Although Sen Gupta expends much energy in redirecting us from Tillyard and other earlier critics, he offers relatively little to replace them in the way of a coherent approach to *Henry V*. His book is perhaps more important within *Henry V*'s critical history for the direction in which it points rather than the path that it takes, reminding us of questions that need to be asked of both historicist and New Critical interpretations of the play.

ROBERT ORNSTEIN

Sen Gupta's anti-historicist approach is pursued at greater length by Robert Ornstein in *A Kingdom for a Stage* (1972) and he too raises questions about the perceived orthodoxy and conventionality of the histories, observing that it is actually very difficult to make generalizing comments about the plays taken together since they vary greatly in form, mood, characterization and scope.[31] He notes again the inherent reductivism of historicism and how the persistent focus on the histories' conventionality 'threatens to turn living works of theatre into dramatic fossils or repositories of quaint and dusty ideas'.[32] Historicist scholarship refuses to grant that 'the ultimate standard for the interpretation of art is aesthetic' or, recognize that writers may actively contribute to and shape, as well as draw upon, the thought of their day.[33] Ornstein does not reject the historicist approach outright but calls for a more rigorous methodology, one that offers a sensitive conjunction of historical and aesthetic interpretation. It is wrong, he argues, to characterize Elizabethan England as a unified community of shared values and beliefs that excluded oppositional perspectives and voices, and naive to assume that intelligent writers and playwrights could not discern 'the contradictions and expediencies of Tudor royalism'.[34] Therefore, continues Ornstein, it is the critic's job to investigate how Shakespeare's artistry exhibits a 'unique insight and intuition' about historical and political concerns rather than simply to 'square his plays with a hypothetical norm of Elizabethan attitudes'.[35] Shakespeare's plays are more exploratory than affirmatory. Instead of hunting in the histories for evidence of orthodoxy, Ornstein details the extent to which Shakespeare (and his sources) were as much concerned with disorder and legitimacy as they were with order and providential retribution: '[t]he fact remains that no other Elizabethan writer so acutely and extensively portrays the weakness, folly, incompetence, and wickedness of English kings'.[36] Like many of the critics discussed in Chapter 4, Ornstein recognizes that Shakespeare had no illusions about the pragmatic realities of medieval and early modern kingship.

Ornstein's interpretation of *Henry V* itself begins by countering those who discount its value as a work of dramatic art:

■ Annoyed that Shakespeare was willing to write a patriotic pageant, readers are not inclined to see what is thoughtful and serious in *Henry V*, and as a result their impressions of it are likely to be shallow and their memories of it mistaken.[37] □

Like Goddard, Ornstein identifies that one's intuitive impression of *Henry V* is frequently dominated by war and triumph, even though such elements are conjured up largely by allusive and rhetorical means. The Chorus plays a large role in leading one to form such impressions, putting us in mind of what we are never actually shown. The Chorus also provides a clue to Shakespeare's artfulness in the play, as it reveals the playwright's inclination towards the use of ironic juxtapositions, ironies that can be overlooked not because they are hidden in the text 'but because they are so obvious that one can hardly believe Shakespeare intended them'.[38] Ornstein maintains that the play's irony was identified as much by Elizabethan audiences as it was by modern audiences and critics. The key to understanding the play, argues Ornstein, is to acknowledge its complex, multifaceted nature, and the way to start doing this is to observe how the Chorus creates the impression of one version of events which is then complicated by the main scenes. Echoing Goddard once more, Ornstein suggests that the Chorus is in one aspect the average Elizabethan audience-member 'whose eyes moisten at the thought of his nation's triumphs' and in another he is an author-surrogate through which Shakespeare meditates upon both history and historical drama.[39] Rather than reading the Chorus's professions of inadequacy as Shakespeare's modest response to the gravity of his epic theme, Ornstein highlights the Chorus's highly suggestive, incredibly playful nature. The Chorus is, after all, the greatest reminder that we have of the play's performative dimension, of the fact that Shakespeare is playing with history. Ornstein does not go as far as he could in applying the implications of his opening chapter (entitled 'The Artist as Historian') to *Henry V*. Despite his insightful comments on the Chorus and his statements on the need to reconcile historicist and aesthetic critical modes, he fails to provide any form of context for irony and ambivalence in the play. Ornstein could even be seen to embody the kind of aestheticist approach to Shakespeare's histories, against which Tillyard and other historicists had reacted in the 1940s, which had once again become popular by the 1970s.[40] On the other hand, Ornstein remains important for *Henry V* criticism in that he identifies the potential for a critical methodology that *could* begin to combine an appreciation of a work's language and artistry in relation to the historical context of its production and reception, an approach that would be developed from the 1980s onwards by the New Historicists.

Before moving to the next chapter to concentrate on New Historicism and its legacy, it is necessary to discuss a critic of the late 1970s whose treatment of *Henry V*'s conscious ambivalence and playfulness underpins many of the ideas developed in subsequent criticism: Norman Rabkin.

NORMAN RABKIN

Rabkin's essay, 'Rabbits, Ducks, and *Henry V'*, begins by acknowledging the prevalence of binary approaches to the play and the frequently reductive way in which previous critics have offered relatively 'simple and whole-hearted' responses seeking to characterize Henry either as a hero or villain.[41] As we have seen, there have certainly been attempts to conjoin both perspectives on the play and to recognize a conscious ambivalence on Shakespeare's part. For Bradley, Palmer and Ellis-Fermor the truth resides somewhere in between the established binary positions, since Shakespeare comes to realize that the qualities of a good king and a good man are not necessarily the same. Such a realization ultimately led Shakespeare to reject the figure of the public man or politician as suitable hero material in his subsequent plays. There are also critics such as Rossiter, Rabkin continues, who recognize Shakespearean ambivalence but cannot apply it to *Henry V*, treating the play instead as a failure. Rabkin also challenges Ornstein's attempts to read *Henry V* as a complex, though unpolemical synthesis of positive and negative responses. Such a mixed view of Henry seems something of a 'fudge', writes Rabkin, as it sees 'complication and subtlety where Shakespeare's art forces us to demand commitment, resolution, answers'.[42] For Rabkin, there cannot be a compromise solution because the play purposively presents such polarized extremes and compels the audience to choose a particular interpretative line:

■ In *Henry V* Shakespeare creates a work whose ultimate power is precisely the fact that it points in two opposite directions, virtually daring us to choose one of the two opposed interpretations it requires of us.[43] □

Rabkin compares the play to the rabbit-duck drawing used in Gestalt psychology that can be viewed as either animal though never both simultaneously.[44] One can never escape, he argues, from adopting a partisan position on the play and its hero. From the outset, Rabkin's argument places great emphasis on audience expectation as he attempts to recreate the interpretative problems faced by those that watched the second tetralogy for the first time. *Richard II* had already explored the right-versus-might question in juxtaposing the issue of the king's legitimacy to rule with Bolingbroke's obvious political acumen and initial popularity. It also asked whether 'the manipulative qualities that guarantee political success [can] be combined in one man with the spiritual qualities that make one fully open and responsive to life and therefore fully human?'[45] *1 Henry IV* 'moves the question to a new generation' by asking whether these qualities, thus far divided between Richard and

Bolingbroke, can be united in Prince Hal.[46] Part one suggests that they can, through the play's festive tone and sustained intermingling of knockabout comedy with Hal's early admission that he merely uses his tavern fellows during the dilatory period prior to his accession. Part two, however, soon quashes this comic optimism through the emphasis placed on ruthless political pragmatism (embodied most dramatically by Henry's brother Prince John), the king's growing scepticism towards his office and title and, of course, the rejection of Falstaff. A sickly, autumnal tone pervades much of *2 Henry IV*.

This is the rather complicated starting point for audiences attending a performance of *Henry V* in 1599. The two parts of *Henry IV*, maintains Rabkin, establish different expectations and as the final play of the tetralogy commences 'we are ready for one of two opposed representations of the reign of the fifth Henry'.

■ Perhaps we hope that the play now beginning will resolve our doubts, set us right, give us a single gestalt to replace the antithetical images before our mind's eye. And that, as is demonstrated by the unequivocal interpretations good critics continue to make, is exactly the force of the play. We are made to see a rabbit or a duck. In fact, if we do not try obsessively to cling to memories of past encounters with the play, we may find that each time we read it, it turns from one shape to the other, just as it regularly does in production.[47] □

Rabkin then invites us to view *Henry V* as an extension of *1 Henry IV*, as a celebratory, heroic piece very much in the mould of Olivier's cinematic production, a thrilling, engaging culmination of every virtue praised and prized by the second tetralogy.[48] The contemplation of the relationship between king and man reaches its climax on the night before Agincourt and in Henry's exculpatory soliloquy on ceremony. The final stage in presenting a fully rounded, human Henry is his attainment of 'mature sexuality', something noticeably absent in the earlier portraits of Hal but now realized in the wooing of Katherine.[49] However, if we view *Henry V* as the sequel to *2 Henry IV*, we are led in a far darker direction. The play's first act, depicting covert political machinations and a problematic construction of a justification for war, raises questions about the royal cause that are never fully resolved in Henry's interaction with Williams. Rabkin also refers back to Goddard's characterization of Shakespeare's Agincourt and the distaste left by the killing-of-prisoners scene.[50] Pistol's inglorious description of his plan to steal back to England (5.1.73–82) undercuts the triumphant scene of the king's return imagined by the Chorus's preceding speech. The Chorus's closing speech in turn subverts the nuptial conclusion of comic convention by reminding the audience of Henry and Katherine's failure to secure the stability of future generations through the birth of their son.

Much of Rabkin's essay, it must be admitted, simply revisits by-now familiar ground and summarizes the constituents for both positive and negative interpretations that others have discussed at greater length. However, the juxtaposition of each reveals just how much of the play needs to be excluded from our consideration if we decide to pursue either interpretation to extremes. For any kind of complete and nuanced understanding of *Henry V*, we are therefore required to hold both views balanced in our mind.[51] Rather than simply suggesting that the adoption of multiple perspectives on the play automatically leads to subversion, with the ironic, negative interpretation forever undercutting the heroic, Rabkin argues that Shakespeare appears to grasp the fact that the perception of reality itself is always 'intransigently multivalent' and that this may be harnessed for productive aesthetic ends.[52] This is a slightly different kind of 'two-eyed' view to those proposed by Rossiter or Goddard as it suggests that ambivalence need not always be linked with irony and indeed questions whether ambivalence can always be explained away by identifying the presence of irony. *Henry V* thus exemplifies a mode of drama that thrives upon conflict and irresolution and requires the presence of an audience to interpret and evaluate the multiple perspectives presented.

■ The clash between the two possible views of the world in *Henry V* suggests a spiritual struggle in Shakespeare that he would spend the rest of his career working through. One sees a similar oscillation, magnified and re-emphasized, in the problem plays and tragedies, and one is tempted to read the romances as a last profound effort to reconcile the irreconcilable. The terrible fact about *Henry V* is that Shakespeare seems equally tempted by both its rival gestalts. And he forces us, as we experience and re-experience and reflect on the play, as we encounter it in performances which inevitably lean in one direction or the other, to share its conflict.[53] □

Such a view has several implications. For a start, it offers an interpretative framework for situating *Henry V* in relation to Shakespeare's subsequent plays and implies that 1599 was a transitional moment in the playwright's dramatic career, as indeed James Shapiro's account of this particular year in Shakespeare's life maintains.[54] Rabkin also highlights the importance of our own perception of the play and the issues that it raises. *Henry V* offers a profound insight into the divided nature of the self, particularly as it relates to political power:

■ Shakespeare reveals the conflicts between the private selves with which we are born and the public selves we must become, between our longing that authority figures can be like us and our suspicion that they must have traded away their inwardness for the sake of power.[55] □

Rabkin thus relates *Henry V* back to many of the earlier debates about the distinction between kingship and humanity that were discussed in Chapter 4. As several of the critics considered in the next chapter argue, ambiguity itself plays an important role in Henry's exercise of royal power. Furthermore, Rabkin begins to suggest more complex ways of exploring how the play reminds us of its own theatricality, and the moment at which one engages with the performance, by placing so much emphasis on an audience's personal expectations and cognitive reactions: how they respond to *Henry V* and construct a particular reading of the king or version of events.

Rabkin's conception of the play as an instrument for juxtaposing alternative, equally viable perspectives begins to broaden the possibilities offered by Shakespearean ambivalence. His essay underlies the work of many later critics, including Larry Champion, Phyllis Rackin and Paola Pugliatti, who continue to advance dialectical readings of *Henry V* in order to examine the different ways in which Shakespeare interrogates the provisional, positivist nature of historiography itself.[56] All three of these critics offer nuanced appreciations of Shakespeare's artistry though they make the same essential observation as Rabkin: that through offering multiple perspectives simultaneously *Henry V* denies the possibility of a coherent, finished thesis and its dialectical nature leaves the audience or critic with the task of interpreting and assessing the information presented.

This chapter has shown the different ways in which critics have identified that ambiguity, scepticism and doubleness are built into the play itself and are not merely the product of *Henry V*'s rich critical tradition. Largely taking for granted that the play offers conflicting visions of the king as both hero and villain, *Henry V* criticism by the 1970s starts to bifurcate in a different way. On the one hand there is the historicist tradition that continues to explore how the play may be unlocked, or at least better understood, by reference to some contemporary, extra-dramatic component. On the other, there is the aestheticist tradition that seeks to redirect us from Tillyard and his heirs by prioritizing the play's structural, thematic and ironic aspects. Richard Levin, indeed, argues in *New Readings vs. Old Plays* (1979) that all criticism on English Renaissance drama written during the 1950s–70s adopts the thematic, ironic or historicist mode; he enumerates the limitations of each and criticizes the predominantly descriptive emphasis that they share.[57] Edward Berry even goes as far as to suggest that there is a certain stalemate or, indeed, staleness in criticism of *Henry V* and the histories by the early 1980s:

■ The controversy over *Henry V*, it seems, has reached the point of diminishing returns. Although more extreme than most other debates about the plays, it can be taken as illustrative, for it proceeds from assumptions that have long dominated studies of the [history play] genre. Bounded by the history of ideas on one side and the 'new criticism' on the other, for the most part, criticism of the histories has remained within a relatively narrow range of interests. If criticism of *Henry V* stands at an *impasse*, it is because the genre as a whole requires new approaches.[58] □

By the time Berry's essay appears, however, new approaches had already begun to emerge, which reconceived and reformulated the relationship between history and aesthetics, and proposed (as Ornstein tentatively suggested) that there should be some form of balance between the historical and aestheticist traditions. In the next chapter, we will examine a number of critics who attempt to draw on the best of each tradition by synthesizing formal appreciation of *Henry V* with a sustained sensitivity to the historical context of both the dramatist and the critic.

CHAPTER SEVEN

The Later Twentieth Century and Beyond: Power, Subversion and Masculinity

During the early 1980s, critics of early modern literature began to re-evaluate the assumptions and practices used by previous generations of commentators and academics when considering how historical context relates to the production and reception of literary works. Practitioners of New Historicism and Cultural Materialism sought to deconstruct the Old Historicist principle that a text can be understood simply by situating it passively against its historical background. They also challenged the whole hierarchy that privileges so-called literary texts over non-literary sources previously used to constitute and delineate that background. New Historicists afforded the same weight to literary and non-literary texts, viewing them as equally complicit in both forming and recording a given historical moment, and drew attention to what Louis Montrose called the 'textuality of history and the historicity of texts'.[1] Such a method obviously has potentially great implications for broadening the canon of texts forming the focus of critical studies. Tillyard's concept of an Elizabethan world picture that could be used to explain the philosophical and ideological workings of a text, which informs earlier historicist readings, subsequently came in for repeated criticism for being an anachronistic contrivance that excluded and effectively silenced marginal and subordinate aspects of Tudor and Stuart culture.[2] New Historicism and Cultural Materialism also challenged ahistorical, purely aestheticist interpretations that were founded on essentialist, humanist assumptions about the universality of human nature or the possibility of a singular, monolithic response to literary texts. The aestheticist emphasis on close reading and identification of irony or fault-lines was, however, integrated with, rather than supplanted by, materialist critical methods. The critics discussed in the next two chapters frequently draw together many of the different techniques for interpreting *Henry V* practised throughout the play's critical history, as well as remaining alert to their own subjective interaction with that history. Drawing on a range of different theorists, ideas and critical vocabularies including Marxism, feminism, psychoanalysis and anthropology, materialist critics from the 1980s onwards investigated how early modern writers intervene in, rather than simply reflect, the historical context in which they work. Materialist criticism has therefore characteristically placed great emphasis on the instrumental role of literary works: how a text actively participates in the wider process of legitimizing the dominant social order and preserving the existing relations of domination and subordination in early modern England.[3] One of the principal tasks of a materialist critic is thus to demonstrate how a text – usually without the author's intention – reveals the ideological structures and beliefs that it sustains.

This is certainly the concern in the earliest New Historicist and Cultural Materialist interpretations of *Henry V*, which has been used as an exemplary test case in some of the seminal, foundational expositions of both methodologies, starting with Stephen Greenblatt's essay 'Invisible Bullets'.

STEPHEN GREENBLATT

'Invisible Bullets' first appeared in the journal *Glyph* in 1981 and was then revised and published in expanded form in Jonathan Dollimore and Alan Sinfield's Cultural Materialist collection *Political Shakespeare* (1985) and in Greenblatt's own *Shakespearean Negotiations* (1988). Greenblatt's argument is circuitous and seemingly digressive at times but it is worth tracing here in full since both its form and content have subsequently been widely discussed, imitated and criticized. The essay begins with an anecdote concerning charges of atheism made in the 1593 police report on Christopher Marlowe (1564–93) and levelled at the Elizabethan mathematician and geographer, Thomas Harriot (1560–1621), that seems on first reading entirely unrelated to *Henry V*. Citing several shorter examples of similar accusations, Greenblatt characterizes sixteenth-century atheism as being a form of demystification, a sceptical exposure of the temporal trickery and hypocrisy behind supposedly metaphysical concepts or entities.[4] This in turn is quickly associated with a wider current of early modern scepticism exemplified (for Greenblatt's purposes) by Machiavelli, who had written about the political pragmatism of temporal institutions that make recourse to divine authority to support their positions of power.[5] There is little in Harriot's writings to support the atheism charge but Greenblatt uses the accusation as a way into reading Harriot's *Brief and True Report of the New Found Land of Virginia* (1588) – again, a work which seems a long way from Shakespeare's Agincourt – in order to gain insight into a contemporary formulation about the relationship between orthodoxy and subversion that will then allow him to construct an interpretative model for reading Shakespeare's histories. Greenblatt thus uses the fragmentary suggestion of Harriot's atheism as a pretext for looking at the subversive potential of demystification as it appears (or is made to appear) in *A Brief and True Report*. He does so in order to offer a new way of confronting the entrenched pro- and anti-Henry critical positions that we have discussed throughout this Guide so far. The conflict between these positions, Greenblatt maintains, is a product of the histories' 'circumstances of production': the 'ideological strategies that fashion Shakespeare's history plays help in turn to fashion the conflicting readings of the plays' politics'.[6] Before turning to Shakespeare in detail, Greenblatt highlights those points in *A Brief and True Report*, where Harriot appears to be 'virtually testing the Machiavellian hypothesis' mentioned above concerning the role of, in this case, primitive religion to enforce social order among the Algonquian Indians through a process of – as Harriot sees it – deliberate mystification and pretence.[7] Harriot then makes rudimentary attempts to compare this process to the function of religion in the Old World. He is, suggests Greenblatt, engaged in 'the testing upon the bodies and minds of non-Europeans or, more generally, the noncivilized, of a hypothesis about the origin and nature of European culture and belief'.[8] For Greenblatt this constitutes the root of Harriot's alleged atheism and subversion. Harriot further tests and confirms his hypothesis about the function of religion when he records the successes gained in the Virginian colonial enterprise through the imposition of his own religion. Harriot's text is therefore both a tool of the ruling power that he serves and, in some ways promotes, a subversive account of the practical gains achieved in the colony through the use of religion as a mechanism of control.[9]

Harriot exemplifies a further form of subversion when he sets out to record 'alien' interpretations of the dominant culture at a point in his text when the native Virginians attempt to understand the new diseases brought by the colonists that began to decimate the indigenous population. Some Algonquians interpreted the disease along prevailing Christian lines as the work of God acting on the colonists' behalf; others believed that the English were shooting them with invisible bullets.[10] Greenblatt makes much of the fact that Harriot records different forms of explanatory stories, both orthodox and subversive, and this forms the essence of his central, paradigmatic interpretative model. Subversive ideas are tested or voiced, such as Harriot's exposition of how illusion functions in the establishment of religion or how disease's providential causation was displaced momentarily by the invisible bullets theory, only to be contained and suppressed within the reiteration of dominant orthodox ideas.[11] The subversion-containment model came to form a cornerstone of New Historicist rhetorical method and was derived in part from the

French philosopher Michel Foucault (1926–84) who wrote at length on the pervasive, inescapable operation of state power and its capacity to contain or repress all forms of personal subversion or transgression.

Greenblatt now turns the paradigm of a self-undermining authority to Shakespeare and he re-formulates everything discussed so far as a means of addressing the question of Henry's perceived conservatism or radicalism. Shakespeare's plays are located alongside the theatrical strategies of Elizabethan statecraft seen in royal pageants, progresses and entries:

■ Shakespeare evidently grasped such strategies not by brooding on the impact of English culture in far-off Virginia but by looking intently at the world immediately around him, by contemplating the queen and her powerful friends and enemies, and by reading imaginatively the great English chroniclers. And the crucial point is less that he *represented* the paradoxical practices of an authority deeply complicit in undermining its own legitimacy than that he *appropriated* for the theater the compelling energies at once released and organized by these practices. (Greenblatt's italics)[12] □

Greenblatt labours to portray Henry, from his first soliloquy in *1 Henry IV*, as 'a conniving hypocrite' and revisits material familiar from Bradley concerning his evident duplicity.[13] But we should understand Henry's 'greener days' not simply as a dilatory period of distraction and misrule, but as an opportunity to record oppositional voices both at and beyond the margins of Henry IV's realm, particularly those of Falstaff and the Eastcheap contingent. Greenblatt also draws attention to Henry's rhetorical prowess when he demonstrates how Shakespeare foregrounds the linguistic, performative strategies essential to successful rule. The play *1 Henry IV* sees the prince engaged in myriad acts of theatrical improvisation that will become essential once he attains power; the education of a ruler should include mastery of all the languages and voices of those to be ruled. The language games played at the Boar's Head with Francis and Poins in *1 Henry IV* allow Henry to declare with confidence that 'when I am King of England I shall command all the good lads in Eastcheap' (2.5.13–14).[14] Warwick affirms such pragmatism in *2 Henry IV* when identifying that '[T]he Prince but studies his companions, / Like a strange tongue, wherein, to gain the language' (4.3.68–9). Using another oblique contemporary analogy, Greenblatt compares Henry's acquisition of linguistic mastery to Thomas Harman's *A Caveat for Common Cursitors* (1566), a treatise of technical terms and language tricks used by the criminal underworld in Elizabethan London, the compilation of which entailed the author betraying the confidence into which he was professedly taken by the obliging rogues. Harman's broken promises are a necessary evil made for the greater social good and the same principle may be applied to Henry's own pragmatic use of language and the truth:

■ The founding of the modern state, like the self-fashioning of the modern prince, is shown to be based upon acts of calculation, intimidation, and deceit. And these acts are performed in an entertainment for which audiences, the subjects of this very state, pay money and applaud.[15] □

So far, Greenblatt has been assembling the broader interpretative models, using extended analogies from Harriot and Harman, that allow him to situate *Henry V* alongside contemporary articulations of how royal power establishes and sustains itself in the Elizabethan period. In the essay's final section Greenblatt begins to make sense of the somewhat disparate elements that have been discussed:

■ The first part of *Henry IV* enables us to feel at moments that we are like Harriot, surveying a complex new world, testing upon it dark thoughts without damaging the order that those thoughts would seem to threaten. The second part of *Henry IV* suggests that we are still more like the Indians, compelled to pay homage to a system of beliefs whose fraudulence only confirms their power, authenticity, and truth. The concluding play in the series, *Henry V*, insists that we have all along been both colonizer and colonized, king and subject. The play deftly registers every nuance of royal hypocrisy, ruthlessness, and bad faith – testing, in effect, the proposition that successful rule depends not upon sacredness but upon demonic violence – but it does so in the context of a celebration, a collective panegyric to 'This star of England', the charismatic leader who purges the commonwealth of its incorrigibles and forges the martial national state.[16] □

Like Goddard, Rabkin and others, Greenblatt recognizes the play's essential doubleness, but, rather than simply re-affirming the virtues of maintaining a 'two-eyed' view of *Henry V*, he attempts to use the subversion-containment model that he patiently constructed previously to connect the negative perceptions of the king listed above to the positive. He identifies a number of points in *Henry V* where Shakespeare apparently 'records' alien voices prior to suppressing and thus containing them within the bounds of orthodox discourse. The four captains' interaction before Harfleur, for example, sees Henry 'symbolically' taming the 'last wild areas of the British Isles', their linguistic otherness a gesture of regional difference pressed into service of the English cause. A similar moment of potential subversion arises and is then diffused when Fluellen draws a laboured analogy between Henry and Alexander the Great that ends with a reference to the king figuratively 'killing' Falstaff (4.7.40–6). No sooner is the comparison made than Henry enters with a flourish, 'potential dissonance being absorbed into a charismatic celebration'.[17] Further alien voices are recorded and negated in scenes featuring the French, for example, in 3.5 when French aristocratic pride is undercut immediately by reference to the acquiescence of native 'madams' to the 'lust of English youth' (3.5.28–30). As several later critics develop much further, in the two scenes in which Katherine speaks French, she does so while attempting to learn the language of her would-be captors.[18] Greenblatt's argument moves ahead briskly to demonstrate how the subversive act of 'explaining' accompanies that of recording, and starts with the need to assert the French campaign's justice and divine endorsement seen in Act one that continues to Agincourt and beyond in Henry's repeated insistence on the metaphysical agency behind the English victory (4.8.115–17). Henry V, Greenblatt maintains, adopts a pattern of showing us the ideological motives and support for the play's contentious key events (including the claim to France, the Harfleur parley and the killing of prisoners) and the means by which they are publicly presented; 'we witness an anticipatory subversion of each of the play's central claims'.[19] However, rather than such exposures leading us to attack or dismiss Henry as a duplicitous charlatan, doubts and consciously cultivated ambiguity, it is argued, actually enhance our interest in the play's central character. As Greenblatt declares confidently 'the very doubts that Shakespeare raises serve not to rob the king of his charisma but to heighten it, precisely as they heighten the theatrical interest of the play'.[20] The gap between real and ideal is laid bare before us. However, this is not simply ambivalence for its own sake. Shakespeare is offering us an oblique insight into the theatricality of state power, the necessary play-acting undertaken by any monarch to some degree but perfected in particular by Elizabeth and developed in new directions by Stuart court culture and masque.[21] He reveals how all power relies on an audience's imagination and the same kind of manipulation that the Chorus attempts as the play opens. What better way of reflecting contemporary conceptions of the theatricality of monarchy than a dramatic examination of what it means to play at being king? Shortly before Greenblatt's essay first appeared, James L. Calderwood discussed how Henry V anatomizes the rhetorical, linguistic foundation of kingship itself and proposed that '[T]o play the king is to play the actor, for the king must have many roles in his repertoire'.[22] Shakespeare's attention in the play to the language of command remains a recurrent concern in Henry V criticism from the 1980s onwards.[23] It feels like we have come a long way from the opening Marlovian anecdote but Greenblatt makes the connection explicit at the very end of 'Invisible Bullets': 'Like Harriot in the New World, the Henry plays confirm the Machiavellian hypothesis that princely power originates in force and fraud even as they draw their audience toward an acceptance of that power'.[24]

'Invisible Bullets' offers exciting possibilities for breaking the stalemate of pro- and anti-Henry criticism and re-imagining what one can do with both close reading and contextual analysis. Rather than simply identifying individual topical allusions, as Simpson and Campbell had, Greenblatt attempts to locate *Henry V* in relation to Elizabethan strategies of state and to offer a far more complicated elucidation of how the play reflects and supports contemporary political orthodoxy than that proposed by Tillyard. Through his attention to language and rhetoric Greenblatt suggests how *Henry V* reveals its own instrumental, coercive properties. Greenblatt's essay also raises many new lines of enquiry about how the play relates to context, no longer simply arguing that X in the play *is* or reflects Y in Shakespeare's period but exploring how X happens at the same time as Y or how X causes Y. 'Invisible Bullets' is hugely important for *Henry V*'s critical tradition – and early modern studies as a whole – and it informs the work of many subsequent New Historicist treatments of the play. For example, in *Power on Display* (1986) Leonard Tennenhouse maintains that *Henry V* exemplifies the way that the Shakespearean stage both authorizes and shapes the policies of state by presenting patriarchal hierarchy in disorder and then demonstrating how disruptive elements are defeated or assimilated by the representatives of state orthodoxy in the play. Tennenhouse draws on the theories of Mikhail Bakhtin (1895–1975) concerning the political functions of carnival for a model of how social inversion and misrule offer a licensed, momentary safety valve for populist energies which keeps them contained within the bounds of state-controlled orthodoxy.[25] By working through a process of unifying disruptive elements from both inside and outside the realm, *Henry V* reveals how the monarch's power during the Elizabethan period 'achieved legitimacy as recalcitrant cultural materials were taken up and hierarchized within the official rituals of state'.[26] Richard Helgerson's book *Forms of Nationhood* (1992) similarly proposes that Shakespeare's histories are unquestioningly concerned with 'the consolidation and maintenance of state power' and that *Henry V* in particular works to stage social exclusion and suppress or silence popular, demotic voices so as to construct a 'preeminently royal image of England'.[27]

New Historicist readings of *Henry V* are still dogged, however, by many of the same problems as those of the old. Greenblatt's argument rests on a series of analogies that inherently raise questions about the limitations of relevant historical context. Similes and extended analogies do much of the work in Greenblatt's essay and in many subsequent New Historicist studies, as do attempts to interpret certain actions in a text 'symbolically'. In each case, exposition is guided quite forcefully by the critic's act of selection and juxtaposition. Greenblatt moves at speed between each stage of his argument, rarely pausing to develop an analogy or consider fundamental differences or contradictions. He also shifts between different conceptions of authorial intention, at times suggesting Shakespeare consciously acknowledges and highlights the play's relation to contemporary politics – though probably never its affinity with Harriot's text – and at others indicating that the subversion-containment model is the discovery of critical detective work. The words 'power' and 'subversion' are fundamental in New Historicist treatments of *Henry V* but they are used as elastic, catch-all terms and rarely defined with any contextual sensitivity, since this would impede the argument that power and subversion are in fact pervasive and often imperceptible. Many readers and critics may also find that they do *not* feel drawn to Henry despite the fact that they are shown the inherent duplicity of charismatic political play-acting. For all of its attempts to distance itself from Tillyard's methods, Greenblatt's essay is guilty of imposing just as unitary a conception of *Henry V*'s original and modern audience as that proposed by earlier historicists. Greenblatt (together with Tennenhouse and Helgerson) takes for granted the monolithic, all-encompassing power of the Elizabethan state to such a degree that *Henry V* is seemingly compelled into being a patriotic, orthodox text. We appear to have reached the same conclusion as Lee, Marriott and Tillyard, only by a different route. As Graham Bradshaw observes wryly, if subversion in the early modern state was contained as rigorously as New Historicists propose, it is a wonder that the English Civil War ever happened.[28] Greenblatt maintained in his essay that even today 'in the wake of full-scale ironic readings and at a time when it no longer seems to matter very much, it is not at all clear that *Henry V* can be successfully performed as subversive'.[29] By the time the 1988 version of the essay appeared, however, several theatrical productions began to stress just such a subversive interpretation. Adrian Noble's 1984 Stratford production presented the king, played by Kenneth Branagh, as a rather unpredictable political pragmatist. Michael Bogdanov's 1986 touring production went much further in drawing out the play's anti-heroic, anti-war potential by casting the English as jingoistic imperialists and evoking xenophobic tabloid coverage of the 1982 war against Argentina in the Falkland Islands.

In 1989, Branagh's film version of *Henry V* situated itself consciously between the patriotism and sentiment of Olivier's version and more problematic interpretations stressing the human cost, rather than the glory, of war. At several points Branagh includes visual evocations of the earlier film, as in his presentation of the St Crispin's Day speech, and – like Olivier – he uses flashbacks to incorporate pertinent scenes from *Henry IV* depicting the king's riotous past and his eventual rejection of

Falstaff. There is a further poignant reminder of the Eastcheap days in the scene where Bardolph is arraigned for stealing a pax and hanged on-screen. A tearful Henry gives the execution order after recalling (in flashback) the exchange in *1 Henry IV* 1.2.60–2 when he is implored, originally by Falstaff, though Branagh transfers the lines to Bardolph, 'Do not, when thou art king, hang a thief', to which the prince replies solemnly 'No, thou shalt'. Branagh includes many of the more problematic, ambiguous scenes omitted by Olivier, such as the exposure of the traitors, the Harfleur parley and the debate with Williams. Whereas Olivier presented the final battle as a spectacle of colourful pageantry and swordplay fought upon an immaculate, verdant field, Branagh's Agincourt appears as an inglorious mudbath, and his film calls to mind both the trench warfare of the First World War and more recent cinematic treatments of the Vietnam War such as *Apocalypse Now* (1979) and *Platoon* (1986).[30] The English victory provides little occasion for celebration and the Agincourt sequence ends with a four-minute slow-motion tracking shot showing the soldiers processing from the field singing '*Non nobis*' (as ordered in 4.8.121) and Henry carrying the body of the Boy from the Eastcheap contingent who is murdered during the baggage raid. Branagh's film has evident anti-war overtones but it would still be difficult to call it subversive. Henry's campaign clearly requires him to make a series of problematic decisions concerning the treatment of both his army and the enemy, but these are always presented as the agonized-over yet necessary actions of a righteous, responsible king. Branagh does not go as far as to show the killing of prisoners nor does he emphasize the frequent disparity between the Chorus's speeches and the action that follows. Indeed, Derek Jacobi's Chorus often assumes the role of an unironic, pro-Henry narrator or voice-over. The film's final scene sees Branagh's Henry woo Katherine, played by his then-wife Emma Thompson in a sentimental, romantic exchange that not only excludes the bawdy puns about 'maiden cities' (5.2.305–15) but also quickly serves to efface any memory of the blood and mud of the preceding act. Henry's troops can strip their sleeves and reveal their Agincourt scars (4.3.47) but the only reminder of the violence that brought England and France to the negotiating table that we see in Branagh's wooing scene is a small nick, like a shaving-cut, near Henry's ear. Although offering a more realistic depiction of warfare than Olivier's adaptation, Branagh presents a far less ambiguous vision of the king than Noble's 1984 stage production, and his cinematic Henry is still an irresistibly heroic figure with whom the audience is encouraged to empathize.

At around the same time that Greenblatt initially revises 'Invisible Bullets' and the more cynical and subversive stagings of *Henry V* start to appear, the British-based Cultural Materialists Jonathan Dollimore and

Alan Sinfield proposed their own response to Old Historicism and a for-mulation of how the play intersects with Elizabethan strategies of state.

JONATHAN DOLLIMORE AND ALAN SINFIELD

Dollimore and Sinfield first published their essay 'History and Ideology: The Instance of *Henry V*' in the 1985 Cultural Materialist collection *Alternative Shakespeares*, edited by John Drakakis, and then expanded it to include a long discussion about masculinity and miscegenation which appeared in Sinfield's book *Faultlines* (1992). The essay begins with the by-now familiar and, some might say, largely unnecessary dismantling of Tillyard's ideas of a world picture and the Tudor Myth and goes on to highlight the limitations of several earlier critics' own critiques of the Old Historicist method. Dollimore and Sinfield are committed to debunking liberal humanist ideas on the universal, unified nature of both history and human subjectivity and, like Greenblatt, they are interested in situating literary texts in relation to social and political processes. Their essay sets out to use *Henry V* to demonstrate how early modern literary texts reveal these processes at work, exposing the operation of Elizabethan political ideology. Whereas New Historicists are interested in the more abstract notion of power and its exercise, Dollimore and Sinfield use the word 'ideology' to signify the 'beliefs, practices, and insti-tutions that work to legitimate the social order – especially by the proc-ess of representing sectional or class interests as universal'.[31] Although power and ideology may seem synonymous, the latter predicates more of an active, ongoing practice than a static, pervasive state of control. Like every other early modern institution, the theatre functioned to maintain a form of ideological unity, claim Dollimore and Sinfield. The attempt to achieve such unity was not always successful, and it is in literary texts that we can identify traces of the ongoing struggle that it involved. Just as Greenblatt argued in 'Invisible Bullets', a dominant ideology must continually seek to suppress or silence dissent by first recognizing it and then giving it voice: '[t]he more ideology (necessarily) engages with the conflict and contradiction that it is its *raison d'être* to occlude, the more it becomes susceptible to incorporating them within itself'.[32] The act of uncovering the struggle to represent society as uni-fied forms the core of the authors' approach throughout the essay and seems motivated by the exciting possibility that a text might let slip the inner workings of Elizabethan ideology. They duly proceed to demonstrate how *Henry V* registers both the consolidation of ideology whilst simultane-ously betraying its instability.[33]

Once again, national unity is revealed to be only part of the story in *Henry V*. The king faces insurrection from many quarters within the kingdom including the aristocracy, the lower classes and marginal, though distinct, regional groups. Each of these groups, Dollimore and Sinfield remind us, had their counterparts in Elizabethan England and represented a similar potential threat. One of the techniques Shakespeare uses to endorse Henry's legitimacy is the public confession from the traitors Cambridge, Scrope and Grey that offers an effulgent validation of the orthodoxy they challenged.[34] Henry's own attempts at self-legitimation on the night before Agincourt are far more problematic as they open to scrutiny – for the only time in the play – the mixed motives of his concerns about kingship. Rather than seeing Henry's soliloquy as a pious meditation on the status and responsibilities of his office, Dollimore and Sinfield highlight how the preoccupation with ceremony masks the king's real concern with obedience and the deceptive means of preserving it. He envies his subjects in 4.1.234–7 because they are never forced into his own position of having to fear being disobeyed and opposed.[35] He also discloses his anxiety that the ceremony that maintains his position of awe and fear risks generating no more than 'poisoned flattery'.

Drawing attention back to the play's context of production, Dollimore and Sinfield stress that ideology needs perpetual reinforcement and the successive attempts to appease, deceive or suppress forces of potential disorder shown in *Henry V* project an Elizabethan political fantasy, an absolutist world where nothing is allowed to compete with royal authority.[36] This was a far cry from the political reality where the aristocracy retained a great deal of power and unruly nobles, like the Earl of Essex, offered a challenge to the ruling sovereign. The Chorus's final lines reiterate the tragic consequences of divided political power, as seen during the infancy of Henry VI '[W]hose state so many had the managing / That they lost France and made his England bleed' (Epilogue, 11–12). A similar fantasy of national unity exists in the scene of the four captains at Harfleur, which Dollimore and Sinfield claim (without irony) 'seems to effect an effortless incorporation'.[37] Fluellen constitutes a synecdochical reminder of the successful annexation of Wales earlier in the Tudor period while the Irishman Macmorris represents a domesticated projection of the ideal outcome of Essex's 1599 expedition to Ireland, a fantasy of Elizabethan imperialist ambition.[38] The 1985 version of the essay ends at this point with the rather general statement that '*Henry V* can be read to reveal not only the rulers' strategies of power, but also the anxieties informing both them and their ideological representation'.[39] Like Greenblatt, Dollimore and Sinfield raise as many questions about critical methods of approaching *Henry V* as they do about the play itself. The authors spend a lot of time establishing the innovation and necessity of their position but offer relatively little depth when they finally turn to the text. There are frequent gestures towards the broader historical context but there is far less detailed contextual discussion and exposition than in the works of earlier historicist critics.

The situation improves somewhat in the sections added to the essay in 1992. Dollimore and Sinfield introduce a new context for exploring the workings of ideology in the play: the representation of sexuality and gender, and the obstacles these pose to ideological unity. As they explain:

■ That the ideological maneuverings already addressed in *Henry V* are continuous in scope and relevance with sexualities and genders is evident from the way they present similar patterns: potentially insubordinate features are expelled after being demonized, or incorporated after being represented as inherently submissive. Even so, again, state orthodoxy proves unable entirely to banish the spectre of revolt.[40] □

There has been relatively little extended discussion of sexuality and gender in the critical history of *Henry V* charted in this Guide so far and the play has generated comparatively few treatments that competently engage with feminist, psychoanalytic and queer theory.[41] Dollimore and Sinfield's essay, however, offers a productive way of exploring sexuality and gender in relation to the wider discussion of power and subversion in materialist criticism. Just as social and regional disorder requires negotiation at each stage, so sexual 'disruption' has to be excluded throughout the play by suppressing the feminine and female.[42] Such exclusion is similarly fraught with ambiguity and anxiety for when Canterbury establishes Henry's claim to France he does by countering the French Salic law that bars the English title to the throne that derives from Edward III's mother Isabella (c. 1295–1358), daughter of Philip IV of France (1268–1314), an inheritance through the female line about which the archbishop remains silent.[43] As Dollimore and Sinfield assert, masculinity and the attendant need to exclude the feminine are central to Shakespeare's presentation of the inherent might and right of the English: 'In *Henry V*, the superior manliness of the English is so insisted upon that it comes to appear the main validation of their title: because they are more manly than the French, they are more fit to rule anywhere'.[44] Conquest over the French is graphically presented as an aggressive male act of sexual violence over the female, as Lance Wilcox, Jean E. Howard and Phyllis Rackin argue (see the next section of this chapter). But an internal mastery also has to take place to ensure the maintenance of masculine identity. Effeminacy in early modern England encompassed everything that jeopardized the masculine, homosocial community, and this included both excessive devotion to women, with its accompanying risk of emasculation, and undue selfishness or self-love.[45] Falstaff is thus often presented as a threat to the young Henry's masculinity. The English 'band of brothers' are consequently shown to be more masculine than the French who abhor the idea that 'our vulgar drench their peasant limbs / In blood of our princes' (4.7.72–3). As Dollimore and Sinfield show, both the English and French 'figure their countries as women requiring masculine control'.[46] The Dauphin taunts Henry on several occasions that he is not up to the task of mastering the female French body (1.2.251–3; 2.4.26–9). The French, however, are presented as even more effeminate in 3.7, the scene depicting their effete discussion of horses and armour on the night before battle. Frank Benson's early twentieth-century production of *Henry V* included dancing girls in the French camp in this scene to heighten the sense of degeneracy.[47] When the French finally learn of English successes in the field, they cast their losses in terms of power exerted over women (3.5.28–31). Women are afforded a negative value by both sides and are ultimately the real victims of this system of representation.[48]

Masculine qualities are also asserted in those scenes of the play that represent the intensity of same-sex relationships. This should not be construed anachronistically as homosexuality but it walks a fine line between the admired masculine ideal and the dangers of regressing towards effeminacy. The greatest example of this sort of struggle in *Henry V* is Exeter's description of York and Suffolk's death in 4.6.7–32 in which the former kisses the latter's fatal wounds to his face and lips before dying himself. Exeter's response, Dollimore and Sinfield observe, is to 'lose manly control, to surrender himself to the feminine response inherited [so he says] from his mother'.[49] Henry momentarily does likewise before news of another French assault forces him to kill the prisoners. Dollimore and Sinfield do not explicitly suggest this, but perhaps the controversial killing of prisoners could be interpreted as a conscious attempt to ward off connotations of a stultifying, effeminate excess of passion.

The authors conclude their essay by re-examining Henry's wooing of Katherine, a scene long treated with either scorn for its awkwardness or reverence due to the unity between England and France it ultimately enacts. Looking back to their earlier demonstration of how Shakespeare uses effeminacy and the feminine to characterize weakness and disempowerment, Dollimore and Sinfield read the scene as a 'sadistic exercise of power' over Katherine.[50] She is a disruptive force to be negated in the same playful manner as Henry exposed the traitors at Southampton. The authors again highlight the potential for ambiguity and anxiety here, as Henry has to maintain rhetorical supremacy while simultaneously avoiding the potential effeminacy of wooing. Tensions concerning masculinity inform the guarded, workmanlike nature of the suit and, as Dollimore and Sinfield note, 'the peak of personal emotion in the play remains the love-death of Suffolk and York'.[51] The essay raises the possibility of an ambiguous reading of the final scene. Katherine not only

maintains a linguistic resistance to the king through her one-line responses, she is ultimately a necessary part of the treaty that will see Henry
named as heir to the French king. As with Edward III, the royal title
passes through the female.[52] French effeminacy has the last laugh, it is
proposed, when it contaminates Henry's English masculinity in the production from Katherine's blood – so King Charles stresses (5.2.333) – of
their son Henry VI.[53]

Dollimore and Sinfield's treatment of masculinity refers to ideology
far less than the earlier parts of their essay. This consequently makes for
a critique that focuses on the text in greater detail and offers a new
framework for considering and explicating the ambiguity of several key
episodes, including the whole of the scene depicting York and Suffolk's
death and the killing of prisoners, and the final wooing of Katherine.
There is also a little more openness in the later sections to the possibility
of alternative readings that expose contradictions, and a hesitancy about
proposing a monolithic conception of how *Henry V* would have appeared
to all of its initial audience members – though not to the privileged view
of well-informed Cultural Materialists, as the 1985 version of the essay
suggests. There are clear signals here of recognition that the projection
of a singular, collective contemporary response to *Henry V*, such as the
New Historicists conceive, is as much of a contrivance as the Old Historicists' world picture. As identified above, Dollimore and Sinfield use
the discussion of sexuality and gender in *Henry V* as further evidence for
their model of how the play reveals its troubled relationship with dominant ideological structures. Their essay also engages most fruitfully
with the contemporary feminist interpretations advanced by Lance
Wilcox, Jean E. Howard and Phyllis Rackin.

LANCE WILCOX

Although, as we have seen, the two episodes that include the French
princess have attracted extended, often quite scathing criticism, there
are relatively few critical treatments of Katherine herself and those in
which she does feature substantively – perhaps rather tellingly – tend to
use her as a foil when examining the other (male) characters. Lance
Wilcox's essay 'Katherine of France as Victim and Bride' (1985) likewise
begins in this fashion as he attempts to intervene in the long-running
pro- / anti-Henry debate using the personality and situation of the princess to illuminate several different aspects of the king's character. Despite
the fact that she was one of Elizabeth's direct female ancestors and sufficiently well known to audiences to be mentioned in the epilogue to
2 Henry IV as one of the promised principal features of Shakespeare's next
play, she is sketched out in functional terms as 'practically the stereotype

of an Englishman's fantasy of a French debutante'.[54] Katherine's 'innocence and delicacy' contrasts greatly with the rest of the play's cast that otherwise consists almost entirely of warriors, statesmen and bellicose ecclesiastics.[55] Her thematic function, Wilcox argues, needs to be set against Shakespeare's preoccupation in the play with the brutal effects of war on a civilian population, which is emphasized on several occasions by Williams, Burgundy and Henry himself. In particular, war is portrayed as the occasion for sexual aggression, in essence, as rape: 'Widespread sexual violence not only represents one of the commoner afflictions of war on a civilian populace; it comes to stand as a symbol for invasion itself'.[56] Nowhere is this made more apparent than in the Harfleur parley:

■ What is't to me, when you yourselves are cause,
If your pure maidens fall into the hand
Of hot and forcing violation? □

(3.3.99–101)

Henry's speech is of course rhetorical in that this is a threat made so that violence and violation can be spared, though his profession of innocence for the abusive actions of his soldiers is certainly questionable. The Duke of Bourbon similarly compares the prospect of a French defeat at Agincourt to a rape in which they themselves are complicit (4.5.10–15). The metaphoric link of war and rape re-appears in the final scene in the bawdy play between Henry and King Charles about the parity of 'maiden cities' and the inviolate princess (5.2.305–15). Wilcox is unequivocal in maintaining that because this is Henry's war, and because rape is both the actual and figurative implication of war, it follows that Henry is 'the king of rapists'.[57]

Such an extreme position is ameliorated in the play, Wilcox continues, by the fact that the 'assailant' and his 'victim' eventually enter into a nuptial relationship where the concept of rape is effectively negated. Furthermore, this is a process in which the princess herself is complicit: 'Katherine does her part to redeem Henry's image by apparently collaborating in his conquest of her; and Henry in part redeems himself by his oddly chivalrous treatment of the princess, once she is indisputably his prize'.[58] Wilcox reminds us that Katherine's first scene immediately follows the threatened sexual violence of the Harfleur parley and the Chorus's admission that the princess has already been offered to Henry as part of a (rejected) ambassadorial agreement (3.0.28–31). Katherine's body is already implicated in the war and its imagined conclusion. Wilcox interprets Katherine's desire to learn English from her attendant Alice as 'an almost conscious design' to meet Henry halfway and prepare herself for conquest. The language-learning episode that accentuates her body and culminates with a pun on the French word for 'cunt' reveals the 'first stirrings of Katherine's sexual awareness'; it prepares the princess and audience 'for the meeting of the representative aggressor and victim later in the play'.[59] When the meeting occurs, Katherine's English has improved dramatically and Henry's own bilingual wooing is depicted as clumsy and continually self-effacing. Henry thus meets Katherine halfway as Shakespeare presents both king and princess as 'possessed of almost identical degrees of competence'; professed linguistic inadequacy veils the physical reality of actually taking Katherine as his bride and, by implication, sexual partner.[60] Shakespeare legitimizes this latter act further through reference to the production of an heir (5.2.199–208). The final wooing scene, in Wilcox's analysis, is thus a necessary means of downplaying associations of Henry's conquest with sexual assault.

The essay concludes with the view that Shakespeare ultimately fails in fully dispelling such associations, in part perhaps because the 'courageously honest and powerful portrait of the conqueror in the earlier, grislier scenes proves too impressive for the charming but shallow conclusion ever to conceal entirely'.[61] This does not really tell us as much about Henry as was promised at the essay's outset and never fully addresses the important, far more complex question of how much this would have mattered to Shakespeare's initial audience. Wilcox never sufficiently develops his suggestion that Katherine's acquisition of English is part of a 'conscious design' to prepare for her conquest and he misses the opportunity to set out a coherent psychoanalytic critique of Katherine. Wilcox is also guilty of failing adequately to historicize his central theme within the context of early modern sexuality; Sarah Werner has argued that the language lesson is more about the anatomy and eroticization of boys – given the gender of the actor originally playing Katherine – than the seduction of women.[62] Wilcox's essay nevertheless draws attention to the dominant literal and figurative presence of sexual violence in *Henry V*, a concept that is commonly avoided or negotiated in pro-Henry, patriotic readings and still seldom accentuated even in the more sceptical theatrical productions of the last decade.

JEAN E. HOWARD AND PHYLLIS RACKIN

In their groundbreaking feminist study of Shakespeare's histories, *Engendering a Nation* (1997), Howard and Rackin explore links between Wilcox's interpretation and early modern conceptions of masculinity that are revealed in the play along the lines discussed above. Their chapter on *Henry V* argues that the play marks a significant point of transition in Shakespeare's representation of patriarchy and masculinity:

■ Here, unlike Shakespeare's earlier history plays, the trappings and ideology of chivalry and hereditary nobility are identified as French and gendered feminine, and the decisive Battle of Agincourt is represented as a communal enterprise, the triumph of a ragged band of Englishmen over a well-equipped French enemy obsessed with the accoutrements that mark their place in a hierarchical culture.[63] □

Howard and Rackin proceed to develop their distinction between different conceptions of masculine identity. The first is based on the biological, essentialist fact of patrilinear inheritance; the other formed by personal achievement, a form of performative, literally 'man-made' masculinity. (It is here that Howard and Rackin implicitly draw on New Historicist theories about performative and self-fashioned identity advanced by Greenblatt and others.) Both models of masculinity, the authors point out, require that women assume their proper place.[64] But what does performative masculinity entail? By *Henry V*, Howard and Rackin argue, the active, chivalric ideal of the warrior engaged in single combat has been reduced to parody by Hotspur's martial bluster in *1 Henry IV*. His apparent lack of 'real' masculinity is revealed, as his wife complains, by the fact that it is only dreams of battle that seem to satisfy Hotspur at night (*1 Henry IV*, 2.4.39–63).[65] Henry finds it equally awkward to unite the register of chivalry and soldiery with that of wooing, as Dollimore and Sinfield observed. We have already discussed how early modern masculinity could be consistent with male homoerotic desire but Howard and Rackin again emphasize that '*Henry V* is the only Shakespearean history play where male authority is demonstrated in modern terms, by the hero's sexual conquest of a desirable woman'.[66] The Chorus to Act three suggests that the whole of the sexually mature male population of England will have followed Henry to fight in France leaving behind only 'grandsires, babies, and old women' (3.0.20).[67] The St Crispin's Day speech emphasizes the masculine nature of the 'band of brothers' and, indeed, the equation of masculinity and patriotism.[68] There are no longer female warriors upon the battlefield of the likes of Eleanor of Aquitaine in *King John*, Joan of Arc in *1 Henry VI* or Margaret of Anjou in *3 Henry VI*, though Shakespeare is obviously constrained by his historical subject matter to a large degree.[69] Howard and Rackin reiterate how Shakespeare devalues any trace of the feminine on the battlefield through stressing the effete inactivity of the French. In doing so, they maintain, Shakespeare also discredits the Dauphin's patrilinear claim to the French throne.[70]

The authors then develop Wilcox's argument about the conflation of military conquest with rape and revisit the same textual evidence before going on to demonstrate how Pistol's contentious marriage to Mistress Quickly and his acquisition of her tavern parodies Henry's conquest of Katherine and France.[71] In *Henry V*, performative masculinity is therefore both figured and enacted as the sexual possession of women and it is this conception of male identity, rather than those of patrilinear inheritance or even same-sex comradeship, that provides and reinforces the play's modernity and consequent potency for modern audiences. This explains, Howard and Rackin suggest, the effectiveness of Branagh's cinematic version, 'a film which reveals how thoroughly Shakespeare's play anticipates the terms in which we have come to think about sexuality and its relationship to male and female identities'.[72] It is also proposed that potential tension concerning Henry's suit of Katherine was mitigated in the film by the audience's knowledge that the actors playing the roles (Branagh and Thompson) were married in real life when it was made.[73] *Henry V* constitutes a significant moment in the history of early modern sexuality, though the authors conclude by offering little more than a gesture towards the wider dimensions of this historical context and its intersection with later twentieth-century feminist theories on marriage:

■ The images of rape that characterize Henry's acquisition of a wife establish, almost at the moment of its conception, the connection between the nascent bourgeois ideal of heterosexual marriage and the savage fantasies of rape that attend it.[74] □

Wilcox, Howard and Rackin offer new ways of advancing an anti-Henry reading and identify a character who is even less attractive than the pragmatic political actor proposed by Greenblatt, Dollimore and Sinfield. The last two critics discussed in this chapter – Graham Bradshaw and Tom McAlindon – endeavour to preserve a more balanced response to the play and its hero. They take pains to establish their interpretations in relation to the pervasive currents of materialist criticism on *Henry V* but also go much further in attempting to establish a framework for appreciating the play's complex, conditional nature.

GRAHAM BRADSHAW

In *Misrepresentations: Shakespeare and the Materialists* (1993), Bradshaw situates his treatment of *Henry V* within a much more wide-ranging examination of the limitations of New Historicist and Cultural Materialist interpretations of Shakespeare. Given the important role played by the essays of Greenblatt, Dollimore and Sinfield in mapping out the techniques and priorities of both methodologies, it is no surprise that Bradshaw engages with *Henry V* at length in establishing his own response to materialist criticism. Bradshaw begins by enumerating the shortcomings of 'prematurely politicized' readings that appropriate the play in an overly partial manner. Materialist critics frequently commit the Tillyardian sin of accepting the words of particular characters in Shakespeare's plays as an unmediated window onto authorial intention and suggesting that the 'real' Shakespeare always speaks via orthodox figures such as Henry or the Chorus, rather than through someone like Williams.[75] Bradshaw takes Greenblatt to task for relying on a monolithic, collective conception of the audience and an aesthetic response wholly governed by a singular inescapable political vision. Such a conception, as we have seen, risks returning to the essentialist humanism of Tillyard and others; 'old historicism with a Foucauldian facelift', as Bradshaw puts it.[76] Clearly subversion was not always contained in the Elizabethan state else Essex's supporters would never have considered the viability of staging *Richard II* on the night before the abortive 1601 coup.[77] Although Dollimore and Sinfield undertake to view *Henry V* as an interrogation of Elizabethan ideology they are restricted, writes Bradshaw, by the assumption that Shakespeare never intended to reveal the 'strategies and anxieties of power' and it follows that the essay's governing logic will be the critics' revelation of information rather than the play's own means of exploring ideology.[78] The dangers of this approach are clearly put into relief when Bradshaw highlights how little (or selective) textual evidence is relied upon to support Dollimore and Sinfield's claim both that the four captains' scene 'seems to effect an effortless incorporation' of disparate regional identities (discussed above) and that *Henry V* might represent 'the fantasy of a successful Irish campaign'.[79]

Bradshaw opposes critical attempts to establish what the play is 'really' trying to say – whether this is revealed by Shakespeare or the critic – and responses that 'short-circuit the genuinely exploratory process of Shakespeare's dramatic thinking'.[80] Bradshaw is certainly not the first critic to recognize Shakespeare's profound interest in the writing of history but he highlights that the play engages us in a 'complicated experiential process' of exploring fundamental questions about historiographical perspectivism.[81] As Goddard and Ornstein observed somewhat earlier (see Chapter 6), the Chorus plays a key role in such exploration. We should thus remain sensitive to the partial, selective nature of the Chorus's information and to the disjuncture between what we are told and what we are shown.

Bradshaw then revisits several familiar sites of critical controversy starting with the complicated sequence of events in Act one leading to the declaration of war and he makes the not entirely original claim that the play's first scene works to promote, rather than resolve, uncertainty about Henry's motives for war.[82] Shakespeare invites our interrogation of historical representation by complicating the apparent order in which things take place in Act one. On a first reading we might imagine, particularly if desirous of seeing Henry as the naive victim of scheming churchmen, that 1.1 presents the pragmatic financial motive behind the genealogical pretext expounded upon in the following scene. But as is always perforce the case in Shakespeare's histories the play begins some way into an ongoing series of events: Henry has already made claims to the French king concerning 'his true title to some certain dukedoms,/ And generally to the crown and seat of France' (1.1.88–9) prior to Canterbury's establishment of the king's rights and promise of support. Henry indeed appears to employ Canterbury to provide the supportive voice of conscience.[83] The Dauphin's taunts and mocking gift therefore furnish Henry with 'retrospective justifications for what he has already determined to do', something that Bradshaw identifies as one of the king's characteristic attributes.[84] (As discussed in Chapter 5, Dover Wilson and Walter similarly argued against seeing Henry as the hapless victim of scheming churchmen.) Further questions are provoked in Act two when the Chorus refers to 'all the Youth of England' preparing for war, a spurious vision of national unity undercut both by the Eastcheap scene immediately following and by the Elizabethan audience's knowledge that contemporary musters and conscription were very different to the idealistic reported narrative.[85] It had been known, indeed, for civilian audiences to be conscripted from the theatres directly, as they were in May 1602.[86] In Act five Shakespeare again plays with different levels of knowledge about post-Agincourt events. On the one hand, the Chorus presents the linear, annalistic report of the king's return home and the topical point of comparison, while on the other 5.1 begins in France as if nothing has taken place since 4.8. Rather than seeing this simply as authorial inconsistency – as also occurs in the Chorus to Act two – and ignoring the question of differences between the play's Quarto and Folio versions, Bradshaw argues that 5.1 functions as a demotic counterpoint to the final scene: a 'highly organized design or poetic-dramatic conceit, in which the two final scenes make up an ironic diptych of "low" and "high" conclusions framed by the Chorus's protesting prologue and still more discontented epilogue'.[87] Bradshaw's final section begins to suggest ways in which a more sympathetic view of the king could be snatched from the jaws of a potential anti-Henry reading. While many critics have read the wooing scene as an attempt to dress-up in romantic terms the inevitable exercise of a victor's power over Katherine, Bradshaw interprets Henry's use of the pose of a Petrarchan lover as a more sincere appeal to the princess 'to recognize that their respective situations make it necessary – or impossible, unless she reciprocates – to create a space for the "good Heart" [5.2.160] in a marriage wholly determined by political necessity'.[88]

Bradshaw's interpretation of *Henry V* is fundamentally reactive against the materialist critics' shortcomings though his central point is relatively simple: Shakespeare's drama is 'demonstrably more genuinely "interrogative", more "radical" and above all, far more intelligent than they allow'.[89] Bradshaw's argument that the play reveals an ongoing exploratory process on Shakespeare's part involves looking at many of the same scenes and ideas examined by those critics of the 1950s–70s discussed in Chapter 6, though he goes much further than merely pro- posing an ironic view or suggesting that *Henry V* offers incompatible alternatives. Indeed, Bradshaw rejects the usefulness of Rabkin's rabbit- duck analogy as it limits the exploratory process to a series of either/or choices and does not fully describe what takes place when we watch a play: 'We can't take a play in at a glance, like a visual image; it unfolds in time, like music, and our responses also unfold, in an experiential process that follows the dramatic process'.[90] Bradshaw could be seen as offering an interpretative principle more than a fully worked-out, origi- nal interpretation of *Henry V* to replace that of Greenblatt or Dollimore and Sinfield. However, he retains an important place in the play's critical tradition since he demonstrates that there was something of a backlash during the early 1990s against New Historicist and Cultural Materialist interpretations of *Henry V*. This was prompted by recognition of a need for greater analytical rigour and textual sensitivity than that practised by Greenblatt, Dollimore and Sinfield, and took the form of a renewed attention to the play's artistry and inherent, rather than latterly imposed, ambiguity. The reaction against materialist critics' limitations also informs Tom McAlindon's chapters on Greenblatt and *Henry V* in his book *Shakespeare Minus 'Theory'* (2004).

TOM McALINDON

Before McAlindon offers his own interpretation of *Henry V*, he sets out (like Bradshaw) to dismantle Greenblatt's influential subversion-containment argument. Working through each of the contextual analogies used to interpret Henry in 'Invisible Bullets', McAlindon demonstrates convinc- ingly and decisively how Greenblatt manipulates the work of Harriot, Machiavelli and Harman in order to fit his broader thesis and frequently takes the authors' words out of context to identify apparent deceit where it is not present.[91] The essay's power and unity, writes McAlindon, rest more on Greenblatt's rhetoric and powers of syncretism and juxta- position than on a logic derived from the texts themselves.[92] McAlindon also attacks Greenblatt's selective recourse to authorial intention and the way that 'testing' and 'explaining' appear initially as conscious strategies on the part of Harriot and others but are then attributed to a more nebulous concept of state power, of which the author is an unconscious agent.[93] We are also urged to be wary of the New Historicist tendency automatically to equate theatricality with political duplicity when examining a culture 'obsessed with the idea that all the world's a stage'.[94] McAlindon rightly observes that although countless critics throughout the twentieth century have advanced interpretations of *Henry V* committed to discovering its ambivalence, the enthusiasm of the pursuit of subversive irony has by now weighted the critical consensus predominantly towards negative readings of Henry.[95] Others have pushed the play's ambivalence to the point of paradox so that any apparent positive qualities have to be read as negative political pragmatism, perhaps because modern conceptions of heroism are themselves more ambiguous.

Lost from all of this, McAlindon believes, is the possibility of

■ an affirmative but complex picture of a hero; one which celebrates greatness while allowing for aspects of character or conduct which we would normally reprehend or rather wish away, but which are somehow intrinsic to heroic achievement or arguably unavoidable in the circumstances in which greatness is achieved.[96] □

This begins to sound like Dover Wilson's comment (quoted in Chapter 5) on how civilian critics and peacetime audiences often cannot handle the unpalatable truth about the qualities and values deemed necessary for successful rule in wartime. Indeed, McAlindon's approach to *Henry V* is not unlike that of Dover Wilson and Walter who set out to defend some of the play's more problematic scenes or concepts, and he too begins by negotiating some of the potential sticking-points for an affirmative interpretation. Rather than reading Shakespeare's allusions to the horrors of war as an ironic undermining of Henry's perceived heroism, McAlindon maintains that early modern audiences, particularly those familiar with Holinshed, would have viewed violence as an accepted reality of Henry's campaign in France.[97] Just cause is equally important, and again it is suggested that Shakespeare's audience would have been aware of the far more complex implications of Henry's claim that date back over a century and place the actions shown in the play within a larger, international dynastic context.[98] The scheming churchmen in the play's first act also need to be read in a sixteenth-century context as a jibe at the ecclesiastical powers that persecuted the proto-Protestant Lollards during Henry's reign: 'the intention is not to question Henry's integrity or independence but to depict the prelacy of Henry's time as a Reformation audience would expect to see it'.[99]

Whereas Greenblatt and others saw paradox and oxymoron in *Henry V* as inherently subversive elements, McAlindon argues that we should recognize these as integral, constitutive parts of Shakespeare's design. War should be seen as inexorably connected with peace, unity with disunity, order with disorder.[100] Evoking a faintly Tillyardian construct of an early modern pattern of thought, McAlindon expounds on Shakespeare's use of the philosophical and political doctrine of *discordia concors*, the idea that there is an inherent stability or harmony achieved in all things by perpetual change and opposition. Such a doctrine informs Shakespeare's use of imagery in the play and the Chorus's attempt to register both unity and disharmony. Act two opens, for example, with the Chorus's reference to both the supposedly universal preparations for war and the faults of the traitorous English nobles discovered and exploited by the French.[101] Readiness for war can take many forms. McAlindon thus counters the theories of Goddard, Ornstein and Bradshaw regarding the Chorus's distance from the actions subsequently presented in each act. He also shows how the conscious pairing of opposites is central to the conception of Henry's character: his wildness and responsibility, his daunting yet amiable nature, his ferocious yet noble conduct, and his ability to express both compassion and pragmatism, as in 4.6 or in Falstaff's rejection.[102] Henry's violent address to Harfleur's governor has to be viewed alongside his desire to forestall actual bloodshed and the fact that Shakespeare changes his source so as to show the king sparing the town from sacking. Henry's apparent tolerance of his soldiers' abuse of Harfleur's civilian population is incompatible with his laws of clement occupation that see Bardolph executed for stealing a pax.[103] Further paradoxes deriving from the notion of good that comes from evil inform the representation of Agincourt and its aftermath. Life and death are consistently compared both before and after the battle, as when Montjoy envisions the festering bodies of the English dead only for Henry to retort that their names will live on 'in brass' or in memory wherever they lie (4.3.83–101).[104] Images of blood form another paradox in the play and are used to suggest, not merely violence, but fraternal community, genealogical continuity and international unity, though the spectre of miscegenation accompanies the last of these, as Dollimore and Sinfield argued.[105]

Perhaps the most original example of paradox that McAlindon produces, and one that confronts a host of earlier negative interpretations, is in his reading of the Chorus's Epilogue. As we have seen, the Chorus's closing speech has often been seen to undercut Queen Isabel's equally paradoxical closing image of the English and French 'two' becoming 'one' and to thus reinforce an anti-heroic view of the play. France *was* lost because England lacked a leader who could successfully manage its many competing factions, but such an admission does not invalidate

Henry's undeniably heroic endeavours.[106] Furthermore, the Tudors relied on the historical fact that Henry not only conquered much of France and married Katherine, but that he died and his widow married Owen Tudor.[107] The play's closing lines present the paradox of a *felix culpa*, a fortunate fall that precipitated the Tudor ruling dynasty and perhaps prompted Shakespeare's audience to remember the link between Elizabeth and her great-great-grandmother. This last example typifies how McAlindon's reading of *Henry V* is valuable for the very reason that it refuses to concede to easy answers or over-arching explanatory paradigms that require us to solve the problems that the play presents by selecting which version of Henry we would like to find. His chapter on *Henry V* concludes with a positive declaration of the rich interpretative possibilities that remain if we continue to resist reductive readings:

■ The extreme prominence in the play of paradoxical and oxymoronic expression, combined with forceful allusions to *discordia concors*, constitute clear signs of thinking in terms of resolved opposites while retaining full awareness of the grim realities involved – an awareness which provides much material for negative and radically ambivalent criticism to work on.[108] □

McAlindon's demonstration of how we might preserve an affirmative interpretation of Henry has implications that go beyond individual questions about the king's reputation or the degree to which Shakespeare endorses or critiques Tudor orthodoxy, for it highlights that the whole issue of our ability to understand and appreciate the play's artistic complexity is still at stake.

Whether or not one agrees with their individual methods and conclusions, all of the critics examined in this chapter offer valuable contributions to *Henry V*'s critical history through their continued interrogation and frequent rejection of the pro- or anti-Henry positions that have been discussed extensively throughout this Guide. As we have seen, binary approaches fail to account satisfactorily for the full range of potential responses to the play and its hero that Shakespeare inculcates and manipulates, and the identification of subversion frequently complicates earlier critical considerations of irony and ambivalence. The New Historicists and Cultural Materialists, for example, identify an ambiguous, potentially unattractive king but one that ultimately affirms and endorses the ideology of Tudor orthodoxy and looks dangerously like the hero of countless patriotic interpretations. The dilemma is then thrown back to audiences and critics to decide whether the kingly qualities revealed in a potentially negative reading are in fact a necessary evil to be endured, perhaps even admired in a successful ruler. Many of the critics discussed in Chapter 4 had already explored this question but the very fact that it still occupies such a central place in the play's critical tradition testifies to the overall complexity and intractability of the political and ethical debates in which *Henry V* intervenes, and that it continues to perpetuate. As Bradshaw and McAlindon illustrate, we should resist the lure of reductive explanatory frameworks and ignore at our peril those critics that remain sensitive to the play's challenging, exploratory nature. Bradshaw and McAlindon demonstrate that character-oriented, Henry-centred readings are still possible but question whether the methodological tools currently used in such interpretations are fit for the purpose. *Henry V* criticism by this point is of course not solely preoccupied with assessing the degree to which the play may or may not be subversive and in the next chapter we will consider a number of critics of the 1990s and beyond who explore how the play interrogates early modern conceptions of nationhood, memory and the justification of war.

CHAPTER EIGHT

A Play for the New Millennium: Nationhood, Memory and Just War

We have seen that throughout the play's critical history, commentators and editors have sought to explain and understand *Henry V* by making recourse to the formal and political contexts in which it was produced and first performed. As seen in the previous chapter, New Historicists and Cultural Materialists also attempted to identify the linguistic, symbolic and imaginative operations of Elizabethan state-power using insights revealed, both consciously and unconsciously, by Shakespeare himself. By the 1990s, materialist criticism formed the basis of the accepted consensus approach to Shakespeare and early modern literature as a whole. Purely aestheticist readings of *Henry V* are by now the exception to the rule, and those that do appear are frequently prefaced by an exculpatory justification of method. Indeed, there are even traces of such sentiments in the long explanatory methodological discussions of Bradshaw and McAlindon. As we saw earlier, self-conscious expositions of critical methods form an inseparable part of earlier materialist discussions of *Henry V*, but still leave more detailed questions unresolved when it comes to the play's instrumental effect, the perceived homogeneity of its audience and Shakespeare's motives for writing such a potentially subversive work. Broad comparative gestures and analogies often falter when confronted with sustained textual evidence, and the relentless hunt for the revelation of ideology at work can tell us as much about modern critical and political paranoia as it can about Shakespeare.

Henry V criticism of the late twentieth and early twenty-first century remains as politically and contextually alert as that of previous generations, but there seems to be less of a preoccupation with the shibboleth of subversion per se and more detailed exploration of how Shakespeare engages with emerging notions of nationhood in early modern England and the importance of language and the imagination in this process. All of the critics surveyed in this chapter contribute to ongoing dialogues regarding how *Henry V* intersects with the fictions and techniques used by the Elizabethans to define their nation, to recall and record its history and to justify the expansion of its territory and dominion. They also demonstrate how *Henry V* continues to relate to early twenty-first-century political concerns such as national identity and racial diversity, the legacy of imperialism, regional self-consciousness and devolution and the justice of overseas military intervention.

NATIONHOOD AND HISTORICAL MEMORY

Critics, directors and audiences have long recognized the patriotic potential of *Henry V* and we have examined how the play has been deployed and interpreted at different times to rouse an English nationalist spirit. However, over the last decade critics and historians have begun to ask far more questions about how early modern audiences would have conceived and understood the concept of nationhood and the nation, and indeed whether such concepts are more rightly the product of post-Enlightenment thinking. There has also been extensive exploration in recent criticism of Shakespeare's histories of how the nation itself is not simply an accepted, clearly recognizable given, a physical, essentialist entity constituted of land and people, but a negotiated construct assembled collectively through a combination of linguistic, imaginative and creative resources. Critics have made frequent recourse to the theories of the twentieth-century historian Benedict Anderson concerning how the nation can best be understood as an 'imagined community'. For Shakespeare and his contemporaries, staging nationhood therefore entails, to quote Patricia Cahill, the 'envisioning of a collectivity': an ongoing process of both discerning who is in and who is out, and establishing the discourses used to make such distinctions including race, class, gender and sexuality.[1] When it comes to studying how *Henry V* engages with early modern constructions of English nationhood, critical attention now turns not only to the synecdochical figure of the king but also to potentially disenfranchised groups in the play that are equally implicated in constituting the imagined community of the English nation. Modern critics of the play also emphasize the importance of selective memory in constructions of the national imagined community. Henry himself recognizes this when he imagines how Agincourt veterans will remember their experience of battle 'with advantages' every St Crispin's Day (4.3.50). Selective acts of forgetting can be equally as significant, and James Baldo has examined how *Henry V* participates in a struggle to consolidate national memory through effacing uncomfortable historical realities such as the loss of Calais in 1558, the colonization of Ireland and traditional tensions between church and state.[2]

In *The Poetics of English Nationhood* (1996), Claire McEachern draws attention to the rhetorical techniques employed in *Henry V* to cultivate the 'corporate feeling' of national identity and identifies that Shakespeare uses the trope of *prosopopoeia* (personification) to give the nation an identifiable, personable voice and the basis for a national community imagined using the terminologies of fellowship.[3] McEachern thus forces us to re-examine the character-oriented readings of Henry in the light of the analogy widely found in Tudor political theory that conceived the state as a person or body. Early modern audiences would have also encountered symbolic bodies within the Reformed Eucharistic liturgy and the figurative identification of the communion bread with Christ's body. They were thus well prepared, argues McEachern, for imaginative constructions of the body politic – both individual and collective – when they came to *Henry V*. It is revealed, however, that 'every form of fellowship the play offers seems to inevitably turn out to really be a hierarchy'.[4] The scene with the four captains is an obvious starting-point for any discussion of nationhood in *Henry V* but it is here that hegemony can be seen to coincide with collectivity. Despite the appearance of a unified British army, there is still a pecking order between the captains since racial caricature isolates Macmorris, and Fluellen 'clearly ranks as the favoured subcultural exponent' through claims of ethnic kinship with the king (4.7.100–2).[5] Henry himself offers the greatest 'fantasy of collectivity' in the play in his St Crispin's Day speech that collapses all social distinctions and re-imagines the army as a 'band of brothers' (4.3.60–3), though its hollowness and pragmatism are exposed after the battle when the list of the dead is recounted in strict hierarchical order (4.8.100–4).[6] Falstaff's rejection and subsequent death exhibit a similar failure of royal fellowship.[7] The play thus records the paradox of the body politic, the coincident familiarity and distance of charismatic leadership. It also reveals a 'simultaneous distrust of and a yearning for community and, concomitantly, a nostalgia for and a suspicion of hierarchy'.[8] Such ambivalence towards community informs the use of multiple languages and registers in *Henry V*, with characters' tongues divided by nation, status, gender, region and 'relative urbanity'.[9] As McEachern observes, 'the failures of these languages to intersect frequently produce conflict' yet communications are maintained through translations, gestures and actions, and indeed she deems linguistic contest preferable to a common, transparent language that risks obscuring crucial differences between sovereign, subject and enemy.[10] Henry further distances his own language from that of his subjects when he refuses to acknowledge the oath given to Williams whilst disguised as a commoner about a duel that is prompted (ironically) by an argument over the king's promise never to be ransomed (4.1.182–211).[11] A common language would seem to offer the ideal basis for establishing a shared national identity and community but, as McEachern demonstrates, it is never as common as it appears nor is it as practical or expedient as one might initially think since it risks demystifying the 'official' language of state and inviting potentially dangerous or discomforting dialogues, as in 4.1. 'Social commonality', McEachern concludes, 'is best imagined rather than enacted'.[12] *Henry V*'s ambivalence rests on its shifting attitudes to social collectivity and union and not on perceptions of the king's character.[13]

Alison Thorne adopts a slightly different perspective on the play's ambivalence towards collective national identity in an essay published in *Shakespeare Studies* in 2002. Rather than believing that *Henry V* unconsciously reveals the fault-lines in the ruling ideology, as Dollimore and Sinfield maintained, Thorne proposes that Shakespeare deliberately interrogates the history play form with which he works and that

■ through a process of internal mirroring, the ideology of this particular form is opened up to critical inspection in ways that expose both the latent ambiguities and the coerciveness implicit in its discourse of native heroism.[14] □

The play also raises questions about the persuasive potential of history itself by revealing how

■ the past is deployed to manipulate audiences (both on- and offstage) into identifying with a political enterprise founded upon a value system and material interests that must, in many cases, have been fundamentally at odds with their own.[15] □

Henry V thus complicates the dramatic cultivation of a collective national identity as it forces us to consider whose nation and whose history it really stages. Thorne begins by revisiting the four captains scene and reminds us that although there is relative amity between the representatives of each nation as they besiege Harfleur, elsewhere in *Henry V* both the Scots and Irish appear as enemies of the English and are kept at a distance (1.2.166–73; 5.0.30–4).[16] Thorne then proceeds to explore one of the seeming contradictions of Elizabethan historical drama: despite its attempt to imagine an aggrandized, gentle audience, as the Chorus implies in the Prologue to *Henry V*, the form was aimed primarily at a demotic, citizen audience whose principal point of identification with the kings and nobles on stage was their shared nationality.[17] A play like *Henry V* indeed invites an audience to focus on their proximity with historical figures brought back to life on stage rather than on the distance or otherness of the past. The 'affective charge' generated by identification with dead English heroes is then compromised, writes Thorne, by the play's self-reflexive exposure of persuasive and interpellative techniques used by Henry and the Chorus, the modes of address of both being 'quite blatantly directed at getting others (mostly representatives of the lower orders) to labour on behalf of the king's cause'.[18] *Henry V* thus also encourages criticism of the imaginary versions of the nation that it articulates and particularly exposes the coercive use of history and memory.

This is first prominent in 1.2 in Canterbury's evocation of the Salic law and the repeated exhortations to Henry that he should imitate the famed success of his great-uncle Edward the Black Prince (1330–76) at the battle of Crécy in 1346 (1.2.102–10). King Charles's respect for Henry derives from a similar memory of that battle and the fact that the English king descends from the same 'stock' as the victor (2.4.48–64). When Henry accepts the challenge to emulate the victories of the past he immediately signals that conquering France offers him the means of securing his place in history since it constitutes an act worthy enough to be remembered and spoken of in the future. The lure of glorious posterity proves too much for Henry and in the rest of the play he then 'redirects the rhetorical strategies used so effectively on him at the plebeian subject, with the aim of eliciting superhuman exertions from his troops'.[19] He repeatedly offers his low-born troops an ennobling fantasy that the entire English army will be remembered as an egalitarian community, as in the rousing Harfleur and Agincourt orations. In each case, Thorne reveals, Henry dexterously manipulates language used to designate class and status, such as that relating to nobility and blood, to suggest the possibility of a national, fraternal common ground:

■ Previous hints that the ordinary conscript, 'be he ne'er so vile', will 'gentle his condition' by his valiant deeds and earn the right to partake of the fame normally reserved for patrician warriors, are restated more baldly in an attempt to bribe him into action.[20] □

The feudal cult of honour is seemingly on offer to all and the prospect of a shared memory of Agincourt extends the imagined fraternity beyond the day of battle 'to the ending of the world' (4.3.58). However, as Thorne demonstrates, Shakespeare also undermines the egalitarian fantasy in scenes that stress Henry's difference and distance from his men, as in the largely unsuccessful nocturnal visit in 4.1 and in the final tally of the English dead that records the aristocratic names and excludes the nameless 'five-and-twenty' from posthumous historical recognition.[21]

The Chorus offers a similar collective fantasy to Shakespeare's audience and establishes a 'reflexive, metacritical framework for the dramatic action by foregrounding the difficulties posed by historical representation and the theatrical medium through which the past must be brought back to life'.[22] The Chorus appeals to the audience's imagination to aid in his project but the social origins of the average playgoer were more likely to be closer to those of Williams than to Henry and at least some may have resisted the invitation to share the king's viewpoint.[23] The same applies to female playgoers; how might they have reacted to encouragements to identify with an imagined community that defines itself in terms that exclude them?[24] Thorne thus offers a corrective to many of the critics discussed in the previous chapter whose argument relied on a unitary conception of Shakespeare's audience. She also demonstrates how *Henry V* provokes an ambivalent response by getting the audience to consider their own social status relative to the vision of a national community presented on stage. Thorne's argument, of course, assumes that early performances would have included the Chorus, which as Gurr maintains is certainly not a given (see Chapter 1). If *Henry V* invites one to react to the coercive use of history, it may well have first had this effect on readers of the 1623 Folio version. Nevertheless, Thorne's essay valuably suggests how, through self-reflexivity and generic self-consciousness, the play raises the possibility of resisting the ideological coercion that so preoccupies the New Historicist and Cultural Materialist critics by exposing the contradictions behind projections of a national imagined community and offering a range of possible responses to royal rhetoric. As she concludes:

■ Like the disaffected conscripts of 4.1 who, despite being suspicious of Henry's fraternal rhetoric, resolve to 'fight lustily' for him, we may thus move between – or even experience at one and the same moment – a critical distantiation from, and emotional identification with, the royal myth of Englishness.[25] □

For Philip Schwyzer, Englishness is only part of the story in *Henry V*; he is one of a number of recent critics committed to investigating how national identity and consciousness in Tudor England was 'largely "British" rather than narrowly "English" in its content and character'.[26] In *Literature, Nationalism and Memory in Early Modern England and Wales* (2004) Schwyzer draws attention to the rather surprising fact that at no point in *Henry V* does the king actually identify himself unambiguously as English, although he calls himself Welsh on two separate occasions.[27] The first is in his disguised meeting with Pistol (4.1.52); the second in his exchange with Fluellen following the battle (4.7.100). Fluellen refers to his majesty's Welsh blood but the historical Henry, though born at Monmouth, had no such heritage. We are once more in the realm of imagined communities and histories, as Henry effectively inherits his Welshness from his Tudor successors rather than from his ancestors.[28] Schwyzer encourages us to read *Henry V* in the light of British nationalism and considers the different means by which the concept of Britain is contrived in the play in references to 'Arthur's bosom' (2.3.9–10) and in the king's exhortations to his troops to identify with the spirits of their fallen countrymen. He also reminds us that in one of Shakespeare's sources for the names of Crispin and Crispianus, *The Gentle Craft* (1597) by Thomas Deloney (c. 1543–1600), the saints are ancient British princes who opposed Roman persecution.[29] Schwyzer demonstrates that the concept of nationalism is wider and more complex than has previously been assumed in the many patriotic interpretations of *Henry V* and indicates that the play's perceived Britishness forces us to de-centre any form of critical focus on Englishness alone in order to appreciate fully the multiple regional voices that Shakespeare brings together. The Irishman Macmorris obviously represents one such voice and his taunting question offered in reply to Fluellen, 'What ish my nation?' (3.3.63), has attracted a range of critical responses over the last decade.

THE QUESTION OF IRELAND

We have already seen how *Henry V* was written and first performed during an expectant period in which Essex attempted to quell Tyrone's rebellion in 1599, and how critics such as Dollimore and Sinfield have discussed the play in relation to the Elizabethan colonization of Ireland.[30] Although there appears to have been a form of state censorship in force during the summer of 1599 forbidding anyone, on pain of death, 'to write or speak of Irish affairs', allusions to the crisis in Ireland nevertheless subtly emerge in imaginative literature of the period.[31] Joel Altman has examined how Shakespeare plays upon and harnesses contemporary anxieties and aggressive energies experienced by his audience during the Irish crisis in order to heighten their identification with, and indeed their participation in, the kind of English victories represented in *Henry V*.[32] Shakespeare himself provides the first historicist reading of Henry's campaign when he encourages the audience to imagine the 'General of our gracious Empress' – most likely Essex – returning from Ireland so as better to picture celebrations for the victor of Agincourt (5.0.30). This is only one example of what Taylor identifies as Shakespeare's preoccupation with Irish affairs in *Henry V*.[33] In addition to featuring Shakespeare's only Irish character, Macmorris, the play includes a disparaging reference to Irish foot-soldiers or 'kerns' (3.7.51), Pistol's use of a corrupted refrain (*'Calin o custure me!'*) from an Irish song (4.4.4), and an apparent Freudian slip on the playwright or compositor's part in 5.2.12, where Queen Isabel addresses Henry as 'brother Ireland' rather than 'brother England'. Ironically, there is even a literal Irish backdrop to Olivier's patriotic *Henry V* film as the Agincourt scenes were shot in County Wicklow.

During the 1990s, a number of critics began to try to make sense of the Irish context and allusions in *Henry V* and to offer a more immediately relevant colonial point of reference than that proposed by Greenblatt. (At around the same time there is an explosion in the number of critical investigations of Spenser's experience as a colonial administrator in Ireland and its impact upon his writings.) David J. Baker is one of the first to locate Shakespeare's treatment of Ireland in *Henry V* in relation to postcolonial theory. His essay '"Wildehirissheman": Colonialist Representation in Shakespeare's *Henry V*' (1992) confronts the overly simplistic interpretations of Dollimore and Sinfield who assume that the four captains' exchange before Harfleur models an idealized, 'effortless' integration of regional differences under the English banner. As postcolonial theorists such as Homi K. Bhabha assert, colonialist discourse involves a continual re-negotiation of perceptions not only of difference and otherness, but also of similarity and proximity. The colonized must become 'like' or mimic the colonized but this inherently predicates a form of hybrid identity for the colonized that causes difficulties when attempting to pigeonhole or represent the latter.[34] Such taxonomic and ascriptive difficulties certainly applied in Elizabethan Ireland where perceptions of difference were complicated by the presence of the so-called Old English, descendants of the twelfth-century English conquerors who by the sixteenth century had, to a degree, integrated with the indigenous Irish and formed an established political and cultural identity of their own. Baker uses Bhabha's terms to explicate the colonial context of *Henry V*: 'the hybrid – either the degenerate Englishman or the incompletely assimilated Irishman – could become, for colonial power, a figure of threatening ambiguity, and his language the site of unsettling contradictions'.[35] Both Macmorris and Fluellen assume different forms of hybrid identity in the play, their otherness from English signalled by their stereotyped regional accents. Their exchange in 3.3, argues Baker, interrogates both Macmorris's national identity and the status of that identity relative to others, including both Welsh and English. Indeed Macmorris repeats the word 'nation' so many times in his reply to Fluellen that it forces us to begin to question what it actually means.[36] It is also unclear exactly where Macmorris situates himself when he either appears to respond to the assumption that others will vilify those of his nation as 'a villain and a bastard and a knave and a rascal' or claims that those who defame his nation are such (3.3.63–5).[37] Macmorris's interrogative reply to Fluellen's seemingly innocuous initial enquiry serves only to perpetuate debate about the nature of Irish nationhood and forestall any 'final meaning'.[38] For Baker, *Henry V* exemplifies a colonialist text as it reveals the apparent impossibility of establishing a practical, static model of 'them' and 'us' in Elizabethan Ireland. He also responds to Greenblatt's argument about how Elizabethan texts attempt to speak for the colonial 'Other' by using theories on hybridity and the permeability of cultural boundaries to offer a more nuanced understanding of how Shakespeare conceives of national differences and the constitutive role they play in consolidating English national identity.[39]

Not surprisingly Macmorris continues to preoccupy critics investigating how *Henry V* engages with one of the greatest and gravest political crises of the late Elizabethan era. For Michael Neill in 'Broken English and Broken Irish: Nation, Language and the Optic of Power in Shakespeare's Histories' (1994), Macmorris's ambiguous position as an Irishman in Henry's English army reflects the wider uncertainty and anxiety about the status of Elizabeth's Irish subjects. In 1541, Henry VIII (1491–1547) made himself 'King' and not simply 'Lord' of Ireland, and, as Neill writes, with this new form of authority 'a systematic war of subjugation could be presented not as the aggressive conquest of an alien people but as a defensive operation designed to secure the good order of the realm against rebels'.[40] Ireland was conceived as something previously owned that had fallen into a degenerate (and for the initial conquerors degenerating) state rather than as a completely new world to claim for the first time. Elizabethan descriptions of Ireland represented it repeatedly as a degenerate, though potentially ideal garden, echoing Burgundy's conceit used with reference to France in 5.2.29–67.[41] The Elizabethan colonial enterprise was thus often envisioned as a civilizing process of recovery and correction. Macmorris consequently occupies a liminal space that is emblematized by his 'broken English', initially a phrase Henry uses to describe Katherine's knowledge of his language (5.2.236) though one which appositely captures the inchoate, unfinished nature both of Macmorris and the (re)conquest of Ireland.[42]

In 'Shakespeare's Irish History' (1996) Andrew Murphy offers a more detailed contextual parallel to Macmorris's liminal or hybrid status by way of comparison with the Irish 'rebel' leader Tyrone himself. Tyrone was born in Ireland of Gaelic parentage but was fostered by an Anglo-Irish family 'in the expectation that he would one day be inserted back into his native Ulster in order to assist his English patrons gain some purchase on that impenetrable Gaelic stronghold'.[43] He obliged initially during the 1570s, though as his relations with the English became strained, he began to exploit his knowledge of the 'sign system of English civility' and complicate perceptions of the distance between the colonizer and colonized, the ruling power and the traitor.[44] Both Tyrone and Macmorris demonstrate the inadequacy of the stereotypical depiction of the Irish as an uncivilized, barbarous Other. Although Shakespeare's Irishman reveals his eagerness to commence the business of throat-cutting at Harfleur, he is also referred to as 'a very valiant gentleman' (3.3.12) and assigned the rank of captain, and his peers are clearly willing to engage him in discourse on military theory. Ultimately, the enigma of Macmorris and his questions can no more be solved by modern critics than they could by Elizabethan writers, audiences and statesmen.

Christopher Highley's chapter on *Henry V* in *Shakespeare, Spenser and the Crisis in Ireland* (1997) goes further than Baker or Neill in challenging suggestions that the play presents a 'fantasy' about English hegemony in Ireland and argues that it 'begins forcefully to register Shakespeare's disillusioned ambivalence about the reasons behind and the consequences of English empire-building'.[45] Highley begins by demonstrating how the play 'both stages and resists the allure of militarism surrounding Essex and his Irish expedition' by juxtaposing the Chorus's reference to Henry's army as 'English Mercuries' (2.0.7) with the Eastcheap rabble shown in the next scene.[46] He then explores how Shakespeare's use of imagery connected with food and hunger intersects with contemporary concerns about the inadequate provisioning of Essex's massive army: '[a]gainst the backdrop of these conditions of extreme hardship in Ireland, the reiterated image in *Henry V* of an English army starving and sick in the field had an inescapable topical valence'.[47] Henry can only offer his troops the 'largesse' of his presence on the night before Agincourt and the promise of future sustenance should they survive the battle and celebrate at the feast of St Crispin.[48] Famine is listed as one of Henry's weapons in the play's prologue and had been used against the indigenous Irish in the 1580s but it now also complicates the distinction between conqueror and conquered.[49] Highley offers a historically nuanced examination of Macmorris's hybridity that identifies him with the Old English,

■ many of whom changed their name's original prefix 'Fitz' to the Gaelic 'Mac'. Macmorris's insecurities about his nation are thus typical of a group seen by the Elizabethan New English as 'more Gaelic than English, and by the Gaels as more English than Gaelic'.[50] □

Unequivocal distinctions between English and Irish are further complicated by similarities between Macmorris's apparently savage threats of throat-cutting and Henry's own 'necessary' barbarity revealed within the same scene in the Harfleur parley; Macmorris and Henry, albeit momentarily, share the same violent lexicon.[51] Highley proposes that Essex himself obscured the perceived distinction between the English colonizer and Irish colonial subject since he used the 1599 expedition as an opportunity to consolidate his own powerbase and authority. Fears of possible betrayal and treason by Essex were current at court during the earl's expedition and are perhaps recorded in the analogy drawn by the Chorus to Act five between Henry, the 'General' and Julius Caesar (100–44 BC). Caesar's return from conquering Gaul in 49 BC initiated civil war and precipitated his eventual assumption of effective control of Rome. Elizabethans already made great play of comparisons between Essex and Caesar and, as Highley argues, the association 'resonates' with Shakespeare's *Julius Caesar* which was performed immediately before Essex's scheduled return.[52] Reference to the 'General' bringing 'rebellion broached on his sword' is thus highly ambiguous: does Essex return as the conqueror of a rebellion or, like Tyrone, has he already set himself in opposition to the English queen, as he would in 1601? As Highley notes, Essex and Tyrone came to occupy the same 'symbolic position' in parliamentary speeches and trial documents following the unsuccessful coup, and Essex's fate further confirmed popular opinion concerning the degenerative influence of Ireland.[53]

The ambiguous, potentially unwritable nature of Elizabethan Ireland – a term which itself encodes the apparent contradictions and complexities inherent in colonial discourse – also has serious implications for conceptions of English nationhood. An imagined community constitutes itself through establishing criteria for inclusion and exclusion, but the Irish liminality and hybridity identified above cannot help but complicate the process of national self-definition. Ireland functions, as Neill writes, 'as the indispensible anvil upon which the notion of Englishness was violently hammered out'.[54] As we have seen, it is difficult to talk about Macmorris without considering his national status relative to Fluellen and, in turn, to the English characters. Critical exploration of the presence of Ireland in *Henry V* certainly appears to underwrite ongoing arguments about the play's inevitable, inescapable Britishness.

JUSTIFYING WAR

Controversy concerning the justice and conduct of the king's campaign has long informed *Henry V* criticism and frequently underpinned potential anti-Henry interpretations. Critics such as Campbell and Gurr have also demonstrated how the play intersects with sixteenth-century debates about just war and the pacifist arguments of humanists such as Erasmus and More. But at the very start of the twenty-first century, Shakespeare's extended interrogation of the arguments and techniques that Henry uses to justify the conquest of a foreign sovereign power gained added resonance and urgency in the wake of the terrorist attacks of 11 September 2001, and inception of the so-called War on Terror. Following the invasion of Afghanistan by US and UK forces in October 2001 and the relatively swift defeat of the ruling Taliban regime held responsible for supporting terror networks behind the 9/11 attacks, Iraq was judged to pose an equally significant threat to international security and – so intelligence sources warned – to be capable of initiating hostilities using 'Weapons of Mass Destruction'. Despite United Nations inspectors failing to locate said weapons, a US-led coalition force invaded Iraq in March 2003. Within little over a month it had toppled Iraq's leader Saddam Hussein and set about the long and – at the time of writing – ongoing process of reconstructing the country's political and economic infrastructure. In the months after the invasion, the intelligence underwriting military action was increasingly called into question and led to widespread international condemnation of the pretexts for the Iraq war and subsequent coalition occupation. When read within the active, controversial context of the war, *Henry V* cannot help but assume a renewed topicality, and the critical debates that the play continues to raise in the future about justifying war are likely to be conditioned by twenty-first-century experiences of warfare and political information management.

To date, critics have been rightly cautious about drawing direct parallels between Shakespeare's Agincourt and modern-day Iraq, and it would be inaccurate at present to identify a tradition of explicitly post-9/11 *Henry V* scholarship. However, a number of commentators have offered accounts of how Shakespeare explores the justification of war in *Henry V* that may provide the groundwork for topical studies by future critics and students. For example, in *Henry's Wars and Shakespeare's Laws* (1993), the lawyer and president of the International Criminal Tribunal for the former Yugoslavia, Theodor Meron, provides a commentary on the laws-of-war issues arising in Shakespeare's presentation of Henry's campaign. Meron notes how close Shakespeare kept to his sources in the opening act which establishes Henry's claim and sees him emphasize the core concern: 'May I with right and conscience make this claim?' (1.2.96). He also demonstrates how Henry's violent address to Harfleur's governor is supported – though not ameliorated – by medieval martial codes based on Deuteronomy 20:10–14 that shift responsibility for any subsequent atrocity onto the inhabitants of a besieged city should they refuse to surrender to an attacker's terms.[55] The historical Henry made a similar appeal to Deuteronomic law in a letter to Charles VI prior to his 1415 expedition.[56] Meron goes on to explain how just cause concerned both *jus ad bellum* (the right to wage war) and *jus in bello* (the law governing conduct in war), and demonstrates how the decision made in the first act affects the relative validity of every action of the English in France, just as Williams insists to the disguised king.[57] Just cause legitimized acts otherwise judged to be criminal if perpetrated in peacetime. According to late medieval and early modern laws of war the baggage train attacked by the French in 4.7 was a valid military objective, contrary to Fluellen's pronouncement (4.7.1–2).[58] Does this therefore make Henry a war criminal for ordering the killing of prisoners that is often construed (including by Gower) as a reprisal for the

French attack? Not if it can be shown that the order actually resulted from tactical necessity prompted by a report of another French assault (as suggested in 4.6.36); for according to the laws of war, 'it cannot be concluded that Henry clearly violated contemporary standards'.[59] Meron concludes that Shakespeare was certainly aligning himself in *Henry V* with 'the advocates of greater adherence to humane laws of war', and, in his accompanying study on Shakespeare's shifting attitude to chivalry, he argues that the playwright is not against war per se, but against abuses in the laws governing its conduct.[60]

This contrasts with the views of Steven Marx in 'Shakespeare's Pacifism' (1992), who similarly sees the playwright engaged in a debate between militarist and pacifist perceptions of warfare, though he argues, after acknowledging his debt to Greenblatt, that the play provides 'pragmatic rationales for war that recognize, answer and contain the pacifist objections that keep cropping up'.[61] In 1.2.13–28, for example, Henry momentarily adopts an anti-war position in his evocation of the imagined brutality of conquest so as to elicit pro-war justifications from the churchmen and nobles. As Marx goes on to contend, *Henry V* and *Troilus and Cressida* represent the turning point for Shakespeare between a pro-war and pro-peace stance in response to shifts in foreign policy at the close of Elizabeth's reign and the emergence of the Stuart culture of pacifism.[62] Marx identifies similar pragmatic appropriation of religious discourse to support the declaration and conduct of war in his essay 'Holy War in *Henry V*' (1995) and re-examines Canterbury's use of Numbers 27:8 to strengthen his bolstering of the king's conscience (1.2.98–100).[63]

R. A. Foakes counters some of Marx's conclusions in his book *Shakespeare and Violence* (2003) and argues that Shakespeare was far from resolved about war and violence while writing *Henry V*. On the one hand, the play depicts divine sanction and ascription for war, by means of the revelation of the traitors prior to the expedition and in how victory in battle apparently confirms for Henry that his prayer of the night before had been answered. The king stresses this point four times in 20 lines and calls for *Non nobis* and *Te Deum* to be sung (4.8.104–24).[64] On the other hand, Shakespeare retains an awareness of the king's burden of responsibility and of how the war's just cause rests in turn upon the contentious issue of Henry's title to the English crown. The Quarto version omits the king's problematic conversation with Williams but it preserves the prayer that begs forgiveness for his father's deposition of Richard II.[65] Within the logic of events shown in the play, victory seemingly affirms divinely sanctioned just title. Foakes also looks to late sixteenth-century tracts on the justification of war (like Campbell before him) and uses contemporary notions of divine ascription to counter Greenblatt's resilient argument concerning Henry's hypocritical attempts to obscure his violent acts.[66] Rather than proving Greenblatt's 'Machiavellian hypothesis' by subverting royal power, the play (Foakes concludes) preserves a heroic concept of Henry's war by contrasting the unruly, covetous violence of Pistol and the Eastcheap contingent with the king's divinely sanctioned cause.[67]

John S. Mebane in '"Impious War": Religion and the Ideology of Warfare in *Henry V*' (2007) returns to the militarist versus pacifist debate and attempts to balance aestheticist and historicist methods by proposing that *Henry V* undercuts the ideology of just war 'by emphasizing the fear that all warfare is damnable'.[68] He falls into the trap, to some degree, of simply re-packaging old critical methods and textual evidence in a new guise when he then examines Shakespeare's ironic deflation of patriotic rhetoric, the comic parody of partisan characters, and contradictions in Henry's advocacy of the conquest.[69] Mebane's essay exemplifies, however, how the customary pursuit of irony and ambivalence in *Henry V* may be re-cast in the light of the urgent topical debate about just war. It offers us a way of re-imagining a play so long connected with militarism and patriotism in the light of both early modern and modern pacifist discourse. Mebane's closing sentence cannot but allude, however obliquely, to the ongoing present-day experience of war:

■ If we read *Henry V* simply as a reflection of cultural conflicts, we fail to appreciate Shakespeare's artistic deflation of the rationalizations for warfare that all too frequently have masked the self-interest of those whose purpose in going to war is to maintain their own power and prestige.[70] □

The twenty-first-century stage has gone much further than academic criticism in drawing comparisons between Henry's campaign and the Iraq war. Nicholas Hytner's 2003 production at London's National Theatre is full of topical allusions and stresses how the play centres on 'a charismatic young British leader who commits his troops to a dangerous foreign invasion for which he has to struggle to find justification in international law'.[71] The opening scene is set in the Cabinet room of 10 Downing Street, and throughout the play there are references to the partial representations of war provided by the contemporary media. Not for the first time, the play has also been used by active servicemen themselves and was quoted for inspiration and emulation during the Iraq campaign.[72] Tentative moves have been made by critics to explore how Shakespeare's work relates to the modern military. A session at the annual conference of the Shakespeare Association of America addressed this topic in April 2006 and stimulated further discussion about the distribution of Armed Service Editions of *Henry V* to US troops posted in the Middle East, and on perceived similarities between Shakespeare's Henry and George W. Bush.[73] There are episodes of riotousness in the 'greener days' of both men, and the former was cited by several political commentators as offering a positive model for the latter of a leader who finds renewed purpose on coming to power and redeems his father's reign through pursuing an extended foreign war.[74] (As discussed in Chapter 2, Charles II's contemporaries viewed Henry as a similarly exemplary precedent for their new ruler.) Critics of the Iraq war, and of claims made by coalition leaders concerning its religious sanction, might also recall Hazlitt's infamous description of Henry's exercise of 'brute force, glossed over with a little religious hypocrisy'. Comparisons between Henry and Bush inevitably highlight essential differences more than similarities between both the leaders (not least in their respective oratorical prowess) and their political and military contexts. Analogies drawn between Agincourt and Iraq are complicated immeasurably in the present-day literal theatre of war that again sees a well-equipped, technologically and numerically superior army pitched against a fragmented force prepared to die for the honour of their chosen cause or beliefs. But with whom now are we supposed to compare Shakespeare's 'happy few'? Ultimately, *Henry V* will continue to have topical relevance and to intersect with running debates about militarism, patriotism, pacifism and just cause for as long as wars are declared, fought and endured.

Conclusion

This Guide has demonstrated just how many interpretative questions and problems *Henry V* has raised since it was first staged over four centuries ago. During the course of its reception history, almost every aspect of the play and its hero has stimulated fruitful debate and further analysis, and we have charted the major trends and paradigm shifts in scholarly opinion. Up until the early nineteenth century commentators were particularly interested in the play's formal properties and discussed its unity, genre and perceived dramatic limitations. It was during the nineteenth century that character-centred criticism came to the fore and one sees a proliferation of evaluative interpretations of the king's person and conduct, a preoccupation that exists for critics, albeit in different guises, to the present day. Character criticism is certainly not outdated and literary critics and theorists continue to explore the structures through which subjectivity and identity were formulated and articulated in the early modern period. The twentieth century saw both the emergence of detailed studies of *Henry V*'s historical context and, at the same time, sustained attention to the play's aesthetic qualities and formal interpretative cruces. As discussed above, Shakespeare's employment of ambivalence and irony has become the customary focus for critics grappling with questions that the play raises about war and conquest. Twentieth- and twenty-first-century critics of *Henry V* have continually shifted and re-negotiated the balance between historicist and aestheticist analysis and the most successful scholarship has remained sensitive to the nuances of both approaches. *Henry V* criticism of the future seems likely to continue to explore the challenges of situating and understanding the play in its late sixteenth-century context, while staying alert to Shakespeare's choice of dramatic medium and the fact that this is a play both of and with history.

Historicism raises its own problems and critical attempts to draw abstruse contextual analogies between *Henry V* and both the early modern and modern world risk replicating the kind of laboured, partisan historicism practised by Fluellen, who forms comparisons based on the juxtaposition of selected points of similarity but ignores glaringly obvious differences and inconsistencies.[1] Future critics should also beware of fetishizing the rather defeatist poststructuralist line which maintains that, because we will never truly or fully know the depth of Shakespeare's patriotic or subversive intentions in *Henry V*, the play can really mean anything we like or, alternatively, nothing at all.[2] This is the view of Terence Hawkes, which is exemplified in relation to *Henry V* by his short essay 'Wittgenstein's Shakespeare' (1988), and it informs many of the 'presentist' interpretations currently in vogue that border on 'Fluellenism' or, indeed, a new ahistoricism.[3] It will also be productive for future criticism to examine in far more detail what else Shakespeare and his fellow playwrights were doing and writing at the time of *Henry V*'s composition. James Shapiro has begun to pursue this kind of lateral contextual study in his book on 1599 but, rather surprisingly, there has still been comparatively little critical attention paid to how *Henry V* relates to historical drama written by Shakespeare's contemporaries. Perhaps we should also question whether traditional Shakespearean genre ascriptions offer the best or only way of approaching *Henry V*, and revisit some of the earlier criticism (discussed in Chapter 5) regarding the play's epic qualities. As seen in the last chapter, there is still most promising further work to be done addressing how the play encodes and responds to emerging conceptions of nationhood and the beginnings of British imperialism, and how Henry's anxieties about 'impious war' intersect with concerns about modern international conflicts.

The Chorus has featured in this Guide almost as much as the king himself and we have seen the vastly divergent opinions on its utility and desirability in the play. Although eighteenth- and nineteenth-century critics and directors found it difficult fully to account for or defend the Chorus's function in both the read and performed text, twentieth-century commentators have identified that it provides a key to unlocking the play's latent ambivalence and subversion. As we saw in Chapter 1, however, the Chorus is only present in the Folio version and thus any hypotheses proposed about the creation of irony or multivocality in *Henry V* need to first consider the bibliographic evidence. This has potentially vast revisionary implications since many modern critics still work with a monolithic idea of what 'the play' actually constitutes. *Henry V* as a textual object would have meant something different to Shakespeare, to late sixteenth-century audiences, to readers of the early seventeenth-century Quartos and to late Jacobean readers of the First Folio. The question 'what is my text?' must surely underlie all future studies of *Henry V*'s subversive potential.

In many ways, the Chorus's Epilogue provides a useful indication of what critics and students of *Henry V* should keep in mind as they continue to approach the play. It reminds us firstly of the positivist, 'man-made' nature of history (and, for that matter, critical history) and the presence of an author figure 'mangling' his narrative materials. Through reference to Shakespeare's earlier representation of Henry VI and the eventual loss of France, it also forces us to situate the play in its much wider historical and dramatic contexts. In doing so, the Chorus invites us to look back and reconsider what we have been shown, and to use the juxtaposition of the past and present to form a more balanced, nuanced understanding of the whole. It therefore emphasizes, like this Guide, the value of critically revaluating what has gone before, and how knowledge of the past informs and inflects present-day practice and experience.

Notes

INTRODUCTION

1 Edward Berry, 'Twentieth-Century Shakespeare Criticism: The Histories', in Stanley Wells (ed.), *The Cambridge Companion to Shakespeare Studies* (Cambridge: Cambridge University Press, 1986), p. 255.

2 Sir Walter Ralegh, *The History of the World*, ed. C. A. Patrides (London: Macmillan, 1971), p. 80.

3 Quoted in Annabel Patterson, *Censorship and Interpretation* (Madison: University of Wisconsin Press, 1984), p. 47.

4 Ivo Kamps, *Historiography and Ideology in Stuart Drama* (Cambridge: Cambridge University Press, 1996), p. 2.

5 Paola Pugliatti, *Shakespeare the Historian* (Basingstoke: Macmillan, 1996), pp. 140–50.

6 Keith Dockwray, *Henry V* (Stroud: Tempus, 2004), p. 14.

7 Quoted in Dockwray (2004), pp. 24–5.

8 Helen Barr (ed.), *The Piers Plowman Tradition* (London: Dent, 1993), p. 206 (line 36).

9 Joseph Candido and Charles R. Forker, *Henry V: An Annotated Bibliography* (New York: Garland, 1983), p. vii.

10 Gary Taylor (ed.), *Henry V*, The Oxford Shakespeare (Oxford: Oxford University Press, 1982), p. 1.

11 See for example M. M. Reese, *The Cease of Majesty: A Study of Shakespeare's History Plays* (London: Arnold, 1961); James Winny, *The Player King: A Theme of Shakespeare's Histories* (London: Chatto and Windus, 1968); Moody E. Prior, *The Drama of Power: Studies in Shakespeare's History Plays* (Evanston: Northwestern University Press, 1973); Michael Manheim, *The Weak King Dilemma in the Shakespearean History Play* (Syracuse: Syracuse University Press, 1973).

12 James Loehlin, *Shakespeare in Performance: Henry V* (Manchester: Manchester University Press, 1996); Emma Smith, *King Henry V*, Shakespeare in Production (Cambridge: Cambridge University Press, 2002).

13 John Dover Wilson (ed.), *Henry V* (Cambridge: Cambridge University Press, 1947), p. viii.

CHAPTER ONE

1 Thomas Nashe, *The Unfortunate Traveller and Other Works*, ed. J. B. Steane (Penguin: Harmondsworth, 1971), p. 113.

2 James Shapiro, *1599: A Year in the Life of William Shakespeare* (London: Faber, 2005), p. 23.

3 Hal's corpulent companion is named Sir John Oldcastle in *1 Henry IV* but in the sequel Shakespeare was compelled to change the name to Falstaff following objections in 1596 from the new Lord Chamberlain, William Brooke, Lord Cobham (1527–97), a descendent of the historical Oldcastle (d. 1417).

4 Andrew Gurr (ed.), *King Henry V*, The New Cambridge Shakespeare (Cambridge: Cambridge University Press, 2005), p. 1.

5 Gary Taylor (ed.), *Henry V*, The Oxford Shakespeare (Oxford: Oxford University Press, 1982), p. 7.

6 Gurr (2005), pp. 242–6.

7 John Dover Wilson (ed.), *Henry V* (Cambridge: Cambridge University Press, 1947), p. xiii.

8 Gurr (2005), p. 40.

9 Steve Sohmer, *Shakespeare's Mystery Play: The Opening of the Globe, 1599* (Manchester: Manchester University Press, 1999), pp. 8–9. Evelyn May Albright, 'The Folio Version of *Henry V* in Relation to Shakespeare's Times', *Publications of the Modern Language Association of America* 43 (1928), pp. 722–56, argues unconvincingly that a pro-Essex version of *Henry V* was staged by the earl's supporters immediately prior to his return in 1599 in a similar spirit to the production of *Richard II* staged before the 1601 coup.

10 Warren D. Smith, 'The *Henry V* Choruses in the First Folio', *Journal of English and Germanic Philology* 53 (1954), pp. 38–57; Richard Dutton, '"Methinks the Truth should live from age to age": The Dating and Contexts of *Henry V*', *Huntington Library Quarterly* 68 (2005), pp. 173–204.

11 Geoffrey Bullough, *Narrative and Dramatic Sources of Shakespeare*, 8 vols (London: Routledge, 1962), volume 4, pp. 378–81, 399–400; Taylor (1982), pp. 34–7.

12 David Norbrook, '*Macbeth* and the Politics of Historiography', in Kevin Sharpe and Steven Zwicker (eds), *Politics of Discourse: The Literature and History of Seventeenth-Century England* (Berkeley: University of California Press, 1987), pp. 78–116.

13 Norbrook (1987), p. 79.

14 Michael Tomlinson, 'Shakespeare and the Chronicles Reassessed', *Literature and History* 10 (1984), p. 52.

15 Annabel Patterson, *Reading Holinshed's Chronicles* (Chicago: University of Chicago Press, 1994), p. 6.

16 Patterson (1994), pp. 131–53.

17 Andrew Gurr, '*Henry V* and the Bees' Commonwealth', *Shakespeare Survey* 30 (1977), pp. 61–72.

18 Bullough (1962), volume 4, pp. 361–3. See also George R. Price, 'Henry V and Germanicus', *Shakespeare Quarterly* 12 (1961), pp. 57–60.

19 Quoted in Taylor (1982), p. 52.

20 Taylor (1982), pp. 53–4.

21 T. W. Craik, (ed.), *Henry V*, The Arden Shakespeare, Third Series (Walton-on-Thames: Nelson, 1997), pp. 10, 36–9.

22 Anne Barton, 'The King Disguised: Shakespeare's *Henry V* and the Comical History', in Joseph G. Price (ed.), *The Triple Bond: Plays, Mainly Shakespearean, in Performance* (University Park: Pennsylvania State University Press, 1975), p. 93.

23 Barton (1975), p. 101.

24 Barton (1975), p. 102.

25 Barton (1975), p. 115.

26 Stanley Wells, Gary Taylor, John Jowett and William Montgomery (eds), *The Oxford Shakespeare: The Complete Works*, 2nd edn. (Oxford: Oxford University Press, 2005), p. lxxi.

27 Alexander Pope (ed.), *The Works of Shakespear in Six Volumes*, 6 vols (London, 1725), volume 1, p. xx.

28 A. W. Pollard, 'The Foundations of Shakespeare's Text' [1909], in J. W. MacKail (ed.), *Aspects of Shakespeare* (Oxford: Clarendon Press, 1933), pp. 1–22; E. K. Chambers, *William Shakespeare: A Study of the Facts and Problems*, 2 vols (Oxford: Clarendon Press, 1930), volume 1, pp. 388–96; G. I. Duthie, 'The Quarto of Shakespeare's *Henry V*', in Duthie (ed.), *Papers, Mainly Shakespearian* (Edinburgh: Oliver and Boyd, 1964), pp. 106–30.

29 Taylor (1982), p. 22.

30 Stanley Wells and Gary Taylor, *Modernizing Shakespeare's Spelling, with Three Studies in the Text of Henry V* (Oxford: Clarendon Press, 1979), p. 110.

31 Wells and Taylor (1979), pp. 72–111.

32 Taylor (1982), p. 23.

33 Graham Holderness and Bryan Loughrey (eds), *The Cronicle History of Henry the Fift* (Hemel Hempstead: Harvester Wheatsheaf, 1993), p. 2.

34 Holderness and Loughrey (1993), p. 13.

35 Holderness and Loughrey (1993), p. 26.

36 Andrew Gurr (ed.), *The First Quarto of King Henry V* (Cambridge: Cambridge University Press, 2000), p. 9.

37 Gurr (2000), p. 1.

38 Gurr (2005), p. 61.

39 Gurr (2000), p. 10.

40 Gurr (2005), p. 63.

41 Gurr (2005), p. 63.

42 Lukas Erne, *Shakespeare as Literary Dramatist* (Cambridge: Cambridge University Press, 2003), p. 174.

43 Gurr (2000), p. ix.

44 Annabel Patterson, *Shakespeare and the Popular Voice* (Oxford: Blackwell, 1989), pp. 73–5.

45 Patterson (1989), p. 87.

46 Sir Philip Sidney, *The Major Works*, ed. Katherine Duncan-Jones (Oxford: Oxford University Press, 2002), p. 224.

47 Patterson (1989), p. 81.

48 Patterson (1989), p. 72.

49 Taylor (1982), pp. 292–5.

50 Lewis Theobald (ed.), *The Works of Shakespeare in Seven Volumes*, 7 vols (London, 1733), volume 4, pp. 30–1.

51 Joseph Candido and Charles R. Forker, *Henry V: An Annotated Bibliography* (New York: Garland, 1983), pp. 382–423.

52 Candido and Forker (1983), p. xxiii.

CHAPTER TWO

1 Ben Jonson, *Every Man in His Humour*, ed. Martin Seymour-Smith (London: Benn, 1966), p. 7 (Prologue, line 15); Francis Beaumont and John Fletcher, *Dramatic Works*, ed. Fredson Bowers, 10 vols (Cambridge: Cambridge University Press, 1966–98), volume 3, p. 167 (3.4.95–111).

2 Emma Smith, *King Henry V*, Shakespeare in Production (Cambridge: Cambridge University Press, 2002), p. 10.

3 J. W. H. Atkins, *English Literary Criticism: 17th and 18th Centuries* (London: Methuen, 1951), pp. 11–12.

4 John Dryden, *Selected Criticism*, ed. James Kinsley and George Parfitt (Oxford: Clarendon Press, 1970), p. 42.

5 Dryden (1970), p. 44.

6 See Sir Philip Sidney, *The Major Works*, ed. Katherine Duncan-Jones (Oxford: Oxford University Press, 2002), p. 243.

7 Scott Paul Gordon, 'Endeavouring to be the King: Dryden's *Astraea Redux* and the Issue of "Character"', *Journal of English and Germanic Philology* 101 (2002), p. 221.

8 Gordon (2002), pp. 216–18.

9 John Dryden, *Selected Poems*, ed. Steven N. Zwicker and David Bywaters (Harmondsworth: Penguin, 2001), p. 15 (lines 169–70).

10 Jonathan Bate, *Shakespearean Constitutions: Politics, Theatre, Criticism 1730–1830* (Oxford: Clarendon Press, 1989), pp. 75–87.

11 Michael Dobson, *The Making of the National Poet: Shakespeare, Adaptation, and Authorship, 1660–1769* (Oxford: Oxford University Press, 1992), pp. 2–3.

12 See, for example, John Dennis, *On the Genius and Writings of Shakespeare* (1712), in D. Nichol Smith (ed.), *Eighteenth-Century Essays on Shakespeare*, 2nd edn. (Oxford: Clarendon Press, 1963), pp. 23–43.

13 Nicholas Rowe (ed.), *The Works of Mr. William Shakespear: Revis'd and Corrected, with an Account of the Life and Writings of the Author*, 7 vols (London, 1709–10), volume 1, p. vii.

14 Rowe (1709–10), volume 1, p. xvii.

15 Rowe (1709–10), volume 1, p. xvii.

16 Brian Vickers (ed.), *Shakespeare: The Critical Heritage: Volume 3: 1733–52* (London: Routledge, 1975), p. 226.

17 Rowe (1709–10), volume 7, pp. 346–7.

18 Rowe (1709–10), volume 7, p. 347.

19 Rowe (1709–10), volume 7, p. 350.

20 Alexander Pope (ed.), *The Works of Shakespear in Six Volumes*, 6 vols (London, 1725), volume 1, p. vi.

21 Pope (1725), volume 1, p. xxiii.

22 John Hughes (ed.), *The Works of Mr. Edmund Spenser*, 6 vols (London, 1715), volume 1, pp. lx–lxi.

23 Lewis Theobald (ed.), *The Works of Shakespeare in Seven Volumes*, 7 vols (London, 1733), volume 1, p. xxx.

24 See Hayden White, *Tropics of Discourse: Essays in Cultural Criticism* (Baltimore: Johns Hopkins University Press, 1978), pp. 81–100.

25 Smith (2002), p. 153. Predictably, the scene was also cut from Thomas Bowdler's notoriously censored *Family Shakespeare* (1807).

26 Quoted in Nichol Smith (1963), p. 86.

27 Quoted in Nichol Smith (1963), p. 198.

28 H. R. Woudhuysen (ed.), *Samuel Johnson on Shakespeare* (Harmondsworth: Penguin, 1989), p. 122.

29 Woudhuysen (1989), p. 136.

30 Woudhuysen (1989), p. 136.

31 Woudhuysen (1989), p. 206.

32 Woudhuysen (1989), p. 211.

33 Woudhuysen (1989), pp. 207–8.

34 Woudhuysen (1989), pp. 208–9.

35 Woudhuysen (1989), p. 210.

36 Woudhuysen (1989), p. 207.

37 Roger Boyle, *The History of Henry the Fifth* (London, 1668), p. 6.

38 Gordon (2002), p. 205.

39 Quoted in Joseph Candido and Charles R. Forker, *Henry V: An Annotated Bibliography* (New York: Garland, 1983), p. 366.

40 Christine Gerrard, *Aaron Hill: The Muses' Projector, 1685–1750* (Oxford: Oxford University Press, 2003), pp. 56–7.

41 Smith (2002), p. 13.

42 Aaron Hill, *King Henry the Fifth: Or, the Conquest of France, By the English: A Tragedy* (London, 1723), sig. A6v.

43 Hill (1723), p. 22.

44 Hill (1723), p. 57.

45 Gerrard (2003), p. 60.

46 Anthony Brennan, *Henry V* (Hemel Hempstead: Harvester Wheatsheaf, 1992), p. xv.

47 See Smith (2002), pp. 15–18.

48 Smith (2002), p. 15.

49 Gary Taylor, *Reinventing Shakespeare: A Cultural History from the Restoration to the Present* (London: Hogarth, 1989), pp. 121–2; Bate (1989), p. 124.

CHAPTER THREE

1 Quoted in Michael Taylor, *Shakespeare Criticism in the Twentieth Century* (Oxford: Oxford University Press, 2001), p. 1.

2 Jonathan Bate (ed.), *The Romantics on Shakespeare* (Harmondsworth: Penguin, 1992), p. 11.

3 Terence Hawkes (ed.), *Coleridge on Shakespeare* (Harmondsworth: Penguin, 1969), p. 261.

4 A. W. Schlegel, *Lectures on Dramatic Art and Literature*, trans. John Black. 2 vols (London, 1815), volume 2, pp. 94–5.

5 Bate (1992), p. 5.

6 Bate (1992), pp. 12–13.

7 Schlegel (1815), volume 2, p. 217. Such a view is echoed in the twenty-first century in Nicholas Grene, *Shakespeare's Serial History Plays* (Cambridge: Cambridge University Press, 2002).

8 Schlegel (1815), volume 2, p. 231.

9 Schlegel (1815), volume 2, p. 231.

10 Schlegel (1815), volume 2, pp. 231–2.

11 Schlegel (1815), volume 2, p. 232.

12 Schlegel (1815), volume 2, p. 232.

13 Schlegel (1815), volume 2, p. 233.

14 Schlegel (1815), volume 2, p. 234.

15 Schlegel (1815), volume 2, pp. 138–9.

16 Schlegel (1815), volume 2, p. 234.

17 Schlegel (1815), volume 2, p. 235.

18 Schlegel (1815), volume 2, p. 236.

19 Emma Smith, *King Henry V*, Shakespeare in Production (Cambridge: Cambridge University Press, 2002), p. 21.

20 Smith (2002), pp. 21–35.

21 Schlegel (1815), volume 2, p. 238.

22 William Hazlitt, *Characters of Shakespear's Plays*, 2nd edn. (London, 1818), pp. vii–viii.

23 Hazlitt (1818), p. xviii.

24 Hazlitt (1818), p. xix.

25 Bate (1992), pp. 7–8.

26 Hazlitt (1818), p. 203. See also Schlegel (1815), volume 2, p. 231; Nathan Drake, *Shakspeare and his Times*, 2 vols (London, 1817), volume 2, p. 426.

27 Hazlitt (1818), p. 203.

28 Hazlitt (1818), pp. 204–5.

29 Bate (1989), p. 168.

30 Hazlitt (1818), p. 205.

31 Hazlitt (1818), pp. 205–6.

32 Hazlitt (1818), p. 206.

33 Hazlitt (1818), p. 206.

34 Hazlitt (1818), p. 209.

35 Hazlitt (1818), p. 214.

36 Richard Levin, 'Hazlitt on *Henry V*, and the Appropriation of Shakespeare', *Shakespeare Quarterly* 35 (1984), pp. 134–41.

37 Hermann Ulrici, *Shakspeare's Dramatic Art* (London, 1846), p. 379; Tom McAlindon, *Shakespeare's Tudor History: A Study of Henry IV, Parts 1 and 2* (Aldershot: Ashgate, 2001), p. 6.

38 Ulrici (1846), p. 379.

39 Ulrici (1846), pp. 384–5.

40 Ulrici (1846), p. 385.

41 Hermann Ulrici, *Shakspeare's Dramatic Art*, 2 vols (London, 1876), volume 2, p. 257.

42 Ulrici (1846), p. 380.

43 Ulrici (1846), p. 383.

44 Ulrici (1846), p. 383.

45 Ulrici (1846), p. 384.

46 McAlindon (2001), p. 8.

47 McAlindon (2001), p. 8.

48 Paul N. Siegel, *The Gathering Storm: Shakespeare's English and Roman History Plays: A Marxist Analysis* (London: Red Words, 1992).

49 G. G. Gervinus, *Shakespeare Commentaries*, trans. F. E. Burnett. 2 vols (London, 1863), volume 1, pp. 347–8.

50 Stephen Greenblatt, *Shakespearean Negotiations: The Circulation of Social Energy in Renaissance England* (Berkeley: University of California Press, 1988), pp. 6–7.

51 Gervinus (1863), volume 1, p. 487.

52 Gervinus (1863), volume 1, p. 358.

53 Gervinus (1863), volume 1, p. 484.

54 Gervinus (1863), volume 1, p. 485.

55 Gervinus (1863), volume 1, p. 345.

56 Gervinus (1863), volume 1, p. 473.

57 Gervinus (1863), volume 1, p. 473.

58 Richard Simpson, 'The Politics of Shakspere's Historical Plays', *Transactions of the New Shakspere Society* 1 (1874), p. 417.

59 Simpson (1874), p. 418.

60 Simpson (1874), p. 419.

61 Simpson (1874), p. 419.

62 McAlindon (2001), p. 11.

63 Simpson (1874), p. 438.

64 McAlindon (2001), p. 12.

65 Adrian Poole, *Shakespeare and the Victorians* (London: Thomson, 2004), p. 225.

66 Edward Dowden, *Shakspere: A Critical Study of his Mind and Art* (London, 1875), p. v.

67 Dowden (1875), p. 163.

68 Dowden (1875), p. 221.

69 Dowden (1875), p. 166.

70 Dowden (1875), p. 169.

71 Dowden (1875), p. 74.

72 Dowden (1875), p. 75.

73 Dowden (1875), pp. 212–13.

74 Dowden (1875), p. 215.

75 Dowden (1875), p. 219.

76 Thomas Carlyle, *On Heroes, Hero-Worship and the Heroic in History*, ed. George Wherry (Cambridge: Cambridge University Press, 1914), p. 113.

77 Charles Knight, *Studies of Shakspere* (London, 1849), p. 183.

78 R. G. Moulton, 'On Character-Development in Shakspere as Illustrated by *Macbeth* and *Henry V*', *Transactions of the New Shakspere Society* 8–10 (1880–6), p. 563.

79 Moulton (1880–6), p. 564.

80 Moulton (1880–6), p. 564.

81 Algernon Charles Swinburne, *A Study of Shakespeare* (London, 1880), p. 115.

82 Swinburne (1880), pp. 68–9.

83 William Watkiss Lloyd, *Critical Essays on the Plays of Shakespeare* (London, 1875), p. 251.

84 Lloyd (1875), p. 252.

85 Lloyd (1875), pp. 252–3.

86 Lloyd (1875), p. 254.

87 Lloyd (1875), p. 254.

88 Lloyd (1875), p. 267.

89 Lloyd (1875), p. 266.

CHAPTER FOUR

1 Quoted in Anthony Brennan, *Henry V* (Hemel Hempstead: Harvester Wheatsheaf, 1992), p. xxi.

2 Quoted in Emma Smith, *King Henry V*, Shakespeare in Production (Cambridge: Cambridge University Press, 2002), p. 38.

3 Quoted in Smith (2002), p. 38.

4 Sidney Lee, *Shakespeare and the Modern Stage* (London: Murray, 1906), p. 187.

5 Quoted in Michael Quinn (ed.), *Henry V: A Casebook* (London: Macmillan, 1969), p. 56.

6 Quoted in Quinn (1969), p. 59.

7 Felix E. Schelling, *The English Chronicle Play: A Study in the Popular Historical Literature Environing Shakespeare* (London: Macmillan, 1902), pp. 119, 122. Shortly before Schelling's book appeared, the historian Charles Kingsford (1862–1926) published perhaps the most celebratory of all scholarly biographies on the historical Henry V, which adopts a eulogistic tone similar to Lee and other late Victorians; see *Henry V: The Typical Medieval Hero* (New York: Putnam, 1901).

8 Schelling (1902), p. 39.

9 Paola Pugliatti, *Shakespeare the Historian* (Basingstoke: Macmillan, 1996), p. 2.

10 Schelling (1902), p. 121.

11 Quoted in Quinn (1969), pp. 55–6. The poets W. B. Yeats (1865–1939) and John Masefield (1878–1967) made several disapproving comments about *Henry V* in passing, though there is little depth to their observations; see Quinn (1969), pp. 54–5, 61–2.

12 A. C. Bradley, 'The Rejection of Falstaff', in Bradley, *Oxford Lectures on Poetry* (London: Macmillan, 1920), p. 255.

13 Bradley (1920), p. 255.

14 Bradley (1920), p. 256.

15 Bradley (1920), p. 257.

16 Bradley (1920), p. 259.

17 Bradley (1920), pp. 260–73.

18 Bradley (1920), p. 249.

19 Bradley (1920), pp. 250–2.

20 Bradley (1920), p. 258. L. C. Knights evokes and rejects such contrivances as offstage family back-stories in his 'How Many Children Had Lady Macbeth? An Essay in the Theory and Practice of Shakespearean Criticism' (1933), in Knights, *Explorations: Essays in Criticism, Mainly on the Literature of the Seventeenth Century* (London: Chatto, 1946), pp. 1–39.

21 Bradley (1920), p. 259.

22 Hugh Grady, *The Modernist Shakespeare: Critical Texts in a Material World* (Oxford: Clarendon, 1991), p. 38.

23 E. E. Stoll, *Poets and Playwrights* (Minneapolis: University of Minnesota Press, 1930), p. 45.

24 John Dover Wilson, *The Fortunes of Falstaff* (Cambridge: Cambridge University Press, 1943), pp. 124–5.

25 Paul Fussell, *The Great War and Modern Memory* (New York: Oxford University Press, 1975), pp. 115–16.

26 Smith (2002), p. 44.

27 Werner Habicht, 'Shakespeare Celebrations in Times of War', *Shakespeare Quarterly* 52 (2001), pp. 452–4.

28 Quoted in Jonathan Bate, *Shakespearean Constitutions: Politics, Theatre, Criticism 1730–1830* (Oxford: Clarendon Press, 1989), p. 124.

29 J. A. R. Marriott, *English History in Shakespeare* (London: Chapman and Hall, 1918), p. 8.

30 Marriott (1918), p. 143.

31 Marriott (1918), p. 136.

32 Marriott (1918), p. 135.

33 Marriott (1918), p. 166.

34 Marriott (1918), p. 147.

35 Gerald Gould, 'A New Reading of *Henry V*', *The English Review* 29 July (1919), p. 42.

36 Gould (1919), p. 42.

37 Gould (1919), pp. 42–3.

38 Gould (1919), p. 44.

39 Gould (1919), p. 45.

40 Gould (1919), p. 48.
41 Gould (1919), pp. 49–52.
42 Gould (1919), p. 52.
43 Gould (1919), pp. 53–4.
44 Gould (1919), pp. 54–5.
45 Gould (1919), p. 55.
46 Gould (1919), p. 55.
47 John Palmer, *Political Characters of Shakespeare* (London: Macmillan, 1945), p. viii.
48 Palmer (1945), p. 182.
49 Palmer (1945), p. 218.
50 Palmer (1945), p. 218.
51 Palmer (1945), p. 220.
52 Palmer (1945), p. 242.
53 Palmer (1945), p. 237.
54 Palmer (1945), p. 247.
55 Poised between the positions adopted by Palmer and Ellis-Fermor is Theodore Spencer's brief discussion of how Henry's character affords Shakespeare an opportunity to explore the ideal relationship between kingship and human nature; see *Shakespeare and the Nature of Man* (Cambridge: Cambridge University Press, 1943), pp. 79–85.
56 Una Ellis-Fermor, *The Frontiers of Drama*, 2nd edn. (London: Methuen, 1964), p. 36.
57 Ellis-Fermor (1964), p. 42.
58 Ellis-Fermor (1964), p. 43.
59 Ellis-Fermor (1964), pp. 43–4.
60 Ellis-Fermor (1964), pp. 44–5.
61 Ellis-Fermor (1964), p. 45.
62 Ellis-Fermor (1964), pp. 46–7.
63 Ellis-Fermor (1964), pp. 47–8.
64 D. A. Traversi, *An Approach to Shakespeare*, 2nd edn. (London: Sands, 1957), p. 42.
65 The best illustration of such a close reading is William Empson's short discussion of a single line from Canterbury's speech on the bees' commonwealth in *Seven Types of Ambiguity* (1930); see Quinn (1969), pp. 68–70.

CHAPTER FIVE

1 For more detailed discussion, see Harry M. Geduld, *Filmguide to Henry V* (Bloomington: Indiana University Press, 1973); James Loehlin, *Shakespeare in Performance: Henry V* (Manchester: Manchester University Press, 1996), pp. 25–48; Emma Smith, *King Henry V*, Shakespeare in Production (Cambridge: Cambridge University Press, 2002), pp. 50–6.
2 Smith (2002), p. 51.
3 Smith (2002), pp. 54–5.
4 G. Wilson Knight, *The Olive and the Sword: A Study of England's Shakespeare* (London: Oxford University Press, 1944), p. 4.
5 Wilson Knight (1944), p. 3.
6 Graham Holderness, 'Agincourt 1944: Readings in the Shakespeare Myth', *Literature and History* 10 (1984), p. 30.
7 Wilson Knight (1944), p. 29.
8 Wilson Knight (1944), p. 30.
9 G. Wilson Knight, *Shakespearian Production* (London: Faber, 1964), pp. 312–14.
10 Wilson Knight (1944), p. 4.
11 Wilson Knight (1944), p. 16.
12 E. M. W. Tillyard, *Shakespeare's History Plays* (Harmondsworth: Penguin, 1969), p. 7.
13 See Edwin Greenlaw, *Studies in Spenser's Historical Allegory* (Baltimore: Johns Hopkins University Press, 1932); 'Sidney's *Arcadia* as an Example of Elizabethan Allegory' [1913], in

Arthur F. Kinney (ed.), *Essential Articles for the Study of Sir Philip Sidney* (Hamden, CT: Archon, 1986), pp. 271–86.
14 E. M. W. Tillyard, *The Elizabethan World Picture* (London: Chatto and Windus, 1943).
15 Tillyard (1969), p. 323.
16 Tillyard (1969), p. 25.
17 Tillyard (1969), pp. 324–5.
18 Tillyard (1969), p. 309.
19 Tillyard (1969), p. 310.
20 Tillyard (1969), p. 310.
21 Tillyard (1969), pp. 311–14
22 Tillyard (1969), pp. 317–18.
23 Tillyard (1969), p. 318.
24 Holderness (1984), p. 43.
25 Holderness (1984), p. 38.
26 Robin Headlam Wells, 'The Fortunes of Tillyard: Twentieth-Century Critical Debate on Shakespeare's History Plays', *English Studies* 66 (1985), p. 396.
27 Henry Ansgar Kelly, *Divine Providence in the England of Shakespeare's Histories* (Cambridge, MA: Harvard University Press, 1970), p. 298, challenges Shakespeare's reliance on Hall and dismisses the providential world picture as the product of Tillyard's 'synthesizing energy'.
28 John Drakakis, 'Introduction', in Drakakis, (ed.), *Alternative Shakespeares* (London: Methuen, 1988), p. 15.
29 John Wilders, *The Lost Garden: A View of Shakespeare's English and Roman History Plays* (London: Macmillan, 1978).
30 Lily B. Campbell, *Shakespeare's Histories: Mirrors of Elizabethan Policy* (London: Methuen, 1964), p. 6.
31 Campbell (1964), p. 15.
32 Campbell (1964), p. 125.
33 Campbell (1964), p. 255.
34 Campbell (1964), pp. 295–305.
35 Campbell (1964), pp. 268–9.
36 Campbell (1964), p. 271.
37 Campbell (1964), pp. 273–5.
38 Campbell (1964), p. 279.
39 Campbell (1964), pp. 279–81.
40 James Shapiro, *1599: A Year in the Life of William Shakespeare* (London: Faber, 2005), pp. 88–96.
41 Dover Wilson (1947), pp. vii–viii. The figure of 130 years correctly dates the anti-Henry critical tradition back to Hazlitt's 1817 essay.
42 John Dover Wilson (ed.), *Henry V* (Cambridge: Cambridge University Press, 1947), p. xxxi.
43 Mark Van Doren, *Shakespeare* (New York: Holt, 1939), pp. 170–9.
44 Van Doren (1939), pp. 170, 174.
45 Dover Wilson (1947), p. xii.
46 Dover Wilson (1947), pp. xii–xiii.
47 Dover Wilson (1947), pp. xiii–xv.
48 Dover Wilson (1947), p. xv.
49 Dover Wilson (1947), p. xvi.
50 Dover Wilson (1947), pp. xvi–xviii.
51 Dover Wilson (1947), pp. xviii–xxiv.
52 Dover Wilson (1947), p. xxiv.
53 Dover Wilson (1947), p. xxiv.
54 Dover Wilson (1947), pp. xxvi–xxvii.
55 Dover Wilson (1947), p. xxvii.

56 Dover Wilson (1947), pp. xxxi–xxxii. *The Battle of Maldon* describes the heroic last stand of the Saxon leader Byrhtnoth against an outnumbering Danish army invading Essex in 991 A.D.

57 Dover Wilson (1947), pp. xxxiii–xxxviii.

58 Dover Wilson (1947), p. xxxvi, note 1.

59 J. H. Walter (ed.), *King Henry V*, The Arden Shakespeare, Second Series (London: Methuen, 1954), p. xvi.

60 Walter (1954), pp. xvi–xviii.

61 Walter (1954), pp. xxi–xxii.

62 Walter (1954), p. xxiv.

63 Walter (1954), p. xxvi. Walter later conjectures that in an earlier draft of the play Falstaff may have accompanied Henry to France but that Shakespeare decided subsequently to kill him off instead, re-assigning much of his part to Pistol (p. xliii).

64 Walter (1954), p. xxxii.

65 Walter (1954), p. xxxii.

CHAPTER SIX

1 John Arden, 'Henry V', *New Statesman* 67 (1964), pp. 946–7. Arden's comments appear in a letter written in response to criticism of Peter Hall and John Barton's 1964 anti-war production of *Henry V* staged at Stratford for the Shakespeare Quartercentenary celebrations.

2 A. P. Rossiter, 'Ambivalence: The Dialectic of the Histories', in Rossiter, *Angel With Horns, and Other Shakespeare Lectures*, ed. Graham Storey (London: Longman, 1961), p. 42.

3 Rossiter (1961), pp. 42–3. The attempt to identify explanatory patterns with which to unlock a work's essence or significance is a common feature of New Critical readings.

4 Rossiter (1961), p. 45.

5 Rossiter (1961), p. 46.

6 Rossiter (1961), pp. 46–7.

7 Rossiter (1961), p. 51.

8 Rossiter (1961), p. 51.

9 Rossiter (1961), p. 59.

10 Rossiter (1961), p. 57.

11 Harold C. Goddard, *The Meaning of Shakespeare*, 2 vols (Chicago: University of Chicago Press, 1960), volume 1, pp. 215–16.

12 Goddard (1960), volume 1, p. 217.

13 Goddard (1960), volume 1, p. 218.

14 Goddard (1960), volume 1, pp. 220–4.

15 Goddard (1960), volume 1, p. 227.

16 Goddard (1960), volume 1, p. 231.

17 Goddard (1960), volume 1, pp. 239, 242, 245.

18 Goddard (1960), volume 1, pp. 261–6.

19 Goddard (1960), volume 1, p. 256.

20 Goddard (1960), volume 1, p. 259.

21 Goddard (1960), volume 1, p. 267.

22 Goddard (1960), volume 1, p. 266.

23 S. C. Sen Gupta, *Shakespeare's Historical Plays* (London: Oxford University Press, 1964), p. vii.

24 Sen Gupta (1964), p. 20.

25 Sen Gupta (1964), p. 115.

26 Sen Gupta (1964), p. 29.

27 Sen Gupta (1964), p. 31.

28 Sen Gupta (1964), p. 141.

29 Sen Gupta (1964), p. 142.

30 Sen Gupta (1964), pp. 143–7.

31 Robert Ornstein, *A Kingdom for a Stage: The Achievement of Shakespeare's History Plays* (Cambridge, MA: Harvard University Press, 1972), p. 2.

32 Ornstein (1972), p. 2.

33 Ornstein (1972), pp. 8–10.

34 Ornstein (1972), pp. 10–11.

35 Ornstein (1972), p. 12.

36 Ornstein (1972), p. 29.

37 Ornstein (1972), pp. 175–6.

38 Ornstein (1972), p. 176.

39 Ornstein (1972), p. 186.

40 Robin Headlam Wells, 'The Fortunes of Tillyard: Twentieth-Century Critical Debate on Shakespeare's History Plays', *English Studies* 66 (1985), p. 399.

41 Norman Rabkin, 'Rabbits, Ducks, and *Henry V*', *Shakespeare Quarterly* 28 (1977), p. 279. The essay is reproduced with minor revisions in Rabkin, *Shakespeare and the Problem of Meaning* (Chicago: University of Chicago Press, 1981), pp. 33–62.

42 Rabkin (1977), p. 295.

43 Rabkin (1977), p. 279.

44 Rabkin (1977), pp. 279–80. E. H. Gombrich discussed the rabbit-duck in his study of the psychology of pictorial representation, *Art and Illusion* (1960).

45 Rabkin (1977), p. 281.

46 Rabkin (1977), p. 281.

47 Rabkin (1977), p. 285.

48 Rabkin (1977), pp. 286–8.

49 Rabkin (1977), p. 288.

50 Rabkin (1977), p. 291.

51 Rabkin (1977), p. 295.

52 Rabkin (1977), p. 295.

53 Rabkin (1977), p. 296.

54 See James Shapiro, *1599: A Year in the Life of William Shakespeare* (London: Faber, 2005).

55 Rabkin (1977), p. 296.

56 Larry Champion, *Perspective in Shakespeare's English Histories* (Athens: University of Georgia Press, 1980), pp. 148, 162–4; Phyllis Rackin, *Stages of History: Shakespeare's English Chronicles* (London: Routledge, 1990), pp. 22–30; Paola Pugliatti, *Shakespeare the Historian* (Basingstoke: Macmillan, 1996), pp. 140–50.

57 Richard Levin, *New Readings vs. Old Plays: Recent Trends in the Reinterpretation of English Renaissance Drama* (Chicago: University of Chicago Press, 1979).

58 Edward Berry, 'Twentieth-Century Shakespeare Criticism: The Histories', in Stanley Wells (ed.), *The Cambridge Companion to Shakespeare Studies* (Cambridge: Cambridge University Press, 1986), p. 255.

CHAPTER SEVEN

1 Louis Adrian Montrose, 'Professing the Renaissance: The Poetics and Politics of Culture', in H. Aram Veeser (ed.), *The New Historicism* (London: Routledge, 1989), p. 20.

2 Jonathan Dollimore, 'Introduction', in Jonathan Dollimore and Alan Sinfield (eds), *Political Shakespeare: New Essays in Cultural Materialism* (Manchester: Manchester University Press, 1985), pp. 5–6.

3 Dollimore (1985), p. 6.

4 Stephen Greenblatt, *Shakespearean Negotiations: The Circulation of Social Energy in Renaissance England* (Berkeley: University of California Press, 1988), pp. 21–2.

5 Greenblatt (1988), p. 24.
6 Greenblatt (1988), p. 23.
7 Greenblatt (1988), p. 26.
8 Greenblatt (1988), p. 28.
9 Greenblatt (1988), pp. 30–3.
10 Greenblatt (1988), p. 36.
11 Greenblatt (1988), p. 39.
12 Greenblatt (1988), p. 40.
13 Greenblatt (1988), p. 41.
14 Greenblatt (1988), pp. 45–6.
15 Greenblatt (1988), pp. 52–3.
16 Greenblatt (1988), p. 56.
17 Greenblatt (1988), p. 58.
18 Greenblatt (1988), p. 59.
19 Greenblatt (1988), p. 62.
20 Greenblatt (1988), p. 63.
21 Greenblatt (1988), p. 64.
22 James L. Calderwood, *Metadrama in Shakespeare's Henriad: Richard II to Henry V* (Berkeley: University of California Press, 1979), p. 170.
23 See David Scott Kastan, 'Proud Majesty Made a Subject: Shakespeare and the Spectacle of Rule', *Shakespeare Quarterly* 37 (1986), pp. 459–75; Dermot Cavanagh, *Language and Politics in the Sixteenth-Century History Play* (Basingstoke: Palgrave Macmillan, 2003), pp. 127–51.
24 Greenblatt (1988), p. 65.
25 Leonard Tennenhouse, *Power on Display: The Politics of Shakespeare's Genres* (New York: Methuen, 1986), pp. 79–80.
26 Tennenhouse (1986), pp. 84–5.
27 Richard Helgerson, *Forms of Nationhood: The Elizabethan Writing of England* (Chicago: University of Chicago Press, 1992), pp. 234, 244.
28 Graham Bradshaw, *Misrepresentations: Shakespeare and the Materialists* (Ithaca: Cornell University Press, 1993), p. 100.
29 Greenblatt (1988), p. 63.
30 Emma Smith, *King Henry V*, Shakespeare in Production (Cambridge: Cambridge University Press, 2002), pp. 71–5. See also James Loehlin, *Shakespeare in Performance: Henry V* (Manchester: Manchester University Press, 1996), pp. 128–45.
31 Jonathan Dollimore and Alan Sinfield, 'History and Ideology, Masculinity and Miscegenation', in Sinfield, *Faultlines: Cultural Materialism and the Politics of Dissident Reading* (Oxford: Clarendon Press, 1992), p. 113.
32 Dollimore and Sinfield (1992), p. 116.
33 Dollimore and Sinfield (1992), pp. 113–14.
34 Dollimore and Sinfield (1992), p. 118.
35 Dollimore and Sinfield (1992), p. 119.
36 Dollimore and Sinfield (1992), p. 121.
37 Dollimore and Sinfield (1992), p. 125.
38 Dollimore and Sinfield (1992), p. 125.
39 Dollimore and Sinfield (1992), p. 127.
40 Dollimore and Sinfield (1992), p. 128.
41 Witness, for example, Richard Corum's disastrous attempt to identify a sodomitic Henry in 'Henry's Desires', in Louise Fradenburg and Carla Freccero (eds), *Premodern Sexualities* (New York: Routledge, 1996), pp. 71–97.
42 Dollimore and Sinfield (1992), p. 129.
43 Dollimore and Sinfield (1992), p. 129. On this form of exclusion, see also Katherine Eggert, 'Nostalgia and the Not Yet Late Queen: Refusing Female Rule in *Henry V*', *ELH* 61 (1994), pp. 523–50.

44 Dollimore and Sinfield (1992), p. 130.

45 Dollimore and Sinfield (1992), p. 131; Rebecca Ann Bach, 'Manliness Before Individualism: Masculinity, Effeminacy, and Homoerotics in Shakespeare's History Plays', in Richard Dutton and Jean E. Howard (eds), *A Companion to Shakespeare's Works, Volume II: The Histories* (Oxford: Blackwell, 2003), pp. 220–45.

46 Dollimore and Sinfield (1992), p. 132.

47 Smith (2002), p. 35.

48 Dollimore and Sinfield (1992), p. 133.

49 Dollimore and Sinfield (1992), p. 136.

50 Dollimore and Sinfield (1992), p. 137.

51 Dollimore and Sinfield (1992), p. 138.

52 Dollimore and Sinfield (1992), p. 139.

53 Dollimore and Sinfield (1992), pp. 140–1.

54 Lance Wilcox, 'Katherine of France as Victim and Bride', *Shakespeare Studies* 17 (1985), p. 62.

55 Wilcox (1985), p. 64.

56 Wilcox (1985), p. 64.

57 Wilcox (1985), p. 66.

58 Wilcox (1985), p. 66.

59 Wilcox (1985), pp. 67–8.

60 Wilcox (1985), p. 70.

61 Wilcox (1985), p. 74.

62 Sarah Werner, 'Firk and Foot: The Boy Actor in *Henry V*', *Shakespeare Bulletin* 21 (2003), p. 23.

63 Jean E. Howard and Phyllis Rackin, *Engendering a Nation: A Feminist Account of Shakespeare's English Histories* (London: Routledge, 1997), p. 187.

64 Howard and Rackin (1997), p. 187.

65 Howard and Rackin (1997), p. 189.

66 Howard and Rackin (1997), p. 196; repeated verbatim on p. 198.

67 Howard and Rackin (1997), p. 199. The Chorus's claim overlooks Canterbury's reference to dividing the army (1.2.213–16).

68 Howard and Rackin (1997), p. 209.

69 Howard and Rackin (1997), pp. 204–5.

70 Howard and Rackin (1997), p. 207.

71 Howard and Rackin (1997), pp. 209–11.

72 Howard and Rackin (1997), p. 215.

73 Howard and Rackin (1997), p. 8.

74 Howard and Rackin (1997), p. 215.

75 Bradshaw (1993), pp. 9, 11, 107.

76 Bradshaw (1993), p. 85.

77 Bradshaw (1993), p. 91.

78 Bradshaw (1993), p. 104.

79 Bradshaw (1993), pp. 106–7; Dollimore and Sinfield (1992), pp. 125–6.

80 Bradshaw (1993), p. 38.

81 Bradshaw (1993), p. 44.

82 Bradshaw (1993), p. 49.

83 Bradshaw (1993), p. 52.

84 Bradshaw (1993), p. 54.

85 Bradshaw (1993), p. 57.

86 Nick De Somogyi, *Shakespeare's Theatre of War* (Aldershot: Ashgate, 1998), p. 6.

87 Bradshaw (1993), p. 63.

88 Bradshaw (1993), p. 121.

89 Bradshaw (1993), p. 112.

90 Bradshaw (1993), p. 80.
91 Tom McAlindon, *Shakespeare Minus 'Theory'* (Aldershot: Ashgate, 2004), pp. 23–32.
92 McAlindon (2004), pp. 32–3.
93 McAlindon (2004), p. 27.
94 McAlindon (2004), p. 37.
95 McAlindon (2004), p. 45.
96 McAlindon (2004), p. 45.
97 McAlindon (2004), pp. 45–6.
98 McAlindon (2004), pp. 49–52.
99 McAlindon (2004), pp. 47–8. Simpson offered a similar interpretation of the churchmen in 1874 (see Chapter 3).
100 McAlindon (2004), pp. 52–3.
101 McAlindon (2004), p. 55.
102 McAlindon (2004), pp. 57–9.
103 McAlindon (2004), pp. 61–2.
104 McAlindon (2004), p. 67.
105 McAlindon (2004), pp. 67–8.
106 McAlindon (2004), p. 75.
107 McAlindon (2004), p. 75.
108 McAlindon (2004), p. 76.

CHAPTER EIGHT

1 Patricia Cahill, 'Nation Formation and the English History Plays', in Richard Dutton and Jean E. Howard (eds), *A Companion to Shakespeare's Works, Volume II: The Histories* (Oxford: Blackwell, 2003), p. 71.
2 James Baldo, 'Wars of Memory in *Henry V*', *Shakespeare Quarterly* 47 (1996), pp. 132–59.
3 Claire McEachern, *The Poetics of English Nationhood* (Cambridge: Cambridge University Press, 1996), pp. 12, 86.
4 McEachern (1996), p. 107.
5 McEachern (1996), p. 107.
6 McEachern (1996), pp. 107–8.
7 McEachern (1996), pp. 109–10.
8 McEachern (1996), p. 111.
9 McEachern (1996), p. 120.
10 McEachern (1996), p. 120.
11 McEachern (1996), pp. 127–8.
12 McEachern (1996), p. 129.
13 McEachern (1996), p. 137.
14 Alison Thorne, '"Awake remembrance of these valiant dead": *Henry V* and the Politics of the English History Play', *Shakespeare Studies* 30 (2002), p. 164.
15 Thorne (2002), p. 164.
16 Thorne (2002), p. 166.
17 Thorne (2002), p. 169.
18 Thorne (2002), p. 172.
19 Thorne (2002), p. 175.
20 Thorne (2002), p. 177.
21 Thorne (2002), pp. 176–9.
22 Thorne (2002), pp. 179–80.
23 Thorne (2002), p. 181.
24 Thorne (2002), p. 181.
25 Thorne (2002), pp. 182–3.

26 Philip Schwyzer, *Literature, Nationalism and Memory in Early Modern England and Wales* (Cambridge: Cambridge University Press, 2004), p. 3.

27 Schwyzer (2004), pp. 126–7.

28 Schwyzer (2004), p. 127.

29 Schwyzer (2004), p. 142. The princes are French in Holinshed.

30 Philip Edwards earlier offers a brief, yet regularly cited discussion of *Henry V* and Ireland in *Threshold of a Nation: A Study of English and Irish Drama* (Cambridge: Cambridge University Press, 1979), pp. 74–86.

31 Willy Maley, 'The Irish Text and Subtext of Shakespeare's English Histories', in Dutton and Howard (2003), p. 95.

32 Joel B. Altman, '"Vile Participation": The Amplification of Violence in the Theater of *Henry V*', *Shakespeare Quarterly* 42 (1991), pp. 1–32.

33 Gary Taylor (ed.), *Henry V*, The Oxford Shakespeare (Oxford: Oxford University Press, 1982), p. 7.

34 David J. Baker, '"Wildehirissheman": Colonialist Representation in Shakespeare's *Henry V*', *English Literary Renaissance* 22 (1992), pp. 39–40.

35 Baker (1992), p. 40.

36 Baker (1992), p. 50.

37 Baker (1992), p. 48.

38 Baker (1992), p. 46.

39 Baker (1992), pp. 54–61.

40 Michael Neill, 'Broken English and Broken Irish: Nation, Language and the Optic of Power in Shakespeare's Histories', *Shakespeare Quarterly* 45 (1994), p. 5.

41 Neill (1994), p. 12.

42 Neill (1994), p. 21.

43 Andrew Murphy, 'Shakespeare's Irish History', *Literature and History* 5 [third series] (1996), p. 40.

44 Murphy (1996), p. 41.

45 Christopher Highley, *Shakespeare, Spenser and the Crisis in Ireland* (Cambridge: Cambridge University Press, 1997), p. 135.

46 Highley (1997), p. 138.

47 Highley (1997), p. 139.

48 Highley (1997), pp. 140–1.

49 Highley (1997), p. 143.

50 Highley (1997), p. 145.

51 Highley (1997), p. 147.

52 Highley (1997), p. 158.

53 Highley (1997), pp. 160–1.

54 Neill (1994), p. 3.

55 Theodor Meron, *Henry's Wars and Shakespeare's Laws: Perspectives on the Law of War in the Later Middle Ages* (Oxford: Clarendon Press, 1993), p. 22.

56 Keith Dockwray, *Henry V* (Stroud: Tempus, 2004), p. 128.

57 Meron (1993), pp. 40–1.

58 Meron (1993), p. 159.

59 Meron (1993), p. 169. John Sutherland and Cedric Watts, *Henry V, War Criminal? and Other Shakespeare Puzzles* (Oxford: Oxford University Press, 2000), pp. 108–16, summarize this debate.

60 Meron (1993), p. 215; Meron, *Bloody Constraint: War and Chivalry in Shakespeare* (Oxford: Oxford University Press, 1998).

61 Steven Marx, 'Shakespeare's Pacifism', *Renaissance Quarterly* 45 (1992), p. 68.

62 Marx (1992), pp. 70–1. See also Robin Headlam Wells, *Shakespeare on Masculinity* (Cambridge: Cambridge University Press, 2000), pp. 31–60.

63 Steven Marx, 'Holy War in *Henry V*', *Shakespeare Survey* 48 (1995), pp. 85–99.

64 R. A. Foakes, *Shakespeare and Violence* (Cambridge: Cambridge University Press, 2003), p. 98.

65 Foakes (2003), pp. 104–5.

66 Foakes (2003), pp. 100–3.

67 Foakes (2003), p. 103.

68 John S. Mebane, '"Impious War": Religion and the Ideology of Warfare in *Henry V*', *Studies in Philology* 104 (2007), p. 252.

69 Mebane (2007), p. 252.

70 Mebane (2007), p. 266.

71 Mark Steyn, 'Henry Goes to Baghdad', *New Criterion* 22 (2003), p. 40.

72 Schwyzer (2004), p. 149, note 41.

73 See Steven Marx, Drafting Shakespeare, http://cla.calpoly.edu/~smarx/Shakespeare/draftingshakespeare2006/index (accessed 18 July 2007).

74 Scott Newstok, '"Step aside, I'll show thee a president": George W as Henry V?', http://www.poppolitics.com/articles/2003/05/01/George-W-as-Henry-V? (accessed 18 July 2007).

CONCLUSION

1 On critical 'Fluellenism', see Richard Levin, *New Readings vs. Old Plays: Recent Trends in the Reinterpretation of English Renaissance Drama* (Chicago: University of Chicago Press, 1979), pp. 209–29.

2 Graham Bradshaw, *Misrepresentations: Shakespeare and the Materialists* (Ithaca: Cornell University Press, 1993), p. 19.

3 Terence Hawkes, 'Wittgenstein's Shakespeare', in Maurice Charney (ed.), *'Bad' Shakespeare: Revaluations of the Shakespeare Canon* (Rutherford, NJ: Fairleigh Dickinson University Press, 1988), pp. 56–60. See also Hawkes, *Shakespeare in the Present* (London: Routledge, 2002).

Select Bibliography

EDITIONS OF *HENRY V*

Craik, T. W. (ed.). *Henry V.* The Arden Shakespeare, Third Series. Walton-on-Thames: Nelson, 1997.

Dover Wilson, John (ed.). *King Henry V.* Cambridge: Cambridge University Press, 1947.

Gurr, Andrew (ed.). *The First Quarto of King Henry V.* Cambridge: Cambridge University Press, 2000.

——. *King Henry V.* The New Cambridge Shakespeare. Cambridge: Cambridge University Press, 2005.

Holderness, Graham and Bryan Loughrey (eds). *The Cronicle History of Henry the Fift.* Hemel Hempstead: Harvester Wheatsheaf, 1993.

Taylor, Gary (ed.). *Henry V.* The Oxford Shakespeare. Oxford: Oxford University Press, 1982.

Walter, J. H. (ed.). *King Henry V.* The Arden Shakespeare, Second Series. London: Methuen, 1954.

ESSAY COLLECTIONS AND REFERENCE WORKS

Candido, Joseph and Charles R. Forker. *Henry V: An Annotated Bibliography.* New York: Garland, 1983.

Dutton, Richard. 'The Second Tetralogy', in Stanley Wells (ed.), *Shakespeare: A Bibliographical Guide.* Oxford: Oxford University Press, 1990, pp. 337–80.

—— and Jean E. Howard (eds). *A Companion to Shakespeare's Works, Volume II: The Histories.* Oxford: Blackwell, 2003.

Quinn, Michael (ed.). *Henry V: A Casebook.* London: Macmillan, 1969.

Smith, Emma (ed.). *Shakespeare's Histories.* Blackwell Guides to Criticism. Oxford: Blackwell, 2004.

MAKING THE TEXT

Barton, Anne. 'The King Disguised: Shakespeare's *Henry V* and the Comical History', in Joseph G. Price (ed.), *The Triple Bond: Plays, Mainly Shakespearean, in Performance.* University Park: Pennsylvania State University Press, 1975, pp. 92–117.

Erne, Lukas. *Shakespeare as Literary Dramatist.* Cambridge: Cambridge University Press, 2003.

Gurr, Andrew. '*Henry V* and the Bees' Commonwealth', *Shakespeare Survey* 30 (1977), pp. 61–72.

Patterson, Annabel. *Shakespeare and the Popular Voice.* Oxford: Blackwell, 1989.

Wells, Stanley and Gary Taylor. *Modernizing Shakespeare's Spelling, with Three Studies in the Text of Henry V.* Oxford: Clarendon Press, 1979.

SEVENTEENTH- AND EIGHTEENTH-CENTURY CRITICISM

Boyle, Roger. *The History of Henry the Fifth.* London, 1668.

Dryden, John. *Of Dramatic Poesy,* in *Selected Criticism,* ed. James Kinsley and George Parfitt. Oxford: Clarendon Press, 1970.

Gordon, Scott Paul. 'Endeavouring to be the King: Dryden's *Astraea Redux* and the Issue of "Character"', *Journal of English and Germanic Philology* 101 (2002), pp. 201–21.

Hill, Aaron. *King Henry the Fifth: Or, the Conquest of France, By the English: A Tragedy.* London, 1723.

Nichol Smith, D. (ed.). *Eighteenth-Century Essays on Shakespeare.* 2nd edn. Oxford: Clarendon Press, 1963.

Pope, Alexander (ed.). *The Works of Shakespear in Six Volumes.* 6 vols. London, 1725.

Rowe, Nicholas (ed.). *The Works of Mr. William Shakespear: Revis'd and Corrected, with an Account of the Life and Writings of the Author.* 7 vols. London, 1709–10.

Theobald, Lewis (ed.). *The Works of Shakespeare in Seven Volumes.* 7 vols. London, 1733.

Woudhuysen, H. R. (ed.). *Samuel Johnson on Shakespeare.* Harmondsworth: Penguin, 1989.

NINETEENTH-CENTURY CRITICISM

Bate, Jonathan (ed.). *The Romantics on Shakespeare.* Harmondsworth: Penguin, 1992.

Dowden, Edward. *Shakspere: A Critical Study of his Mind and Art.* London, 1875.

Gervinus, G. G. *Shakespeare Commentaries*, trans. F. E. Burnett. 2 vols. London, 1863.

Hazlitt, William. *Characters of Shakespear's Plays.* 2nd edn. London, 1818.

Moulton, R. G. 'On Character-Development in Shakspere as Illustrated by *Macbeth* and *Henry V*', *Transactions of the New Shakspere Society* 8–10 (1880–6), pp. 563–78.

Schlegel, A. W. *Lectures on Dramatic Art and Literature*, trans. John Black. 2 vols. London, 1815.

Simpson, Richard. 'The Politics of Shakspere's Historical Plays', *Transactions of the New Shakspere Society* 1 (1874), pp. 396–441.

Swinburne, Algernon Charles. *A Study of Shakespeare.* London: 1880.

Ulrici, Hermann. *Shakspeare's Dramatic Art*, trans. A. J. W. Morrison. London, 1846.

——. *Shakspeare's Dramatic Art*, trans. A. J. W. Morrison. 2 vols. London, 1876.

Watkiss Lloyd, William. *Critical Essays on the Plays of Shakespeare.* London, 1875.

EARLY TWENTIETH-CENTURY CRITICISM

Bradley, A. C. 'The Rejection of Falstaff', in Bradley, *Oxford Lectures on Poetry.* London: Macmillan, 1920.

Gould, Gerald. 'A New Reading of *Henry V*', *The English Review* 29 July (1919), pp. 42–55.

Lee, Sidney. *Shakespeare and the Modern Stage.* London: Murray, 1906.

Marriott, J. A. R. *English History in Shakespeare.* London: Chapman and Hall, 1918.

Schelling, Felix E. *The English Chronicle Play: A Study in the Popular Historical Literature Environing Shakespeare.* London: Macmillan, 1902.

MID- TO LATE TWENTIETH-CENTURY CRITICISM

Campbell, Lily B. *Shakespeare's Histories: Mirrors of Elizabethan Policy.* London: Methuen, 1964.

Ellis-Fermor, Una. *The Frontiers of Drama.* 2nd edn. London: Methuen, 1964.

Goddard, Harold C. *The Meaning of Shakespeare.* 2 vols. Chicago: University of Chicago Press, 1960.

Levin, Richard. *New Readings vs. Old Plays: Recent Trends in the Reinterpretation of English Renaissance Drama.* Chicago: University of Chicago Press, 1979.

Ornstein, Robert. *A Kingdom for a Stage: The Achievement of Shakespeare's History Plays.* Cambridge, MA: Harvard University Press, 1972.

Palmer, John. *Political Characters of Shakespeare.* London: Macmillan, 1945.

Rabkin, Norman. 'Rabbits, Ducks, and *Henry V*', *Shakespeare Quarterly* 28 (1977), pp. 279–96.

Rossiter, A. P. 'Ambivalence: The Dialectic of the Histories', in Rossiter, *Angel With Horns, and Other Shakespeare Lectures*, ed. Graham Storey. London: Longman, 1961, pp. 40–64.

Sen Gupta, S. C. *Shakespeare's Historical Plays*. London: Oxford University Press, 1964.

Tillyard, E. M. W. *Shakespeare's History Plays*. Harmondsworth: Penguin, 1969.

Traversi, D. A. *An Approach to Shakespeare*. 2nd edn. London: Sands, 1957.

Van Doren, Mark. *Shakespeare*. New York: Holt, 1939.

Wilson Knight, G. *The Olive and the Sword: A Study of England's Shakespeare*. London: Oxford University Press, 1944.

LATER TWENTIETH- AND EARLY TWENTY-FIRST-CENTURY CRITICISM

Baker, David J. '"Wildehirissheman": Colonialist Representation in Shakespeare's *Henry V*', *English Literary Renaissance* 22 (1992), pp. 37–61.

Bradshaw, Graham. *Misrepresentations: Shakespeare and the Materialists*. Ithaca: Cornell University Press, 1993.

Dollimore, Jonathan and Alan Sinfield (eds). *Political Shakespeare: New Essays in Cultural Materialism*. Manchester: Manchester University Press, 1985.

——. 'History and Ideology, Masculinity and Miscegenation', in Sinfield, *Faultines: Cultural Materialism and the Politics of Dissident Reading*. Oxford: Clarendon Press, 1992, pp. 109–42.

Foakes, R. A. *Shakespeare and Violence*. Cambridge: Cambridge University Press, 2003.

Greenblatt, Stephen. *Shakespearean Negotiations: The Circulation of Social Energy in Renaissance England*. Berkeley: University of California Press, 1988.

Hawkes, Terence. 'Wittgenstein's Shakespeare', in Maurice Charney (ed.), *'Bad' Shakespeare: Revaluations of the Shakespeare Canon*. Rutherford, NJ: Fairleigh Dickinson University Press, 1988, pp. 56–60.

Highley, Christopher. *Shakespeare, Spenser and the Crisis in Ireland*. Cambridge: Cambridge University Press, 1997.

Howard, Jean E. and Phyllis Rackin. *Engendering a Nation: A Feminist Account of Shakespeare's English Histories*. London: Routledge, 1997.

McAlindon, Tom. *Shakespeare Minus 'Theory'*. Aldershot: Ashgate, 2004.

McEachern, Claire. *The Poetics of English Nationhood*. Cambridge: Cambridge University Press, 1996.

Marx, Steven. 'Shakespeare's Pacifism', *Renaissance Quarterly* 45 (1992), pp. 49–95.

——. 'Holy War in *Henry V*', *Shakespeare Survey* 48 (1995), pp. 85–99.

Mebane, John S. '"Impious War": Religion and the Ideology of Warfare in *Henry V*', *Studies in Philology* 104 (2007), pp. 250–66.

Meron, Theodor. *Henry's Wars and Shakespeare's Laws: Perspectives on the Law of War in the Later Middle Ages*. Oxford: Clarendon Press, 1993.

——. *Bloody Constraint: War and Chivalry in Shakespeare*. Oxford: Oxford University Press, 1998.

Murphy, Andrew. 'Shakespeare's Irish History', *Literature and History* 5 [Third Series] (1996), pp. 38–59.

Neill, Michael. 'Broken English and Broken Irish: Nation, Language and the Optic of Power in Shakespeare's Histories', *Shakespeare Quarterly* 45 (1994), pp. 18–22.

Schwyzer, Philip. *Literature, Nationalism and Memory in Early Modern England and Wales*. Cambridge: Cambridge University Press, 2004.

Thorne, Alison. '"Awake remembrance of these valiant dead": *Henry V* and the Politics of the English History Play', *Shakespeare Studies* 30 (2002), pp. 162–89.

Wilcox, Lance. 'Katherine of France as Victim and Bride', *Shakespeare Studies* 17 (1985), pp. 61–76.

HENRY V ON STAGE AND SCREEN

Geduld, Harry M. *Filmguide to Henry V*. Bloomington: Indiana University Press, 1973.

Loehlin, James. *Shakespeare in Performance: Henry V*. Manchester: Manchester University Press, 1996.

Smith, Emma. *King Henry V*, Shakespeare in Production. Cambridge: Cambridge University Press, 2002.

Steyn, Mark. 'Henry Goes to Baghdad', *New Criterion* 22 (2003), pp. 40–4.

CINEMATIC ADAPTATIONS

Henry V (1944) 137 minutes. Colour. Great Britain. Rank/Two Cities Films. Director: Laurence Olivier.

Henry V (1989) 137 minutes. Colour. Great Britain. Curzon/Renaissance Films. Director: Kenneth Branagh.

INDEX